# The
# School Counselor's
# Guide to
# Special Education

Barbara C. Trolley • Heather S. Haas • Danielle Campese Patti

**CORWIN PRESS**
A SAGE Company

Copyright © 2009 by Corwin Press

All rights reserved. When forms and sample documents are included, their use is authorized only by educators, local school sites, and/or noncommercial or nonprofit entities that have purchased the book. Except for that usage, no part of this book may be reproduced or utilized in any form or by any means, electronic or mechanical, including photocopying, recording, or by any information storage and retrieval system, without permission in writing from the publisher.

*For information:*

Corwin Press
A SAGE Company
2455 Teller Road
Thousand Oaks, California 91320
www.corwinpress.com

SAGE Ltd.
1 Oliver's Yard
55 City Road
London EC1Y 1SP
United Kingdom

SAGE India Pvt. Ltd.
B 1/I 1 Mohan Cooperative
   Industrial Area
Mathura Road, New Delhi 110 044
India

SAGE Asia-Pacific Pte. Ltd.
33 Peking Street #02-01
Far East Square
Singapore 048763

Printed in the United States of America.

*Library of Congress Cataloging-in-Publication Data*

Trolley, Barbara C.
The school counselor's guide to special education/Barbara C. Trolley, Heather S. Haas, and Danielle Campese Patti.
      p. cm.
Includes bibliographical references and index.
ISBN 978-1-4129-6830-0 (cloth)—ISBN 978-1-4129-6831-7 (pbk.)
   1. Counseling in special education—Handbooks, manuals, etc. 2. Special education—Handbooks, manuals, etc. I. Haas, Heather S. II. Patti, Danielle Campese. III. Title.

LC3969.48.T76 2009
371.9—dc22                                    2008034490

This book is printed on acid-free paper.

09  10  11  12  13  10  9  8  7  6  5  4  3  2  1

| | |
|---|---|
| *Acquisitions Editor:* | Jessica Allan |
| *Editorial Assistant:* | Joanna Coelho |
| *Production Editor:* | Amy Schroller |
| *Copy Editor:* | Rebecca Keever |
| *Typesetter:* | C&M Digitals (P) Ltd. |
| *Proofreader:* | Charlotte J. Waisner |
| *Cover Designer:* | Scott Van Atta |

# Contents

# Acknowledgments

Corwin Press acknowledges the following peer reviewers for their editorial insight and guidance:

Waldo V. Alvarado, M.Ed.
Reading School District
Reading Senior High School
Reading, PA

Mary Carlson
Special Education Teacher
Park Hill K–8
Denver, CO

Steven Coats, PhD
Licensed Psychologist
LifeTrek – Psychological Solutions
Houston, TX

Mary Guerrette
Director of Special Education
Maine School Administrative District
No. 1
Presque Isle, ME

Diana Joyce, Ph.D., NCSP
Psychologist/School Psychologist
University of Florida
Gainesville, FL

Brenda Melton, M.Ed., LPC, NBCT
President (2002–2003), American
School Counselor Association
Lanier High School
San Antonio, TX

Sarah Miller
Special Education/
Resource Teacher
Baldwin County Schools
Orange Beach Elementary
Orange Beach, AL

Mary Reeve
SPED Director
Gallup-McKinley County
Public Schools
Gallup, NM

Lee Ann Wischmeyer
Counselor
Woodbrook Elementary
Carmel, IN

# About the Authors

 **Barbara C. Trolley** is a licensed psychologist and certified rehabilitation counselor. She is an Associate Professor at St. Bonaventure University in the Counselor Education program, and the chair of the university's Disability Committee. Editor of the New York State School Counseling Journal, and lead author of two prior books on cyberbullying and school counseling resources, Dr. Trolley has been in the clinical and academic arena for several decades. Her counseling work and research has focused on issues related to children and youth, such as grief, adoption, abuse, and school counseling. She is the mother of five children, ages 6–18.

 **Heather S. Haas, MSEd, CAS** holds a Master of Science in Education and Certificate of Advanced Study from St. Bonaventure University. She is NYS certified in School Building Leadership, School Counseling, and Special Education. Currently, she is an administrator of special education. In the past, she has worked as a special education teacher, school counselor, and chairperson for the Committee on Special Education. Heather has extensive experience with students classified as emotionally disabled and learning disabled, as well as with creating and implementing Individualized Education Programs. She has a current publication with Booklocker.com entitled *A School Counselor's Resource Manual: Practical Tools for the Trade*. Heather served as President of the Buffalo-South Chapter of Phi Delta Kappa for the 2007–2008 school year. She enjoys speaking at local conferences to further advocate for students with disabilities.

 **Danielle Campese Patti** was born and raised in Jamestown, NY. After pursuing a Master's in Education in the field of counseling, she began her career as an elementary school counselor with the Southwestern Central School District. She later moved into a position as a high school counselor within the district to broaden her experience. After obtaining an additional Master's in Education in the field of educational leadership, she transitioned into the role of elementary school assistant principal. Her experiences include presentations to the New York State School Counseling Association on the important role counselors play in the special education process, chairing the Committee on PreSchool Education for Southwestern School District, and operating as past President of the Chautauqua County School Counselor's Association.

Beginning her career as a counselor and later transitioning into administration has provided her with a wide range of experiences and knowledge in the field of human development. She refers to herself as an advocate for children and education. Believing that all students can achieve success is her motivation and she strives to provide exceptional support and educational programming for the families within her school district.

# Introduction

**M**any educational changes have occurred in the past few decades, which have an impact on all students, including those with disabilities. The mandate set forth by No Child Left Behind Act (NCLB) has improved academic performance for all children, and the changes in the reauthorization of the Individuals with Disabilities Act of 2004 suggest that many students with disabilities be held accountable to standardized academic achievement tests and achievement (Hallahan & Kauffman, 2006). In addition, more students are being included as the "least restrictive environment" is being interpreted by many as the regular classroom. Assistive technology is allowing many such students to actively participate, and medical advances and early interventions are helping children and youth with disabilities to better function.

---

### Activity

Read "School counselors making a difference in the lives of students with special needs" (www.counseling.org/Files/FD.ashx?guid=7e6326d2–8c98–45be-af0a-71be7901fa3e), published by NCPSE, the National Clearinghouse for Professions in Special Education (www. special-ed-careers.org). List five of your professional experiences and personal qualities that will enhance your work with students with special needs. Identify five areas of needed improvement, education, and growth.

---

As it has often been said in general, that "it takes a village to raise children," multidisciplinary teams are a crucial part of the educational journey of students with disabilities. In light of all of the aforementioned advancements and changes, it is crucial that professionals assisting students with disabilities have a grasp of the issues and tasks associated with facilitating the educational growth of students with disabilities.

The purpose of this book, therefore, is to provide all professionals, including practicing school counselors, with:

- A better understanding of their role in working with students with special needs
- An overview of pertinent legal and ethical issues
- An exposure to frequently used acronyms in the special education field
- An increased awareness of the special education classifications
- An awareness of assessment procedures and tests
- A clarification of the special education process for school age, preschool, and transitioning students
- A comprehensive source of resources such as assessment tools, activities, Web sites, and books
- Practical, "hands-on forms"
- Study questions for reflection

1

## Activity

View a film on disability listed on the Special Education Web site. (http://special.ed school.virginia.edu/information/film/filmhall.html). Write a brief essay on how people with disabilities are portrayed in the media.

## Questions for Reflection

1. What is the percentage of students with IEP or 504 plans of your caseload? Your colleagues? Your school district? Surrounding school districts?

2. What is your school district policy for school counselors' roles in working with students with special needs?

3. Which professionals are available for collaboration within your school? Within your school district?

4. What type of collaboration exists among these professionals? What is their designated role?

5. What type of continuing education training in the realm of working with children with special needs is available to you in your school? In your school district?

6. What funding is available in your district to service children with special needs? What type of services does the funding provide?

7. How are referrals of children with special needs made to the school counselors in your school? In your school district?

8. What are the expectations of the school counselors when working with students with special needs?

# Special Education Roles

**S**pecial education is a multi-disciplinary effort, involving many professionals completing independent and overlapping tasks. As can be seen in Chapter 4, a gamut of team members and sites may communicate and collaborate in order to best identify and meet the needs of students with disabilities. At the infant and toddler stage, the pediatrician may have the crucial role in being the first to identify a possible disability and to refer the family for outside evaluation and services. Medical specialists, physical therapists, speech and language therapists, social workers, regular and special educators, local education agencies (LEAs), rehabilitation agencies, and psychologists may play a part in servicing students with disabilities from infancy to high school graduation. School psychologists, special educators, and counselors become involved once the child with a disability starts school. The role of the school psychologist is primarily that of assessment and their role is addressed further in Chapter 5. The role of the school counselor is more extensive and more generally stated. While many of the team members may have overlapping roles, it is the purpose of this chapter to further clarify that of the school counselor.

## Activity

Interview several school counselors working with students with special needs. Develop a master calendar in relation to monthly special education tasks.

Recently, an entire publication of the *School Counselor Journal* (ASCA, 2005) was devoted to the issue of working with students with special needs. In the president's address in this journal, the issue addressed was that of expanding the notion of who constitutes children and youth with special needs to include children who are challenged physically, emotionally, and cognitively, including those uprooted by natural disasters. School counselors in general are seeing not only an increase in the size of their student caseloads and in those students with mental health issues, but are also servicing more students with *individualized education plans*

(IEPs) and 504 plans. Coupled with this increase in students with special needs on school counselors' caseloads is increasing academic standards, such as those dictated by NCLB. Few graduate-level academic programs require school counseling trainees to take a course in special education, thereby leaving entry-level counselors in need of developing skills and abilities to work with students in special education programs (Allen & LaTorre, 1998; Bowen & Glen, 1998; Frantz & Prillaman, 1993; Gillam, Hendricks, George, & Baltimore, 2003; Greer, Greer, & Woody, 1995; Korinek & Prillaman, 1992; Scarborough & Deck, 1998; Studer & Quigny as cited in Studer, 2005). For school counselors, the question becomes, "How do I help students with special needs, while at the same time attend to my large number of 'regular' students assigned to me?"

The first step in defining the role of the school counselor is to review the American School Counselor's (ASCA) Position Statement on this topic, which is presented in Table 1.1.

---

### Activity

Review and collate position statements of state school counselor professional organizations (http://www.schoolcounselor.org/content.asp?pl=325&sl=127&contentid=179)  in  relation to working with students with special needs.

---

As can be seen in review of the statements presented in this table, the majority of roles defined, such as individual and group counselor, collaborator, advocate, consultant, team member, and referral agent, are similar to those one would expect in regard to working with children and youth without disabilities. While these roles are important, they are generic, with specific tasks in regard to students with special needs left open to definition. Adding to the complexity of this issue is the fact that the role of the school counselor in general still varies greatly, influenced by factors such as district policy, number and type of professionals within the district, level of school served, geographical location, public versus private nature of the school, number of students, and funding resources. There is clearly a need for further delineation and specification of how school counselors can best meet the needs of students with special needs.

The roles and duties of both general education and special education teachers often work in isolation of one another. Each educator's daily routines, methods of instruction, and responsibilities are quite different from the other. When a student becomes eligible for special education classification, general and special educators can become more independent in their approach to educating and supporting the child. Interventions, modifications, and accommodations that are the responsibility of both educators may create conflict when determining with whom the responsibility lies. Furthermore, the role of the school counselor, as defined by ASCA, also does not provide much mention of the support to students with disabilities.

---

### Activity

Review an educational film on disability and children such as *A Video Guide to (Dis) ability* (*http://www.disabilitytraining.com/avgd.html*) or *Special People, Special Needs* (http://www.cev multimedia.com/fcs/parenting.php). Write a bulleted list of appropriate school counselor tasks in regard to one of the children with special needs identified in the film.

---

The June 2004 "Role of the School Counselor," provided by ASCA, recommends a counselor to student ratio of 1:250 with little mention of the related services provided to students whose IEPs indicate group or individual counseling. It is the responsibility of the school counselor to provide individual and group counseling to students whose lives and

**Table 1.1**    ASCA Position Statement

ASCA Position Statement: Special-Needs Students

http://www.schoolcounselor.org/content.asp?contentid=218

**The Professional School Counselor and Students with Special Needs**

(Adopted 1999; revised 2004)

**American School Counselor Association (ASCA) Position**

Professional school counselors encourage and support all students' academic, personal/social, and career development through comprehensive school counseling programs. Professional school counselors are committed to helping all students realize their potential and make adequate yearly progress despite challenges that may result from identified disabilities and other special needs.

**Rationale**

Professional school counselors have increasingly important roles in working with students who have special needs. State and federal laws require schools to provide an equitable education for all students, including those with special needs. Components of federal laws such as due process, individual educational programs, least restrictive environment, and other plans for students with accommodations and modifications provide opportunities to use the professional school counselor's skills to benefit students with special needs. Professional school counselors work with students with special needs both in special class settings and in the regular classroom, and are a key component in assisting with transitions to post-secondary options. It is particularly important that the professional school counselor's role in these procedures is clearly defined and is in compliance with laws and local policies.

**The Professional School Counselor's Role**

When appropriate, interventions in which the professional school counselor participates may include but are not limited to:

- leading school counseling activities as a part of the comprehensive school counseling program
- providing collaborative services consistent with those services provided to students through the comprehensive school counseling program
- serving on the school's multidisciplinary team that identifies students who may need assessments to determine special needs within the scope and practice of the professional school counselor
- collaborating with other student support specialists in the delivery of services
- providing group and individual counseling
- advocating for students with special needs in the school and in the community
- assisting with the establishment and implementation of plans for accommodations and modifications
- providing assistance with transitions from grade to grade as well as post-secondary options
- consulting and collaborating with staff and parents to understand the special needs of these students
- making referrals to appropriate specialists within the school system and within the community

*(Continued)*

**Table 1.1** (Continued)

The professional school counselor advocates for students with special needs and is one of many school staff members who may be responsible for providing information as written plans are prepared for students with special needs. The professional school counselor has a responsibility to be a part of designing portions of these plans related to the comprehensive school counseling program, but it is inappropriate for the professional school counselor to serve in supervisory or administrative roles such as:

- making decisions regarding placement or retention
- serving in any supervisory capacity related to the implementation of IDEA
- serving as the LEA representative for the team writing the IEP
- coordinating the 504 planning team
- supervising of the implementation of the 504 plan

The professional school counselor continues to seek opportunities for professional development to better understand special needs in regard to assessment, research, and legislation. The professional school counselor also collaborates with members of the community who are providing services to students with special needs.

**Summary**

The professional school counselor takes an active role in providing a comprehensive school counseling program to students with special needs. Professional school counselors advocate for all students and provide collaborative services to students with special needs consistent with those services provided to students through the comprehensive school counseling program.

personal circumstances necessitate emotional support. School counselors are to provide all students with a comprehensive school counseling program, which often includes education on topics including bullying and anger management, in addition to topics of age-appropriate levels for elementary, middle, and high school students. Unfortunately, the 1:250 recommended ratio is often not the case as the 2005–2006 school year national average was 1:476 (NCES Common Core Data (CCD), "State Nonfiscal Survey of Public Elementary/Secondary Education: 2005–2006 School Year"). Those school counselors who are the sole counselor of a school must not only fulfill the expectations of administrators and district mission statements and philosophies, but also the state and federal obligations to students who are classified as having a disability and who have counseling as a related service on their IEP. School counselors are becoming more and more present at child study team meetings, parent conferences, and special education committee meetings; however, their role is not specifically defined by state or federal guidelines. It then becomes the responsibility of the local education agency to provide all educators with specific roles and responsibilities of school counselors in the special education arena.

*Dawson is a ten year old male in fifth grade. He is classified as other health impaired. Dawson has been diagnosed by a psychologist as having attention deficit hyperactivity disorder. His family is currently trying to change his diet, examine research on allergies, and incorporate holistic approaches for treatment. In school, Dawson is rapidly falling behind. Parents have called the counselor complaining about him disrupting their children in class. Group counseling has been attempted in an effort to promote appropriate social skills and build relationships. Recently, Dawson has been acting out and getting into trouble. He has been sent to the principal for the third time in one day. You are the school counselor, and have just been contacted by the principal.*

*She asks for your help in dealing with this situation. You explain the interventions that have been attempted. She asks you to call the parents in for a meeting.*

- What discussion will you have with the parents regarding Dawson?
- Is it appropriate to share information with other parents regarding a disruptive student in the classroom?
- At what point does this situation become an issue for administration to pursue rather than the role of the school counselor?
- Are there other steps that can be taken to help Dawson in the educational setting?

The coordination of general education, special education, and school counseling is not something that can easily be fixed after a day of inservice or conference. Communication is the key to unlocking the barrier. A sharing of duties and responsibilities so that all are aware of one another's roles and strengths begins the dialogue necessary to create a system of educators that work together, not against one another. Providing school counselors with the tools necessary to communicate with a common language is a beginning.

In addition, Erford (2003) described a number of specific tasks that school counselors might undertake, including provision of multiculturally sensitive education about disabilities; education and civil rights information; assistance of families in negotiating educational systems; consultation in terms of medical management; monitoring of progress.

Additional specific tasks that school counselors might undertake include:

## At the start of the school year:

- A clear explanation to colleagues such as special education and regular teachers, and school psychologists, as well as parents of students with special needs, as to the role of the school counselor
- Meeting with regular teachers to address referral process
- Distribution of related forms to teachers regarding classroom assessment, intervention documentation, counseling referrals
- Introduction to/meeting with Committee on Special Education (CSE) Chair to develop rapport, address roles and expectations
- Introduction to/meeting with school psychologist to develop rapport, identify assessment tools utilized, education regarding psychologist reports; understanding of possible test accommodations for various standardized tests
- Identification of students coming with IEPs and 504 plans that are part of the school counselors' caseload

## Ongoing throughout the school year:

- Teacher assistance with identification and documentation of intervention strategies tried; suggestion of alternative interventions
- Assistance in writing specific behavioral counseling goals
- Regular team review of students with IEPs and 504 plans to specifically define needs and counseling expectations; progress
- Education of parents as to the CSE process
- Development of continuing education presentations on topics such as organizational skills, study skills for students, parents, and staff
- Partnership in development of workshops for staff and parents related to specific education topics such as attention deficit disorders and pervasive developmental disorders
- Periodic visits to the resource room, self-contained classes; visits with the Special Education Itinerant Teachers (SEIT)
- Periodic contacts with physical and occupational therapists; speech pathologists
- Attendance at professional conferences on special education

Even when tasks are spelled out, problems can arise when school counselors try to collaborate with others in terms of special education:

- Waste of school counselors' time due to ineffectiveness of team meetings
- Administrative lack of sensitivity to school counselors' caseloads
- School counselors may not be in attendance when they have an assigned task
- Inaccurate belief may exist that school counselors address only social skills
- Inaccurate belief that school counselors only provide behavior modification or social interventions in isolation of the students' program
- False belief that students' academic needs must wait until school counselor magically addresses emotional issues
- Lack of local education agency (LEA), IDEA, and 504 updates to school counselor
- Lack of ability to follow up on counseling interventions due to caseload size
- Other school staff may feel that they don't have to cooperate with counseling part of team plan
- Teams may fail to specify academic and behavioral success outcomes
- Lack of support for proactive interventions for students with mild disabilities who are at risk for eventual academic failure
- Families, advocates, and agencies may have unreal counseling expectations
- Lack of resources, especially alternative placements, for students in extreme need
- Ethical concerns for limited counseling resources being provided to students with the most vocal parents
- Ethical concerns when being required to provide additional services, which warrant more training or supervision (Erford, 2003, p. 372).

Important considerations in assuming these tasks include what school counselors feel is in their professional role to assume, whether or not they have appropriate training in taking on these tasks, contents of their defined job description, and perhaps most importantly, the question of how the completion of these tasks will better serve their students with special needs.

## Questions for Reflection

1. Who are the professionals that work with students with special needs at your school? At your school district?

2. What are their roles?

3. How are the roles communicated?

4. What tasks are unique to certain professionals?

5. What tasks are shared among these professionals?

6. What preparation/training do these professionals have in working with students with special needs?

7. How many students at your school have special needs? How many in your district?

8. What are the services available to students with special needs in your school/district? In your community?

# 2

# Special Education Terminology and Disability Categories

**T**he world of special education can seem like "alphabet soup" with the myriad of acronyms that abound. It is challenging enough for specialists in the field to stay abreast of the terminology, and even more daunting for school counselors and parents to do so. Yet these acronyms stand for key principles in special education, and are commonly utilized within Committee on Special Education (CSE) meetings, IEPs, and assessment reports, to name a few. Numerous Web sites exist, which can be a basic primer and resource, such as:

- Frequently Used Special Education Terms and Definitions
  http://www.mcpherson.com/418/special_ed/terms_defintions.html
- Special Education Dictionary: Parentpals.com Special Education Guide
  http://www.parentpals.com/2.0dictionary/dictnewsindex.html
- Special Education in Plain Language
  http://www.csea7.k12.wi.us/sped/Parents/plintro.htm

In addition, numerous parent friendly documents, including those describing special education needs, statements, step-by-step descriptions of special education, access to education for children and youth with medical illness, support and partnership in special education, and assessments, may be found at: http://www.direct.gov.uk/EducationAndLearning/Schools/Special.

A sampling of the primary acronyms used in special education is presented in Table 2.1. Equally important is comprehension of the thirteen disability classifications used to identify students with disabilities. These classifications are presented in Table 2.2.

There has long been controversy over the use of diagnostic labels, especially as they apply to children and youth. Concern arises over students being stereotyped and perceived as different and less than normal. Such fears extend beyond the social realm to the academic area. Parents fear their child receives a less than quality education, and that long-term goals such as college may be negatively impacted.

Litigation has also arisen in this regard due to bias against non-Caucasian students, that is non-White students being disproportionately or inappropriately classified (Gearheart, Mullen, & Gearheart, 1993). In addition, educators are equally concerned that students are being appropriately identified and instructed.

These concerns should not be taken lightly. However, if students are appropriately referred for assessment, the assessment tools are pertinent and comprehensive, classifications are assigned by qualified and credentialed professionals, communication of assessment results and classification categories are sensitively and clearly explained to parents and students, then this categorization system will benefit the students. Previously unknown problems may be identified, assisting all involved to better define needed educational services. Psychologically, understanding that a disability exists and what it is may help alleviate anxiety and ambiguity, decrease feelings of being "crazy," and correct misinterpretations that the students are simply lazy and unmotivated. Implicit in this classification system is the education of teachers, staff, administrators, parents, and students as to disabilities, as well as to sensitivity training.

---

### Activity

Download special education glossaries, such as those provided by *The Council for Disability Rights* (http://www.disabilityrights.org/glossary.htm) and *Wrights Law* (http://www.fetaweb.com/06/glossary.sped.legal.htm). Or those found at http://www.txbsi.org/docs/SPECIAL%20EDUCATION%20TERMS.doc.

---

### Activity

Attend a CSE meeting. Make a list of all the acronyms mentioned and review after the meeting.

---

Table 2.1 provides a detailed list of typical acronyms used in special education. This list can be helpful for educators, parents, and students.

This list is neither exclusive nor final. Individual districts or states may use acronyms to abbreviate different terms. Check your district or state education Web site for the acronyms and terms used most commonly in your area. In addition to the acronyms of special education, a clear knowledge of the definitions of the classifications is also imperative when talking to and writing documents for students with disabilities. Table 2.2 provides the federal classifications, definitions, and acronyms for the thirteen categories of disabilities

Resource A provides a concise description of the federal definitions of the thirteen disability categories as well as useful information for special education teachers, general education teachers, school counselors, parents, advocates, and students. Although the fact sheets do not contain information that is exclusive, they can be used to provide educators and parents with the necessary information to assist in an appropriate understanding of a child's disability and the behaviors and needs that accompany.

*Jordan is a seven- year-old female in second grade. She has been diagnosed with a learning disability. Currently, her educational program includes the use of a consultant teacher for forty-five minutes per day. She also receives resource room service for thirty minutes a day. Once a week, Jordan goes to occupational therapy with a group of students from her classroom. She holds her pencil with a thumb wrap and frequently adapts her grip to a functional dynamic grasp. She is unable to correctly spell her name, and struggles with formation of most capital letters. The classroom teacher asks you to come in and conduct a brief observation.*

*(Text continued on page 17)*

**Table 2.1**    Special Education Acronyms

| | |
|---|---|
| AAD | adaptive assistive devices |
| ABA | applied behavior analysis |
| ABD | antisocial behavior disorders |
| ABE | adult basic education |
| AD | attachment disorder |
| ADA | Americans with Disabilities Act; average daily attendance |
| ADD | attention deficit disorder |
| ADHD | attention deficit with hyperactivity disorder |
| ADL | activities of daily living |
| AEP | alternative education placement |
| APD | antisocial personality disorder; auditory processing disorder |
| APE | adaptive physical education |
| ASD | autism spectrum disorder |
| ASL | American Sign Language |
| AT | assistive technology |
| BASIS | Basic Adult Skills Inventory System |
| BD | behaviorally disordered; behavior disorders; brain damaged |
| BIA | Brain Injury Association; Bureau of Indian Affairs |
| BIP | behavior intervention plan |
| BOCES | Board of Comprehensive Education Services (New York State) |
| CA | chronological age |
| CAPD | central auditory processing disorders; see also APD (auditory processing disorder) |
| CBA | curriculum based assessment |
| CBM | curriculum based measurement |
| CD | conduct disorder |
| CNS | central nervous system |
| COTA | certified occupational therapist assistant |
| CP | cerebral palsy |
| CPSE | committee on preschool special education |
| CSE | committee on special education |
| DB; DBL | deaf-blind |
| DD | developmental disabilities; developmentally delayed |

*(Continued)*

**Table 2.1** (Continued)

| | |
|---|---|
| DDC | developmental disabilities council |
| DNR | do not resuscitate |
| DOE | Department of Education |
| DSM | Diagnostic and Statistical Manual (for Mental Disorders) |
| EBD | emotional and behavioral disorders |
| EC | early childhood; exceptional child[ren] |
| ECE | early childhood education |
| ECI | early childhood intervention |
| ECSE | early childhood special education |
| ECT | early childhood team |
| ED | emotionally disturbed; emotional disorders |
| EHA | Education for All Handicapped Children Act (since 1990, known as the Individuals with Disabilities Education Act [IDEA]) |
| EI | early intervention |
| EMDR | eye movement desensitization and reprocessing |
| EMR | educable mentally retarded |
| ESE | exceptional student education |
| ESEA | Elementary and Secondary Education Act |
| ESL | English as a second language |
| ESOL | English for speakers of other languages |
| ESY | extended school year |
| EYS | extended year services (ECSE) |
| FAPE | free appropriate public education |
| FBA | functional behavior assessment |
| FERPA | Family Educational Rights to Privacy Act (aka the Buckley Amendment) |
| GT | gifted and talented |
| HI | hearing impaired |
| HOH | hard of hearing |
| HS | head start; high school |
| IASA | Improving America's Schools Act |
| ICDP | individual career development plans |
| ICF | intermediate care facility |
| IDEA | Individuals with Disabilities Education Act |

| IED | intermittent explosive disorder |
| --- | --- |
| IEE | independent education evaluation |
| IEP | individualized education program |
| IEPC | individualized educational planning committee |
| IFSP | individualized family service plan |
| IHO | impartial hearing officer |
| IQ | intelligence quotient |
| ISP | individualized service plan |
| ISS | in school suspension |
| ITP | individualized transition plan (similar to IEP) |
| LD | learning disabilities; learning disabled |
| LDA | Learning Disabilities Association |
| LEA | local education agency |
| LEP | limited English proficient |
| LRE | least restrictive environment |
| LSSP | licensed specialist in school psychology |
| MA | mental age |
| MBD | minimal brain dysfunction |
| MDT | multidisciplinary team; manifest determination team |
| MESC | migrant education service center |
| MD | multiple disabilities |
| MI | multiple intelligences |
| MR | mentally retarded or mental retardation |
| MR/DD | mentally retarded/developmentally disabled |
| NCLB | No Child Left Behind Act |
| NEA | National Education Association |
| OCD | obsessive compulsive disorder |
| ODD | oppositional defiant disorder |
| OHI | other health impairments |
| OT | occupational therapy/therapist |

*(Continued)*

**Table 2.1** (Continued)

| OT/PT | occupational therapy/physical therapy |
|---|---|
| PDD | pervasive development disorder |
| PLEP | present level of educational performance |
| PPD | Preschooler with a disability |
| PPS | pupil personnel services |
| PT | physical therapy/therapist |
| PTSD | post-traumatic stress disorder |
| RAD | reactive attachment disorder |
| REBT | rational emotive behavior therapy |
| RTI | response to intervention |
| SEA | state education agency |
| SECTION 504 | a part of the Rehabilitation Act of 1973 making it illegal for any organization receiving federal funds to discriminate against a person solely on the basis of disability |
| SED | seriously emotionally disturbed; state education department |
| SI | speech impaired |
| SIB | self-injurious behavior |
| SLD | specific learning disability |
| SLP | speech-language pathologist |
| SLPA | speech-language pathologist assistant |
| SPED | special education |
| SSI | statewide systemic initiative; supplemental security income |
| SS | Standard Score |
| SST | student study team; student support team |
| TBI | traumatic brain injury |
| VI | visually impaired |
| VESID | Vocational and Educational Services for Individuals with Disabilities |
| WISC-R | Wechsler Intelligence Scale for Children-Revised |
| WISC-III | Wechsler Intelligence Scale for Children-Third Edition |
| WRAP | wraparound program |

**Table 2.2**    Classification and Definitions of IDEA, Part 300

| | |
|---|---|
| Autism | Part 300 (i) Autism means a developmental disability significantly affecting verbal and nonverbal communication and social interaction, generally evident before age 3 that adversely affects a student's educational performance. Other characteristics often associated with autism are engagement in repetitive activities and stereotyped movements, resistance to environmental change or change in daily routines, and unusual responses to sensory experiences. The term does not apply if a child's educational performance is adversely affected primarily because the student has an emotional disturbance defined in paragraph (b)(4) of Part 300.7.<br><br>(i)  A child who manifests the characteristics of "autism" after age 3 could be diagnosed as having "autism" if the criteria in paragraph (c)(1)(i) of Part 300.7 are satisfied. |
| Mental Retardation<br><br>**MR** | Part 300: Mental retardation means significantly subaverage general intellectual functioning, existing concurrently with deficits in adaptive behavior and manifested during the developmental period, that adversely affects a student's educational performance |
| Learning Disability<br><br>**LD** | Part 300: Specific Learning Disability is defined as follows:<br><br>(i)  *General.* The term means a disorder in one or more of the basic psychological processes involved in understanding or in using language, spoken or written, which manifests itself in an imperfect ability to listen, think, speak, read, write, spell, or do mathematical calculations, including conditions such as perceptual disabilities, brain injury, minimal brain dysfunction, dyslexia and developmental aphasia.<br><br>(ii) *Disorders not included.* The term does not include learning problems that are primarily the result of visual, hearing or motor disabilities, of mental retardation, of emotional disturbance, or of environmental, cultural or economic disadvantage. |
| Emotional Disturbance<br><br>**ED** | Part 300 Emotional disturbance is defined as follows:<br><br>(i)  The term means a condition exhibiting one or more of the following characteristics over a long period of time and to a marked degree that adversely affects a child's educational performance:<br><br>A.  An inability to learn that cannot be explained by intellectual, sensory, or health factors.<br><br>B.  An inability to build or maintain satisfactory interpersonal relationships with peers and teachers;<br><br>C.  Inappropriate types of behavior or feelings under normal circumstances;<br><br>D.  A generally pervasive mood of unhappiness or depression; or<br><br>E.  A tendency to develop physical symptoms or fears associated with personal or school problems.<br><br>(ii) The term includes schizophrenia. The term does not apply to children who are socially maladjusted, unless it is determined that they have an emotional disturbance. |
| Traumatic Brain Injury<br><br>**TBI** | Part 300: Traumatic brain injury means an acquired injury to the brain caused by an external force, resulting in total or partial functional disability or psychosocial impairment, or both that adversely affect educational performance. The term includes open or closed head injuries or brain injuries from certain medical conditions resulting in mild, moderate or severe impairments in one or more areas, |

*(Continued)*

**Table 2.2** (Continued)

| | |
|---|---|
| | including cognition, language, memory, attention, reasoning, abstract thinking, judgment, problem solving, sensory, perceptual and motor abilities, psychosocial behavior, physical functions, information processing, and speech. The term does not include injuries that are congenital or caused by birth trauma. |
| Visual Impairment<br><br>**VI** | Part 300: Visual impairment including blindness means an impairment in vision that, even with correction, adversely affects a child's educational performance. The term includes both partial sight and blindness.<br><br>Legally blind: An individual with a visual acuity of 20/200 or less even with correction or has a field loss of 20 degrees or more.<br><br>Low Vision: A person who is still severely impaired after correction, but whom may increase functioning through the use of optical aide, nonoptical aids, environmental modifications and/or techniques. |
| Hearing Impairment<br>**HI** | Part 300: Hearing impairment means an impairment in hearing, whether permanent or fluctuatinng, that adversely affects the child's educational performance but that is not included under the definition of deafness in Section 300.7. |
| Deafness | Part 300: Deafness means a hearing impairment that is so severe that the child is impaired in processing linguistic information through hearing, with or without amplification, that adversely affects a child's educational performance. |
| Deaf-blindness<br><br>**DB** | Part 300: Deaf-blindness means concomitant hearing and visual impairments, the combination of which causes such severe communication and other developmental and educational needs that they cannot be accommodated in special education programs solely for children with deafness or children with blindness. |
| Speech or Language Impairment<br>**SI** | Part 300: Speech or language impairment means a communication disorder, such as stuttering, impaired articulation, a language impairment or a voice impairment, that adversely affects a child's educational performance |
| Other Health Impairment<br><br><br><br>**OHI** | Part 300: Other health impairment means having limited strength, vitality or alertness, including a heightened alertness to environmental stimuli, that results in limited alertness with respect to the educational environment that<br><br>(i) Is due to chronic or acute health problems such as, asthma, attention deficit disorder or attention deficit hyperactivity disorder, a heart condition, hemophilia, lead poisoning, leukemia, nephritis, rheumatic fever and sickle cell anemia; and<br>(ii) Adversely affects a child's educational performance |
| Orthopedic Impairment<br><br><br><br>**OI** | Part 300: Orthopedic impairment means a severe orthopedic impairment that adversely affects a child's educational performance. The term includes impairments caused by congenital anomaly (e.g., clubfoot, absence of some member, etc.), impairments caused by disease (e.g., poliomyelitis, bone tuberculosis, etc.), and impairments from other causes (e.g., cerebral palsy, amputation, and fractures or burns which cause contractures). |
| Multiple Disabilities<br><br><br><br>**MD** | Part 300: Multiple disabilities means concomitant impairments (such as mental retardation-blindness, mental retardation-orthopedic impairment, etc.), the combination of which causes such severe educational needs that they cannot be accommodated in a special education program solely for one of the impairments. The term does not include deaf-blindness. |

*She feels that Jordan is struggling to make gains, and would like you to assess on task/off task frequency.*

- What will you look for in the classroom to determine whether Jordan's struggles are environmentally related?
- Is consultation necessary with any other school personnel to best meet her needs?
- Discuss the role of the school counselor as part of the educational planning team. How can valuable, useful suggestions be incorporated into her current program?
- What are some struggles that school counselors often face in situations like this?

## Questions for Reflection

1. What acronyms are used most commonly in your school? In your school district?

2. Are the acronyms understood by all of the multidisciplinary team?

3. How are parents educated as to the acronyms?

4. What percentage of students in your school is classified in each of the classification categories? What percentage in your school district?

5. What classification of students with special needs is most frequently included in your school? In your school district? On school counselor caseloads?

6. What classifications of disability categories are most familiar to professionals at your school? At your school district? What classifications are least familiar?

# 3

# Assessment and Referral Processes

**O**nce a regular education teacher has attempted several interventions with a student resulting in little or no growth or success, and has collaborated with colleagues regarding possible additional strategies that could be addressed in the regular classroom, typically the next step in the process is a formal referral for assessment by this team (often called intervention assistance teams, building level teams, child study conferences, Schmidt, 2003; Studer, 2005). Parents need to be notified of and give consent to this assessment referral, the purpose of which is to determine students' eligibility for services and to develop programs for qualified children and youth. Assessment needs to be comprehensive, nondiscriminatory, and multifactored, frequently involving the use of standardized testing. While school psychologists, special educators, and private practitioners typically conduct these assessments, school counselors may also wear many hats in this regard. They may be administrators, designing and managing the testing program. In addition, school counselors may be interpreters, providing information to students, staff, and parents; and consultants, providing meaning of the tests to school staff and families for which they are qualified (Stone & Bradley, 1994). School counselors may administer tests for which they are appropriately trained, such as career tests. They may act as advocates for families during the assessment process, helping them to obtain needed services for their children and youth, or as counselors, working through families' fears and concerns. Erford (2003) summarized the potential assessment functions of school counselors:

- Carry out and/or interpret functional behavioral assessments (FBAs)
- Interpret educational skill assessments
- Carry out and/or interpret curriculum-based assessment
- Explain psychological testing (cognitive ability, emotional status, behavioral profile measures)
- Carry out and/or interpret counseling assessments (social skills, emotional status, behavioral profile measures)
- Carry out structured observations of the student
- Carry out a student records review

- Help stress the need to assess students' strengths
- Assess peer attitudes toward students with disabilities
- Collaborate with others using portfolio-, performance- and curriculum-based assessments (p. 374).

---

### Activity

Search the Web and compile a list of ten Web sites with url addresses and Web site descriptions in regard to assessment. For example, http://specialed.about.com/od/assessment/Special_Education_Assessment.htm and http://www.pearsonassessments.com/k12/index.htm.

---

Implicit in this assessment process is the familiarity of school counselors with various types of assessment tools. In working with children who have special needs, it is important to have this standardized means of evaluation. Many such instruments exist, in terms of general intelligence, achievement, and behavior assessments, as well as specific measures of visual-motor skills, adaptive functioning, and existence of pervasive developmental disorders. As with all standardized testing, it is crucial to choose assessments that best fit the needs of the children and youth, such as norm group referencing and specific test content. Additionally, considerations surrounding test administrations, such as administrator credentials, test time frame, and accommodations should be considered. Most of the tests listed require either a "Level B" {user has completed graduate training in measurement, guidance, individual psychological assessment, or special appraisal methods appropriate for a paRTIcular test} or "Level C" {user has completed a recognized graduate training program in psychology with appropriate coursework and has had supervised practical experience in the administration and interpretation of clinical assessment instruments} qualification standard. Time-frame completions vary among these tests depending on such variables as age of test taker and scales utilized. Most can be completed within an hour or less. Specific accommodations, as with all the test description areas mentioned earlier, can be found in the manuals associated with the specific assessment tool. In addition, a number of Web sites exist, such as www.Psych-EdPublications.com, http://www.assessmentpsychology.com, and www.psychtest.com, which list and describe a gamut of testing tools.

---

### Activity

Interview a school psychologist. Make a list of at least one assessment tool in reference to each of the thirteen special education classifications.

---

# ACADEMIC INTERVENTION SERVICES (AIS)

## Definition of Academic Intervention Services [100.1(g)]

Academic Intervention Services (AIS) are services designed to help students achieve the learning standards in English Language Arts and mathematics in grades K–12 and social studies and science in grades 4–12. These services include two components:

- additional instruction that supplements the general curriculum (regular classroom instruction);

**Figure 3.1**    The Assessment Process

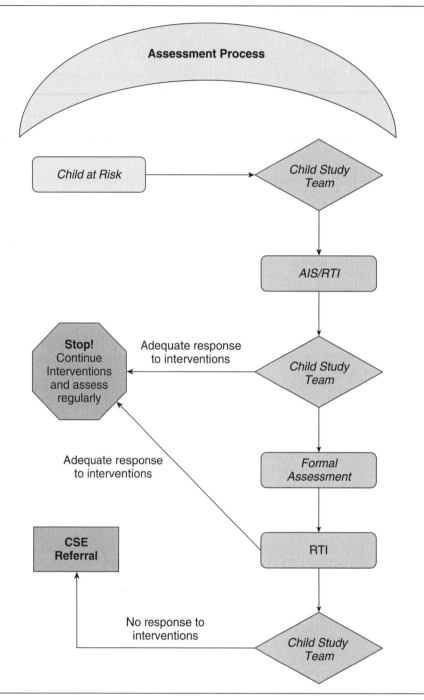

and/or

- student support services needed to address barriers to improved academic performance.

The intensity of such services may vary, but must be designed to respond to student needs as indicated through state assessment results and/or the district-adopted or district-approved procedure that is consistent throughout the district at each grade level.

Academic intervention services are not required in standards areas where there are no state assessments, even though students must earn one or more units of credit for graduation. They are only required in English Language Arts, mathematics, social studies, and science.

*(Text continued on page 28)*

**Table 3.1**    Child Study Team Referral

A complete screening should be completed by the child study team.
Included in the screening/referral:

| | |
|---|---|
| **Parent Conference and Contact Record** | • List contact attempts (date and time) and person attempting contact<br>• List comments on conference and parental input |
| **Records Review and School History** | • Attendance pattern<br>• Past and current subject grades<br>• End of grade test scores |
| **Data Collection** | • Parental notification of screening procedures<br>  a. Sent by<br>  b. Parental invitation/Section 504 information |
| **Classroom Observations** | • Subject observed<br>• Learning situation<br>  a. One-to-one<br>  b. Class<br>  c. Small Group<br>  d. Independent<br>• Student behaviors |
| **General Medical Health Screening** | • Serious illness since birth<br>• Relevant health information<br>• Visual acuity<br>• Hearing<br>• Other |
| **Social Functioning and Environmental and Cultural Status** | • Information concerning the social, environmental, and cultural status of the student has been reviewed |
| **Individual Screening** | • Parental permission for screening received/date<br>• Ability test scores<br>• Achievement test scores<br>• Any previous testing<br>• All information dated and accurately presented |
| **Previous Intervention Strategies Attempted** | • Track dates and results of:<br>  a. Behavioral contract<br>  b. Change in curriculum<br>  c. Change in schedule<br>  d. Change in teachers<br>  e. Community resources<br>  f. Counseling<br>  g. Detention/ISS<br>  h. Modified environment<br>  i. Modified instruction<br>  j. Parental follow-up<br>  k. Praise/attention<br>  l. Specialized instructional equipment<br>  m. Time out<br>  n. Title 1<br>  o. Tutoring/remediation<br>  p. Other |
| **Determine effectiveness of interventions** | • Has learning or behavior not improved as a result of interventions<br>• Describe in behavioral terms the learner's own learning process<br>• Describe the duration, frequency, and intensity of the behavior |
| **Decisions made re: further interventions or CSE referral to be made** | • Be sure to follow district's policy and submit all pertinent information to CSE Chairperson and/or School Principal for CSE Referral |

## GLOBAL CONCEPTS CHARTER SCHOOL
### Student Support Team Referral

Student Name _____ Grade _____ Date _____

### Primary Concern/Key Issue

☐ problems with learning          ☐ vision problems          ☐ physical problems

☐ behavioral/emotional            ☐ speech/language          ☐ parental referral
  problems                          problems

☐ low academic                    ☐ hearing problems         ☐ other:
  performance

☐ comments:

### Student Abilities

☐ works well independently        ☐ creative and curious     ☐ attentive

☐ writes in concise and clear     ☐ reads at or above grade  ☐ receives majority marks of
  style                             level                       A and B

☐ follows instructions easily     ☐ cooperative              ☐ popular with classmates

☐ shows good sportsmanship        ☐ highly developed vocabulary  ☐ completes assigned tasks

☐ does assignments promptly       ☐ motivated to learn       ☐ accepts suggestions/
                                                                criticisms

☐ appears self-confident          ☐ math at or above grade   ☐ frequently contributes to
                                    level                       class

☐ expresses thoughts well         ☐ courteous                ☐ speech flows smoothly

☐ communicates effectively        ☐ achieves at or above grade   ☐ exceptional ability to
  with an individual                level in content areas        organize, store, and
                                                                  retrieve knowledge

☐ proficient in verbal skills     ☐ proficient in language   ☐ communicates basic wants
                                    mechanics                   and needs

☐ communicates effectively in     ☐ skilled in problem solving   ☐ exceptional ability to
  groups                            and reasoning                 acquire knowledge

☐ other:

### Academic Reasons for Referral

☐ difficulty concentrating        ☐ difficulty with written  ☐ abandons difficult tasks
                                    expression

☐ poor reading skills             ☐ frequent reversals of    ☐ deficient in vocabulary
                                    letters/numbers

☐ poor handwriting, organiza-     ☐ difficulty remembering facts,  ☐ difficulty in problem solving
  tion, and legibility              details

☐ difficulty organizing, storing, ☐ deficient in mathematical ☐ achieves below grade level
  or retrieving knowledge           calculations                 in content areas

☐ difficulty acquiring            ☐ difficulty following     ☐ makes excuses
  knowledge                         directions

☐ other:

## Social/Emotional/Behavioral Reasons for Referral

- ☐ excessive daydreaming
- ☐ provokes or aggravates others
- ☐ perseveration
- ☐ poor self-concept
- ☐ requires constant supervision
- ☐ defiant
- ☐ difficulty making transitions
- ☐ disorganized work habits
- ☐ cries easily, oversensitive
- ☐ other

- ☐ ritualistic behaviors— rocking, pacing, etc.
- ☐ irritable or moody
- ☐ fights/bites
- ☐ talks about morbid themes
- ☐ destructive
- ☐ fearful
- ☐ talks excessively, attention seeking, disruptive
- ☐ physically aggressive

- ☐ appears depressed, withdrawn
- ☐ consistent inappropriate emotional responses
- ☐ blames others
- ☐ immature behaviors
- ☐ talks about hurting or killing self or others
- ☐ poor social skills
- ☐ difficulty expressing, demonstrating knowledge
- ☐ temper tantrums

## Physical Reasons for Referral

- ☐ physical complaints
- ☐ chronic allergic conditions
- ☐ impaired hearing
- ☐ impaired vision
- ☐ lacks physical mobility
- ☐ overweight
- ☐ asthma
- ☐ other

- ☐ difficulty copying—paper or board
- ☐ currently takes medication
- ☐ frequently gets hurt
- ☐ seizures
- ☐ lethargic—tired and listless
- ☐ underweight
- ☐ epilepsy

- ☐ wets or soils clothes
- ☐ involuntary muscle spasms
- ☐ lacks age-appropriate self-care
- ☐ poor physical fitness
- ☐ poor gross motor skills
- ☐ poor fine motor coordination

## Referring Person

Print Name _____  Signature _____

Position _____  Date _____

Copyright © 2009 by Corwin Press. All rights reserved. Reprinted from *The School Counselor's Guide to Special Education* by Barbara C. Trolley, Heather S. Haas, and Danielle Campese Patti. Thousand Oaks, CA: Corwin Press, www.corwinpress.com. Reproduction authorized only for the local school site or nonprofit organization that has purchased this book.

FORM 3.2   RTI Form

# GLOBAL CONCEPTS CHARTER SCHOOL

**Response to Intervention**

**Tier 1 Interventions**

Student _____

Teacher _____ Grade _____

| Intervention | Dates Implemented | Results/Comments |
|---|---|---|
| Core Reading Curriculum (Scott Foresman) | | |
| Core Math Program (Scott Foresman) | | |
| Core Science Curriculum (Scott Foresman) | | |
| Core Social Studies Curriculum (McGraw-Hill) | | |
| 90 minutes uninterrupted reading and language instruction 5 days/week | | |
| Parent communication | | |
| Use of and checking planner | | |
| Repeat directions | | |
| Provide extra examples | | |
| Differentiated instruction | | |
| Learning contracts | | |
| Cooperative learning | | |
| Multi-sensory methods | | |
| Consultations among classroom teachers and service providers (specify who, suggestions given, results) | | |
| Curriculum mapping | | |
| Handwriting Without Tears | | |
| Other: | | |
| Other: | | |
| Other: | | |
| Other: | | |

Copyright © 2009 by Corwin Press. All rights reserved. Reprinted from *The School Counselor's Guide to Special Education* by Barbara C. Trolley, Heather S. Haas, and Danielle Campese Patti. Thousand Oaks, CA: Corwin Press, www.corwinpress.com. Reproduction authorized only for the local school site or nonprofit organization that has purchased this book.

**LETTER 3.1**

## PARENTAL CONSENT

**Parental Consent Letter for Initial Student Study Team Review and Testing**

Student: _____

Grade _____ Date _____ Teacher _____

School personnel have recognized the need for gathering more information about your child. The proposed screening(s) and evaluations(s) by qualified personnel will include the use of tests in one or more of the areas below to help determine strengths, areas of concern, and eligibility for special education services.

| Area | Information |
|---|---|
| Physical Health | Basic vision, hearing, motor, medical screening |
| Educational | A variety of assessments measuring academic achievement and special abilities including the Wide Range Achievement Test-4th Edition |
| Social | Social, personal, behavioral, and developmental history including Connor's Rating Scales |
| Communication skills | Understanding and using spoken language—screening |
| Motor | Visual motor integration, eye/hand coordination, gross motor coordination. |
| Adaptive behavior | Behavior that is effective in meeting the natural and social demands in one's environment, including self-help and care |
| Functional Behavioral Assessment | To determine why a student engages in challenging behavior and how the student's behavior relates to the environment. |
| Other: | |

A summary of these evaluations will be shared with you. If you have any questions, please contact: _____
_____ at _____.

## PARENTAL CONSENT

Please sign and return to: _____

___**Yes, I give permission** for my child _____ to receive evaluation services and I understand the description of the tests listed above.

_____     _____     _____
signature                              relationship                              date

___ **No, I do not give permission** for my child _____ to receive evaluation services.

_____     _____     _____
signature                              relationship                              date

Copyright © 2009 by Corwin Press. All rights reserved. Reprinted from *The School Counselor's Guide to Special Education* by Barbara C. Trolley, Heather S. Haas, and Danielle Campese Patti. Thousand Oaks, CA: Corwin Press, www.corwinpress.com. Reproduction authorized only for the local school site or nonprofit organization that has purchased this book.

**FORM 3.3**  SST Intervention Plan

| Student Name | | Date Initiated | |
|---|---|---|---|
| DOB | | Grade | |
| Teacher | | Side | |

☐ BEHAVIORAL    ☐ ACADEMIC    ☐ OTHER _____

**Identified Student Strengths (Use Behavioral Terms):**



**Identified Areas in Need of Improvement (Use Behavioral Terms):**



**Method(s) of data collection (check all that apply):**

| | | | |
|---|---|---|---|
| | Internal Documents | | Classroom Observation |
| | Student Interview | | Parent Interview |
| | Psychological Evaluation | | Reading First Coach Interview |
| | Teacher Consultation | | ESL Teacher Interview |
| | Special Education Consultation | | SST Support Team Consultation |

**Interventions Attempted:**

| | |
|---|---|
| Extended time; shortened tasks; chunking; limited homework; 1:1; small group, etc. | |

☐ BEHAVIORAL    ☐ ACADEMIC    ☐ OTHER _____

| Student | |
|---|---|
| Grade | |
| Date | |

A standard of discipline must be maintained for the protection of all students and to minimize disruption to the educational process.  Nothing in this plan is intended to prevent school authorities from taking whatever emergency or immediate steps necessary to maintain a safe environment.

| Intervention Strategy | Consequences (positive and/ or negative) | Assessment/ Data Collection (method and schedule) | Person(s) Responsible for Implementation | Dates Implemented | Outcome | Continue/ Discontinue |
|---|---|---|---|---|---|---|
|  |  |  |  |  |  |  |
| Differentiated Instruction | Consequences (positive and/ or negative) | Assessment/ Data Collection (method and schedule) | Person(s) Responsible for Implementation | Dates Implemented | Outcome | Continue/ Discontinue |
|  |  |  |  |  |  |  |

**RTI Tier Tracking**

| Date |  |  |  |  |  |  |
|---|---|---|---|---|---|---|
| # of Weeks with SST |  |  |  |  |  |  |
| Tier |  |  |  |  |  |  |
| (C)  Continue with SST services<br>(F)  Continue with SST& a FASST<br>(D)  Discontinue with SST services |  |  |  |  |  |  |

Copyright © 2009 by Corwin Press. All rights reserved. Reprinted from *The School Counselor's Guide to Special Education* by Barbara C. Trolley, Heather S. Haas, and Danielle Campese Patti. Thousand Oaks, CA: Corwin Press, www.corwinpress.com. Reproduction authorized only for the local school site or nonprofit organization that has purchased this book.

## Relationship of AIS to Special Education Programs:

### *Education Law, Sections 4401 (1) (2)*

Academic Intervention Services are additional general education instructional and/or support services that assist students in meeting state learning standards. AIS are provided in addition to, and must not supplant, special education services. Because AIS are general education services, they should not be indicated on the individualized education program (IEP). Special education services are specially designed individualized or group instruction or special services or programs designed to meet the student's unique needs that result from his/her disability and enable the student to participate and progress in the general education curriculum. The Committee on Special Education (CSE), with parental input, makes recommendations for special education and related services that are listed on the student's individualized education program. Examples of special education services include consultant teacher services, resource room, or related services. The CSE cannot recommend that a student with a disability receive AIS.

## Meaning of the Phrase,"To the extent consistent with the Individualized Education Program"

"To the extent consistent with the individualized education program (IEP)" means appropriate accommodations and supports must be provided when AIS are implemented for students with disabilities to assure that these students benefit from AIS. For example, if a student's IEP indicates that a specific adaptive material, assistive technology device, or curriculum modification is to be provided, then these same accommodations or supports must be provided when AIS are delivered.

## Role of the Committee on Special Education in Relation to AIS

The CSE must ensure that staff providing AIS are informed of their responsibilities related to the specific accommodations, modifications, and supports that must be provided for the student in accordance with the IEP. In addition, staff must have access to the student's IEP. This ensures that supports and accommodations listed on the IEP are consistently applied with the provision of AIS. This does not require a meeting of the CSE. If a student is determined to need AIS and has already been identified as a student with a disability, school personnel may determine that a review of the student's IEP by the CSE is needed. For example, a student scores below the designated state performance level in English Language Arts and is receiving special education service to address his/her need in reading. In this case, a review by the CSE of the student's IEP may be warranted to coordinate the additional reading instruction.

## AIS Not on a Student's IEP

AIS are general education services and should not be indicated on the IEP. However, the scores the student received on the local or state assessments that identified a student with a disability as needing AIS may be indicated on the IEP under present levels of performance.

# RESPONSE TO INTERVENTION (RTI)

IDEA 2004 specifically states:

Notwithstanding section 607(b), when determining whether a child has a specific learning disability as defined in section 602, a local education agency shall not be required to take into consideration whether a child has a severe discrepancy between achievement and intellectual ability in oral expression, listening comprehension, written expression, basic reading skill, reading comprehension, mathematical calculation, or mathematical reasoning [20 U.S.C. 1414 (b)(6)(A)].

IDEA 2004 indicates changes that further align the law to No Child Left Behind (NCLB) and states, in part:

In making a determination of eligibility under paragraph (4)(A), a child shall not be determined to be a child with a disability if the determinant factor for such determination is-(A) lack of appropriate instruction in reading, including the essential components of reading instruction (as defined in section 1208(3) of the Elementary and Secondary Education Act of 1965 (which is the NCLB) [20 U.S.C. 1414(b)(5)(A)].

## What is RTI?

"The process of implementing high-quality, scientifically validated instructional practices based on learner needs, monitoring student progress, and adjusting instruction based on the student's response" (Bender & Shores, 2007).

RTI is a problem-solving process with an integrated data collection and analysis system to provide teachers with the necessary tools to improve the delivery of instruction and ensure student success. The primary goal of RTI is to use data to drive instruction, not to classify or label a student. Progress monitoring is a scientifically based practice used to assess student's academic performance and to evaluate the effectiveness of instruction. Data is to be used as a tool to provide appropriate and meaningful instruction. Research-based strategies and interventions rule out inadequate instruction and better determine the presence of a disabling condition. Differentiated instruction is the accommodations provided to students. Instruction strategies and CBM delivery of instruction are the core components of Response to Intervention. Fidelity of instruction ensures that the curriculum-based measurements are delivered accurately and systematically.

RTI is a multi-tiered model of instruction/intervention. Most commonly used is a three-tier model, although some four-tier models are also implemented, with the special education referral beginning at the fourth tier.

RTI measures a student's levels of performance based on comparisons with same age peers. After receiving instruction from highly qualified teachers at the first tier, a student that demonstrates difficulty learning as evidenced by low scores on yearly assessments or at-risk behaviors would be referred to the second tier. At the second tier, students receive remediation in small groups, with curriculum-based measurements to determine if the interventions are successful. If not, the student will move to Tier 3 and receive further differentiated instruction. This new model of assessment provides early services and interventions to students struggling academically that were not necessarily provided in the typical discrepancy model.

According to Barnett, Daly, Jones, and Lentz (2004), the current discrepancy model waits for children to fail before providing appropriate interventions. The RTI model provides meaningful services prior to special education based on scientifically valid interventions and continuous progress monitoring. Fuchs (2003) states,

Perhaps the most feasible way of measuring student responsiveness to intervention is to test students following intervention and then apply a standard to the post-treatment score for differentiating between children who responded to the intervention (thereby showing the absence of disability) and those who proved unresponsive (for whom the presence of disability is inferred)

The goal of the federal government is to have Response to Intervention implemented in all schools by 2012 (Bender & Shores, 2007).

**Figure 3.2**     RTI Pyramid

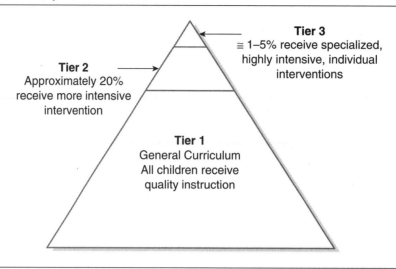

## Core features of RTI

1. high quality classroom intervention
2. research-based instruction
3. classroom performance measures
4. universal screening
5. continuous progress monitoring
6. research-based interventions
7. progress-monitoring during interventions
8. fidelity measures

## RTI process should include the following (2004 Ld Roundtable)

1. high quality, research-based instruction and behavior supports in general education
2. scientific, research-based interventions focused specifically on individual student difficulties and delivered with appropriate intensity
3. use of a collaborative approach by school staff for development, implementation, and monitoring of the intervention process
4. data-based documentation reflecting continuous monitoring of student performance and progress during interventions
5. documentation of parental involvement throughout the process
6. documentation that the timelines described in the federal regulations are adhered to
7. systematic assessment and documentation that the interventions used were implemented with fidelity

# THREE-TIER MODEL

## Tier 1: Research-supported teaching strategies already in place to provide quality instruction to all students:

*All students receive quality instruction with teaching methods such as:*

- Cooperative learning
- Parent communication

- Preferential seating
- Curriculum mapping
- Use of planners/check planners
- Consultations between teachers and related service providers

*Proactive and Preventative*

*Assessments given three times/year to determine
the students in need of more structured interventions*

## Tier 2: Evidence-based teaching strategies provided in the general education curriculum to those students identified as the lowest 20%

*Students who score in the bottom 20% of the general education
assessments receive specialized interventions including, but not limited to:*

- Program monitoring
- Group AIS services
- Modified instruction
- Testing accommodations (except on state-mandated tests)
- Small group instruction
- Individual behavior plan

*Specific instruction for approx. 10 weeks
(generally, not more than a grading period)*

*Students are assessed and data is collected
twice per month (progress monitoring)*

- Students responding to interventions may remain at Tier 2 or return to Tier 1
- Students not responding to the interventions offered at Tier 2 may be eligible to move to Tier 3

## Tier 3: Scientifically based research, intensive, systematic specialized instruction is provided

*Students experiencing difficulties who have
not responded to Tier 1 or Tier 2 interventions*

*Specialized, individual instruction including, but not limited to:*

- Up to 60 minutes supplemental instruction per day, as recommended for reading
- Direct involvement with service providers (e.g., PT, OT, speech, counseling)
- FBA/BIP

*Assessments given and data is collected
one to three times per week (progress monitoring)*

- Students responding to the interventions at Tier 3 may return to Tier 2
- Students not responding to the interventions at Tier 3 may be eligible for a CSE referral through the school's Child Study Team

## Sample ways to increase intensity of interventions or instruction

- Tier three interventions should not be differentiated instruction, but rather more and more intensive instruction.
- Reduce the size of the group

**Figure 3.3**     RTI Flow Chart

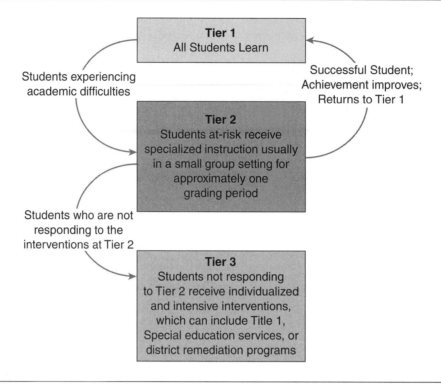

- Increase time spent in intervention instruction
- Change materials so they are more systematic, sequential, multisensory, or provide more repetitions
- Provide more examples
- Provide a wider range of examples
- Break a task into smaller steps
- Spend longer time on a task

## Benefits of RTI

- Preventative and proactive approach means students do not need to wait for interventions
- Can help to reduce the number of referrals to the CSE
- Limits the amount of unnecessary testing that provides little to no instructional support
- Continues to provide quality education for all students
- Engages all stakeholders in providing opportunities for student success—parents, general educators, special educators, related service providers, and school counselors
- Provides multiple means of instruction and assessment for all learners with different strengths

## Goals

- Deliver evidence-based interventions
- Use student's response to interventions as a basis for determining instructional needs and intensity
- Replace, or at the very least, augment the IQ/discrepancy model of classification
- Provide a team-based approach to student success
- Increase the success rate of students in the general education setting

- Provide early intervention to struggling students and reduce the number of referrals to special education
- Allow for and provide differentiated means of assessments to include informal assessments, work samples, report cards that indicate effort, standardized tests, parent, teacher and/or student rating scales, curriculum based measurement, and behavioral and academic logs

## Progress monitoring

- Accurate, current data needed to make important decisions about a student's educational program
- The baseline phase is where data is collected prior to any interventions
- The intervention phase is the time frame of the selected intervention and data collection
- The Response to Intervention phase is where progress is monitored over a predetermined amount of time and after the interventions have been fully implemented

## Curriculum-based measurement

- Standardized tests that meet professional standards for reliability and validity
- Short and inexpensive to administer
- Can be done on a weekly basis
- Measures basic skills such as reading fluency, comprehension, spelling, mathematics, and written expression
- Many online resources, such as:

Dynamic Indicators of Basic Early Literacy Skills (DIBELS) http://dibels.uoretgon.edu
AIMSweb http://www.aimsweb.com
Monitoring Basic Skills Progress (MBSP) http://www.proedinc.com
Yearly Progress Pro http://mhdigitallearning.com

- Intervention Central is a Web-based support that provides countless information on curriculum-based measurement, academic intervention, behavioral intervention, peer-tutoring programs, and user-friendly documents to support your school's RTI program. http://interventioncentral.org

# FUNCTIONAL BEHAVIOR ASSESSMENT

## Definition

Functional behavioral assessment is the process of determining why a student engages in challenging behavior and how the student's behavior relates to the environment. Functional assessments describe the relationship between a skill or performance problem and variables that contribute to its occurrence. Functional behavioral assessments can provide the CSE with information to develop a hypothesis as to:

- why the student engages in the behavior;
- when the student is most likely to demonstrate the behavior; and
- situations in which the behavior is least likely to occur.

This type of assessment often involves reviewing curriculum, instructional, and motivational variables in relation to a student's behavior and/or examining classroom arrangements, individuals present, physical health issues, instructional subject and work demands (NASDSE, 1998).

## Components of a functional behavioral assessment

A functional behavioral assessment should minimally include the following components:

- Identification of the problem behavior.
- Definition of the behavior in concrete terms.
- Identification of the contextual factors that contribute to the behavior (including affective and cognitive factors).
- Formulation of a hypothesis regarding the general conditions under which a behavior usually occurs and probable consequences that serve to maintain it.

## Assessment techniques

A variety of techniques are available to conduct a functional behavioral assessment including, but not limited to:

- indirect assessment (e.g., structured interviews, review of existing evaluation information).
- direct assessment (e.g., standardized assessments or checklists, or observing and recording situational factors surrounding the behavior).
- data analysis (e.g., a comparison and analysis of data to determine whether or not there are patterns associated with the behavior).

# GUIDELINES FOR ASSESSING AND ADDRESSING BEHAVIORS

## Functional behavioral assessment

Develop a plan to conduct a functional behavioral assessment of the student's behavior or review an existing functional behavioral assessment:

- Identify the behavior that needs to be assessed.
- Determine how the function of the student's behavior and the circumstances and factors associated with both the occurrence and nonoccurrence of the behavior will be assessed.
- Determine who will be responsible for conducting the planned assessment.
- Determine who will coordinate the written report of the assessment.
- Establish a date for the assessments to be completed.

## Behavioral intervention plan

Develop or review an existing behavioral intervention plan based on the results of the functional behavioral assessment:

- Identify the behavior.
- Define the behavior in concrete terms.
- Select supports and interventions to address, as appropriate
  - antecedent and setting events
  - alternative skills instruction
  - consequence strategies that build skills and reduce problem behaviors
  - long-term prevention
  - support for team members
- Identify resources available, or that need to become available, to implement the plan.
- Identify who will do what, when, and how.
- Determine a plan for monitoring the effectiveness of the supports and interventions.
- Develop a timetable for the review and monitoring of the plan.

Determine what, if any, changes need to be made to a student's IEP and/or behavioral intervention plan as a result of review. (For samples of completed FBAs, see Resource B. For samples of completed BIPs, see Resource C.)

*(Text continued on page 43)*

## LETTER 3.2

### Sample Consent Letter for FBA

**Consent for Functional Behavior Assessment**

I understand that my child, _____, was referred to the Child Study Team (CST) for determination of interventions strategies to support his/her needs. The team would like to conduct a functional behavior assessment (FBA), and as a result, develop a behavior plan. An FBA is the process of determining why a student engages in challenging behavior and how the student's behavior relates to the environment. This type of assessment often involves reviewing curriculum, instructional, and motivational variables in relation to a student's behavior and/or examining classroom arrangements, individuals present, physical health issues, instructional subject and work demands. The process may involve data collection methods of reviewing records, parent/teacher/student interviews, classroom observations, and/or examining assessment information.

I understand the information presented above, and give consent for—*Enter school name*—to conduct a functional behavior assessment, and to develop a behavior plan. By signing below, I am granting consent for this action:

Student Name _____

Student Date of Birth _____

Parent/Guardian Signature _____ Date _____

*Adapted from Springville Griffith Institute Central School District

**Consent for Functional Behavior Assessment**

I understand that my child, _____, was referred to the Child Study Team (CST) for determination of interventions strategies to support his/her needs, and a functional behavior assessment was recommended. I understand that the team began conducting the functional behavior assessment (FBA), but requests additional time to complete this evaluation and to develop the behavior plan.

By signing below, I am granting consent for this action:

Student Name _____

Student Date of Birth _____

Parent/Guardian Signature _____ Date _____

*Adapted from Springville Griffith Institute Central School District

Copyright © 2009 by Corwin Press. All rights reserved. Reprinted from *The School Counselor's Guide to Special Education* by Barbara C. Trolley, Heather S. Haas, and Danielle Campese Patti. Thousand Oaks, CA: Corwin Press, www.corwinpress.com. Reproduction authorized only for the local school site or nonprofit organization that has purchased this book.

# FUNCTIONAL BEHAVIOR ASSESSMENT

**Global Concepts Charter School**
**1001 Ridge Road**
**Lackawanna, NY 14218**

Student Name _____ Date Initiated _____

DOB _____ Grade/Teacher _____

Classification: _____ Program Placement: _____

**Identified Student Strengths (Use Behavioral Terms):**

**Identified Selected Problem Behavior (Use Behavioral Terms):**

**Identification of Targeted Behavior (observable, measurable, and well defined—what is the specific behavior that you want to increase or decrease):**

**Method(s) of data collection (check all that apply):**

|  | Internal Documents |  | Classroom Observation |
|---|---|---|---|
|  | Student Interview |  | Parent Interview |
|  | Psychological Evaluation |  | Educational Evaluation |
|  | Teacher Consultation |  | Counselor Interview |
|  | Other: |  | Other: |

List target behavior that most interferes with the student's functioning in the educational setting. Estimate or directly observe the frequency, intensity, and duration of each:

**Baseline Data**

| Behavior | Frequency | Intensity | Duration |
|---|---|---|---|
|  |  |  |  |

Observe and identify the environmental factors that seem to cause and maintain the targeted behavior. List the consequences that have been attempted:

| Settings<br>*Where does the target behavior seem to occur* |  |
|---|---|
| Interventions Attempted<br>*Planned ignoring, curriculum modification, classroom modification, time away, reprimands, ISS/OSS, physical intervention, parent conference, superintendent's hearing, etc.* |  |
| Educational Impact<br>*How is the target behavior disrupting the educational process of the student or other students* |  |

**What seems to be the function of the target behavior?**

| | Function | |
|---|---|---|
| | Affective Regulation/Emotional Reactivity<br>*Anxiety, depression, anger, poor self-concept* | |
| | Cognitive Distortion *Distorted thoughts, inaccurate attributions, negative self-statements, erroneous interpretation of events* | |
| | Reinforcement<br>*Antecedent*<br>*Behavior*<br>*Consequence* | |
| | Modeling<br>*Poor decision-making skills, ineffective problem-solving skills, delayed or maladaptive emotional development, insufficient coping strategies* | |
| | Family Issues<br>*Poor social skills* | |
| | Psychological/Constitutional<br>*Physiological, personality characteristics, developmental disabilities, temperament, inadequate attention span, poor impulse control* | |
| | Communicate Need<br>*Inability to communicate with verbal cues* | |
| | Curriculum/Instruction<br>*Instruction, curriculum, environment, poor academic skills, cognitive ability* | |
| | Love and Belonging<br>*The need to be loved and accepted by groups, families, and loved ones* | |
| | Power<br>*The need for achievement and feeling worthwhile; desire for respect and recognition within a group; competitive desire to win* | |
| | Survival/Safety<br>*The need for things that keep us psychologically and physiologically healthy and safe such as food, clothing, shelter* | |
| | Freedom<br>*The need to form our own space; sense of independence and autonomy* | |
| | Fun<br>*The need to enjoy ourselves and seek pleasure* | |

**Hypothesis Statement**

Write a hypothesis regarding the function of the behavior.

*When x (trigger) occurs, the student does y (behavior) in order to z (function).*

Copyright © 2009 by Corwin Press. All rights reserved. Reprinted from *The School Counselor's Guide to Special Education* by Barbara C. Trolley, Heather S. Haas, and Danielle Campese Patti. Thousand Oaks, CA: Corwin Press, www.corwinpress.com. Reproduction authorized only for the local school site or nonprofit organization that has purchased this book.

**FORM 3.5**   Sample BIP

## BEHAVIOR INTERVENTION PLAN

Student: _____

Grade: _____

Date: _____

The team recognizes that this student may manifest behavior that does not conform to the usual rules and regulations of the school. However, it also recognizes that a standard of discipline must be maintained for the protection of all students and to minimize disruption to the educational process. Therefore, this Behavior Intervention Plan has been developed. Nothing in this plan is intended to prevent school authorities from taking whatever emergency or immediate steps necessary to maintain a safe environment.

| Target Behavior | |
|---|---|
| Replacement Behavior | |

| Intervention Strategy | Consequences (positive and/or negative) | Assessment/ Data Collection (method and schedule) | Person(s) Responsible for Implementation | Dates Implemented | Outcome |
|---|---|---|---|---|---|
| | | | | | |
| | | | | | |
| | | | | | |

*Adapted from Global Concepts Charter School

Copyright © 2009 by Corwin Press. All rights reserved. Reprinted from *The School Counselor's Guide to Special Education* by Barbara C. Trolley, Heather S. Haas, and Danielle Campese Patti. Thousand Oaks, CA: Corwin Press, www.corwinpress.com. Reproduction authorized only for the local school site or nonprofit organization that has purchased this book.

**Table 3.2**    Sample Intervention Strategies

- Replace problem behaviors with appropriate behaviors that serve the same function as inappropriate ones
- Increase rates of existing appropriate behaviors
- Make changes to the environment that eliminate the possibility of engaging in inappropriate behavior
- Providing the supports necessary for the child to use the appropriate behaviors

**Academic**

| Intervention Strategy | Consequences (Positive and/or negative) |
|---|---|
| Offer opportunities to assist or mentor peers in classroom setting | Increase peer acceptance and contacts |
| Select one activity where he may provide academic support to a peer | Increase positive social interactions with peers; increase self-esteem |
| Provide choices of classroom assignments | Increase interest in on-task behavior |
| Establish short increments of time to complete tasks | Provide a sense of accomplishment<br>Encourage motivation<br>Provide enjoyable alternative task for reward |
| Shortened tasks | Provide a sense of accomplishment<br>Encourage motivation |
| Modify curriculum for below-average reading skills | Provide opportunity for academic success |
| Encourage student to ask questions, clarify tasks, and immediately ask for teacher support | Avoid becoming overwhelmed with difficult tasks; increase self-control |
| Chunk material into small increments | Provide opportunities for success<br>Provide clear beginning and ending of assignments |
| Have student begin class with a review task that he can be successful with, then have student complete more difficult tasks in progression | Increase sense of accomplishment<br>Increase positive feelings of self |
| Check for understanding | Consistent academic support |
| Modify curriculum to include interesting and challenging activities<br>Provide enhancement work in particular class | Encourage above-average cognitive skills |

*(Continued)*

**Table 3.2** (Continued)

**Behavioral**

| Intervention Strategy | Consequences (positive and/or negative) |
|---|---|
| Reinforce positive behavior by offering frequent praise and encouragement | Decrease the frequency of the possibility of engaging in negative behavior |
| Will be given classroom duties or special tasks on a daily or weekly basis | Positively engaged in classroom activities and positive interactions with peers and staff; increase self-esteem |
| Time out within/outside classroom | Time away to regain control |
| 1:1 academic and behavioral support from staff when needed | Personal attention to meet individual needs |
| Alternate working environment within the school | Time away from environmental stimuli; individual needs met |
| Select student to assist peers or teacher | Avoid negative peers<br>Improve focus on tasks |
| Provide student to be in a positive leadership role | Eliminate following negative peers |
| STOP, THINK, LISTEN—remind student to stop and think about actions and consequences, and listen to and comply with staff requests | Time to process and act upon request or demand |
| Provide skill-building opportunities to model and teach effective problem-solving, communication and conflict resolution skills | Experience more healthy and satisfying interpersonal relationships<br>Develop improved self-esteem<br>Enjoy academic success |
| Discuss healthy methods and times to get emotional and social needs met | Increase self-awareness |
| Provide structured daily activity immediately at the beginning of class (bell work, routine task) | Immediate positive engagement |
| Help student recognize the physical signs of anger | Proactive approach to de-escalation |
| Incorporate relaxation skills; mental imagery; positive self-talk; use of stress balls, counting to 10, etc. | Relax the student<br>Increase self-awareness<br>Increase self-control and coping strategies |
| Provide problem-solving tasks<br>List possible solutions to a problem<br>Determine likely consequences of each solution | Improve internal locus of control<br>Decrease crises |

| Intervention Strategy | Consequences (positive and/or negative) |
|---|---|
| Provide opportunities to practice communication skills, i.e., taking turns, listening, appropriate body language, normal tone of voice, eliminate profanity | Improve interpersonal skills |
| Provide visual cues of goals set by the student | Reminders of goals |
| Physical removal from frustrating peer conflicts<br>Face wall, time away, quiet area | Time and space to calm down |
| Offer clear specific expectations before beginning group work/assignment | Proactive approach to decreasing negative behaviors by providing the students with information |
| Use student name to positively reinforce behavior | Improve self-esteem |
| Planned time-outs with specific counselors, psychologist, or staff | Proactive approach to help student cope with stress and act with self-control |
| Talk to and be listened to by specific staff | Student feels respected |
| Offer choices whenever possible to correct student behavior or class work (i.e., "you can do __ or __ ") | Develop internal locus of control; provide opportunity for academic/behavioral success |
| Provide student 10 min. to calm down and do not talk to student during student time | Emotional space away from conflict/stressor; allows time to identify emotions |
| Weekly 5-minute meetings to check in with student | Reinforcement of achievements<br>1:1 attention<br>Positive reinforcement |
| Acknowledgement of successes | Improve confidence and esteem |
| Discuss with student antecedents and consequences of antisocial behaviors | Decrease antisocial behaviors and increase empathy |
| Model appropriate social skills and assist student in identifying alternatives to the target behaviors | Decrease antisocial behavior<br>Provides alternative methods to get needs met |
| Hold student accountable for behavior | Clear understanding of natural consequences to decrease antisocial behavior |
| Provide opportunities for positive leadership (classroom duties, after-school activities) | Improve opportunities for prosocial behavior |
| Close supervision at all times | Decrease antisocial behavior |
| Gradually increase the time between student's request/demand and the teach student response (i.e., ask student to wait for assistance for 30 sec., then one min., etc., then praise student for waiting appropriately | Increases ability to be patient<br>Encourages internalization of a more positive concept<br>Increases awareness of appropriate social structure<br>Proactive approach to de-escalation |

*(Continued)*

**Table 3.2** (Continued)

| Intervention Strategy | Consequences (positive and/or negative) |
|---|---|
| State request as a directive, not a choice; (i.e., "you need to…" instead of "would you…") | Offers firm, clear expectations<br>Reduces opportunity for debate |
| Allow student to make up work at a later date due to upsetting subject matter | Reduce anxiety while maintaining academic standards |
| Allow student opportunity to contact guidance | Talking to a trusted adult to reduce negative emotions |
| Allow student time away from class and the opportunity to make up class work at a later time if he expresses the need to talk to a trusted adult | Time and space from emotional stressors<br>Time to process difficulties/problems and solve for solutions |
| Give student the choice of time away from the stressor or time to speak with a trusted adult | Time and space to evaluate an appropriate response; improve decision-making skills; improve internal locus of control |
| Provide 2-minute warnings before transitions | Allows time to prepare for transition and process behavioral expectations |
| Teach healthy vs. unhealthy relationships | Clear understanding of appropriate social contacts<br>Improve interpersonal relationships |
| Pair with positive peers | Provide positive peer influences and modeling for behaviors |
| Frequently acknowledge successes | Improve confidence and self-esteem |
| Offer student a laminated pass to guidance or specific staff member | Provide student with an "out" to speak with staff and regain emotional control |
| Structure student self-monitoring | Student can take responsibility for behaviors and feel in control<br>Increase desired behaviors |
| Cool down time after exciting activities (gym, lunch, etc.) | Time and space to regain emotional control |
| Develop classroom-based communication alternatives (hand signals, signs, etc.) | Allow student to communicate needs in an appropriate manner |
| Development of social skills monitoring and reward program to include recognition of performance at school or home | Increase self-esteem<br>Develop internal locus of control |
| Development of social skills program targeting cooperation, assertion, responsibility, empathy, and self-control including:<br>individual coaching<br>classroomwide instruction and activities<br>daily monitoring<br>tangible rewards for achieving daily goals<br>moment-by-moment praise of desired behavior<br>daily reporting of progress | Develop/improve social skills<br>Develop/improve interpersonal skills |

| Intervention Strategy | Consequences (positive and/or negative) |
|---|---|
| Bibliotherapy—provide information regarding specific issues (ADHD, bipolar disorder, learning disability, etc.) | Provide accurate information for student awareness |
| Provision of rewards for meeting work initiation, work completion, attendance, etc. | Encouragement to complete tasks Begin to develop internal motivation by providing external rewards |
| Model appropriate coping skills and assist student in identifying alternatives to the target behaviors | Improved communication of feelings and needs |
| Discuss with student antecedents and consequences of poor decisions | Decrease unsafe behaviors and increase safety |
| Planned time-outs with specific counselors, psychologist, or staff to discuss future goals and consequences of choices | Proactive approach to help student cope with stress and act with self-control |

Note: This list is not exhaustive. Interventions may be altered, changed, or combined to best serve the student's needs.

Reading and interpreting test scores is usually the responsibility of the school psychologist. An understanding of standard scores and percentile rank scores will allow teachers, counselors, and advocates to interpret the meanings for parents and students in a manner that is clear and concise. The following chart explains the types of assessments as well as an explanation of the different types of scores.

*Weekly student support meetings are held to discuss concerns. You are present for a meeting regarding Janet, a sixteen-year-old freshman student. Janet has been retained twice; once in first grade and again in seventh. She struggles in class to keep up with the homework due to a tenacious home life. There has been suspected abuse since she was in elementary school although many calls to report concerns have been deemed unfounded by local authorities. She was referred to the team because she was recently classified as learning disabled and receives the support of a consultant teacher. The consultant teacher feels that she is just wasting time with Janet. She says that Janet is a low-average student but doesn't require special education intervention. At the CSE meeting, people argued because her classification was a result of a discrepancy between her performance IQ and her achievement. The consultant teacher is requesting a functional behavioral assessment be conducted to find the root of Janet's problem. She accuses the CSE as operating like a Band-Aid rather than as a diagnostician.*

- What is the difference between RTI and the discrepancy model?
- A functional behavioral assessment is considered to be an intervention on which tier of RTI?
- What is a counselor's responsibility when it comes to advocating for a student with special needs?
- Discuss the process that Janet's team should have used in determining her educational program.

## Activity

Based on Case "Janet," develop assessment plan.

**Table 3.3**   Common Assessments

---

**Common Assessments Used by School Psychologists,
Classroom Teachers, and Clinicians**

**Intelligence Tests**

**Definitions**:  A test designed to measure a person's mental aptitude or inherent ability. The measure is taken and a numerical score is assigned and then compared to others who've taken the same test. (http://www.alleydog.com)

The first of the standardized norm-referenced tests was developed during the nineteenth century. Traditional psychologists believe that neurological and genetic factors underlie "intelligence" and that scoring the performance of certain intellectual tasks can provide assessors with a measurement of general intelligence. There is a substantial body of research that suggests that IQ tests measure only certain analytical skills, missing many areas of human endeavor considered to be intelligent behavior. IQ is considered by some to be fixed or static; whereas an increasing number of researchers are finding that intelligence is an ongoing process that continues to change throughout life. (http://www.newhorizons.org)

**Achievement Tests**

**Definition**:   An achievement test is a standardized test that is designed to measure an individual's level of knowledge in a particular area. Unlike an aptitude test which measures a person's ability to learn something, an achievement test focuses specifically on how much a person knows about a specific topic or area such as math, geography, or science.(http://www.alleydog.com).

An achievement test measures the individual's level of learning or degree of accomplishments in a subject or task (Aiken, 2000; Erford, 2003).

Both intelligence and achievement assessment scores will be included in a school psychologist's initial report when diagnosing based on the discrepancy model.

| | *Intelligence* | *Achievement* |
|---|---|---|
| **Title** | *Wechsler Abbreviated Scale of Intelligence (WASI)* | *Wechsler Individual Achievement Test – II (WIAT)* |
| **URL** | http://harcourtassessment.com | http://harcourtassessment.com |
| **Description** | Individually administered, standardized, normed, and validated short form of both the Wechsler Intelligence Scale for Children and the Wechsler Adult Intelligence Scale. | Source of information about an individual's achievement skills and problem-solving abilities. Abbreviated form available. High validity and reliability. |
| **Age** | Children–Adult | Elementary through secondary school; Adults |
| **Administration Time** | Approximately 30 minutes | Approximately 60 minutes |

**Table 3.3** (Continued)

|  | *Intelligence* | *Achievement* |
|---|---|---|
| **Areas Measured** | The four subtests of the WASI, i.e., Vocabulary, Block Design, Similarities, and Matrix Reasoning, tap various facets of intelligence, such as verbal knowledge, visual information processing, spatial and nonverbal reasoning, and crystallized and fluid intelligence. | Measures academic achievement abilities in the areas of reading, comprehension, math, spelling, writing, and listening comprehension. |
| **Title** | *Wechsler Intelligence Scale for Children – Fourth Edition (WISC-IV)* | *Woodcock Johnson III (WJ,III)* |
| **URL** | http://harcourtassessment.com | http://www.riverpub.com |
| **Description** | Consists of 10 core subtests each measuring a different facet of intelligence. | Measures academic achievement in 7 areas |
| **Age** | 6–16.11 years of age | 2–90+ |
| **Administration Time** | 65–80 minutes | 55–65 minutes |
| **Areas Measured** | Performance on these various measures is summarized into five composite scores: Verbal Comprehension (measures verbal abilities utilizing reasoning, comprehension, and conceptualization), Perceptual Reasoning (measures perceptual reasoning and organization), Working Memory (measures attention, concentration, and working memory), Processing Speed (measures speed of mental or graphomotor processing), and a Full Scale IQ (measures overall cognitive). | Basic skills, reading fluency, math calculation, math reasoning |
| **Title** | *Stanford-Binet Intelligence Scales (SB5), Fifth Edition* | *Wide Range Achievement Test – 4th edition (WRAT)* |
| **URL** | http://www.riverpub.com | http://www.slosson.com |

*(Continued)*

**Table 3.3** (Continued)

|  | *Intelligence* | *Achievement* |
|---|---|---|
| **Description** | Individually administered assessment of intelligence and cognitive abilities. | A brief, individually administered achievement test containing three subtests: Reading, Spelling, and Arithmetic. Provides standard scores that can be read in correlation with most achievement and cognitive testing. High validity and reliability. |
| **Age** | 2–85+ years old | Ages 5–75 years old |
| **Administration Time** | Approximately 5 minutes per test | Approximately 15 minutes |
| **Areas Measured** | Fluid Reasoning, Knowledge, Quantitative Reasoning, Visual-Spatial Processing, and Working Memory. | Measures academic achievement abilities in the areas of math, spelling, and word reading. |

**Behavior scales**

**Definition:** Rating scales consist of lists of characteristics or behaviors to observe and of evaluative scales on which to indicate the degree to which they occur (Schmidt, 2003).

|  | *Behavior Scale* | *Behavior Scale* |
|---|---|---|
| **Title** | *Conners Comprehensive Behavior Rating Scale (CBRS)* | *Behavior Assessment System for Children – 2nd Edition (BASC-2)* |
| **URL** | www.mhs.com/conners | http://ags.pearsonassessments.com |

|  | *Behavior Scale* | *Behavior Scale* |
|---|---|---|
| **Description** | Direct and clear links to the DSM-IV-TR and the Individuals with Disabilities Education Improvement Act 2004 (IDEA 2004)<br>– Spanish versions are available for parent and self-report forms.<br>– Straightforward administration, scoring, and reports<br>– Excellent reliability and validity | A comprehensive set of rating scales and forms including the Teacher Rating Scales (TRS), Parent Rating Scales (PRS), Self-Report of Personality (SRP), Student Observation System (SOS), and Structured Developmental History (SDH). Together, they help you understand the behaviors and emotions of children and adolescents. |
| **Age** | 6–18 for parent and teacher scales; 8–18 for self report | 2:0 through 21:11 |
| **Administration Time** | varies – 200 questions on a Likert scale – software to score results is user friendly | 10–20 minutes (TRS and PRS), 30 minutes (SRP) |
| **Areas Measured** | Assesses the following disorders:<br>– Generalized anxiety disorder<br>– Separation anxiety disorder<br>– Social phobia<br>– Obsessive compulsive disorder<br>– Major depressive episode<br>– Manic episode<br>– Autistic disorder<br>– Asperger's disorder<br>– Attention-deficit/ hyperactivity disorder<br>– Oppositional defiant disorder<br>– Conduct disorder | aggression, anxiety, depression, conduct disorders, hyperactivity, learning difficulties, social skills, communication, withdrawal |

*(Continued)*

**Table 3.4** Standardized Test Interpretations

**Criterion-Referenced Test**: provides information on a test taker's mastery of a certain skill (e.g., student has mastered algebra skills; student received a 90% on history exam)

**Norm-Referenced Test**: provides information on a test taker's relative rank or standing and is determined by comparing the test taker to a normative sample (small, representative cross section of group being tested) based on the normal curve

| Standard Score | Percentile | Grade Equivalent Scores | Stanines |
|---|---|---|---|
| converted from raw scores to indicate how far above or below the average (mean) that a student's score falls | indicate a student's rank relative to the standard sample, using a hypothetical group of 100—a student who is at the 25th percentile has scored as well as or better than 25% of the students in the norm group | indicate that a student has attained the same score (not skill level) as an average student of that age or grade—this means that a 12th grade student who achieved a Grade Equivalent Score of 7.0 got the same number of questions correct that an average 7th grade student did—this does not mean that the skill level is at 7th grade because the content or type of questions the students could or could not answer is not indicated | essentially a group of percentile ranks, with the entire group of scores divided into 9 parts, with the largest number of individuals falling in the middle stanines and less falling at the extremes |

Wechsler classification for standard scores are as follows (Wechsler Adult Intelligence Scale—Fourth Edition):

| Classification | IQ & Achievement Score (Standard Score) | Percentile Rank | Stanines |
|---|---|---|---|
| Very Superior | 130 and above | 96+ | 9 |
| Superior | 120–129 | 75–95 | 8 |
| High Average | 110–119 | 61–74 | 6–7 |
| Average | 90–109 | 31–60 | 4–5 |
| Low Average | 80–89 | 16–30 | 3 |
| Borderline | 70–79 | 5–15 | 2 |
| Extremely Low or Intellectually Deficient | 69 and below | 1–4 | 1 |

# Questions for Reflection

1. What are the specific steps that need to be taken in your school and by whom before a referral for assessment is made?

2. Who is part of your study team? How is this decided? What are their specific roles?

3. What is the school counselors' role at your school in terms of assessment process?

4. With which assessment tools are you most comfortable?

5. What are the primary concerns that parents typically have in terms of the assessment referral process? How are they alleviated?

6. What aspects of classroom observation are most important to document and why?

7. What part of the assessment process at your school is the weakest? The strongest?

# Process and Services

## *Preschool*

In schools with primary-age children, it is important for school counselors to be involved in the preschool process for special education, the Committee on Preschool Special Education (CPSE).

Important recommendations will be made at meetings regarding placement, services, and interventions. Early interventions are key in helping students achieve success in school. Counselors play a role in delivering these services and in making important recommendations. Often, the arena of CPSE is an area with which school counselors are unfamiliar. Counselors need to be aware of a student's history in order to provide appropriate interventions at the school-age level.

The CPSE serves the educational needs of children ages 3 years until they attend school. This committee differs from the CSE, which serves school-age children. One main difference in these committees is that the governing body for CPSE is the county in which the child resides. Each county has a municipality representative that attends the CPSE meetings. However, the school district in which the child resides is responsible for conducting meetings.

Members of the CPSE include parent(s) of the child, a regular education teacher, a special education teacher or provider, a parent of a child with a disability in the district, a representative of the school district serving as the committee chairperson, a municipality representative, an early intervention representative, and an individual who can interpret evaluation results. CPSE referrals can be made by a parent, staff member, physician, judicial officer, public agency representative, approved preschool special education agencies, or an early intervention official.

Preschool students classified under the CPSE process do not bear individual classifications although they must fit the definition of a student with a disability according to section 200.1 of the Part 200 Regulations of the Commissioner. Following an evaluation by approved site, a student may be referred to the district CPSE. Eligibility criteria are based on evidence of a significant delay or disorder in one or more functional areas. This delay or disorder must indicate one of the following; a 12-month delay, a 33% delay in one area or 25% delay in each of two functional areas, or 2.0 standard deviations below the mean in one functional area or 1.5 standard deviations below the mean in two functional areas. If a student meets the definition according to section 200.1, they will be classified as a preschool student with a disability.

In summary, the role of the CPSE is to identify and determine eligibility for special education programs and services for preschool students. Upon determination of eligibility, the CPSE must identify present levels of performance, strengths, and needs of the child. This information will be compiled into an individual education plan (IEP). A program will be recommended and services will occur in the least restrictive environment.

## Laws That Guide the CPSE Process

IDEA Individuals with Disabilities Act, 2004

No Child Left Behind

---

### Activity

Compare, contrast, and critique early childhood procedures in five different states, such as:

Arizona (http://www.ade.az.gov/earlychildhood/preschool/programs/presch/)

Minnesota (http://education.state.mn.us/MDE/Learning_Support/Special_Education/Birth_to_Age_21_Programs_Services/Early_Childhood_Special_Education/index.html)

Illinois (http://www.isbe.net/earlychi/default.htm)

Wisconsin (http://dpi.state.wi.us/ec/ecspedhm.html)

Virginia (http://www.doe.virginia.gov/VDOE/sped/earlychildhood.html),

---

## Committee on Preschool Special Education (CPSE)

### Each CPSE must include, but is not limited to:

- the parents of the preschool child;
- a general education teacher of the child whenever the child is or may be participating in the general education environment;
- a special education teacher of the child, or, if appropriate, a special education provider of the child;
- a representative of the school district who is qualified to provide or supervise special education and who is knowledgeable about the general curriculum and the availability of preschool special education programs and services and other resources of the school district and the municipality. The representative of the school district shall serve as the chairperson of the committee;
- an additional parent member of a child with a disability residing in the school district or a neighboring school district and whose child is enrolled in a preschool or elementary level education program, except when the parent(s) of the child request that the additional parent member not participate;
- an individual who can interpret the instructional implications of evaluation results, provided that such individual may also be the individual appointed as the general education teacher, the special education teacher or special education provider, the

school psychologist, the representative of the school district or a person having knowledge or special expertise regarding the student when such member is determined by the school district to have the knowledge and expertise to fulfill this role on the committee;

- other persons having knowledge or special expertise regarding the child, including related services personnel as appropriate, as the school district or the parents shall designate;

- for a child in transition from early intervention programs and services, the appropriate professional designated by the agency that has been charged with the responsibility for the preschool child; and

- a representative of the municipality of the preschool child's residence at the discretion of the municipality. In the event the municipality representative does not attend the meeting, the CPSE may proceed as a legally constituted committee, provided the other required members of the committee participate in the meeting.

Check state education agencies for specific guidelines for individual states.

Figure 4.1 outlines the continuum of services for preschool education.

## EARLY INTERVENTION SERVICES

The Committee on Preschool Special Education picks up where Early Intervention (EI) services leave off. Under Part C of IDEA, states must provide services to any child "under 3 years of age who needs early intervention services" [IDEA 2004, §632(5)(A)] because the child:

"(i) is experiencing developmental delays, as measured by appropriate diagnostic instruments and procedures in 1 or more of the areas of cognitive development, physical development, communication development, social or emotional development, and adaptive development; or (ii) has a diagnosed physical or mental condition which has a high probability of resulting in developmental delay" [IDEA 2004, §632(5)(A)].

A state also *may provide* services, at its discretion, to at-risk infants and toddlers. An at-risk infant or toddler is defined under Part C as "an individual under 3 years of age who would be at risk of experiencing a substantial developmental delay if early intervention services were not provided to the individual" [IDEA 2004, §632(1)].

*Joseph is a four-year-old child who attends preschool within your district. He is classified under the committee for preschool special education. As part of your role, you attend CPSE meetings for children that will be transitioning into a school-age program. He will be of compulsory age in July, and his parents are intending he attend school and be in a general education classroom. Currently, his services include special education itinerant services within his home. His cognitive functioning is well below average and he is completely nonverbal. As a school counselor, you are called on to provide your opinion regarding this transition.*

- What are some recommendations that you would make to the parents?
- How will Joseph's needs best be met in a general education setting?
- Are there any assistive devices that you would recommend for communication? How will this recommendation impact your school district?
- If a student is declassified from CPSE, can he be classified under the CSE umbrella once he is school age? What ramifications need to be taken into consideration if the parents are resistant to classification?
- What developmental factors may impact this situation?

*(Text continued on page 59)*

**Figure 4.1**     Continuum of CPSE Services

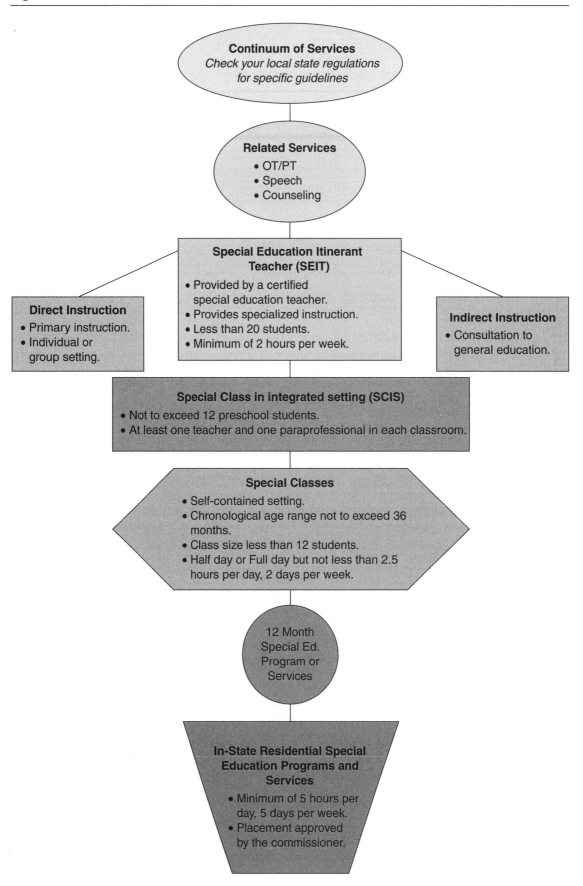

**FORM 4.1**    Sample Preschool IEP

---

### Preschool Individualized Education Program (IEP)
### School District
### Street Address
### City, State, and Zip Code
### Telephone Number

| Student Name: | Date of Birth:  /  / | Age: |
|---|---|---|

**Disability Classification:**
☐ **Preschool Student with a Disability**
☐ **Declassified**

| | |
|---|---|
| **Street:** | **Telephone:** |
| **City:** | **County of Residence:** |
| **Zip:** | Male ☐ Female ☐ |
| **Student ID#:**<br><br>**Medical Alerts:**<br><br>**Surrogate Parent Needed: Yes ☐  No ☐** | **Racial/Ethnic Group of Student: Choose One:**<br><br><br>**Native Language of Student:** |

**Other Information:**

☐ **Child received Early Intervention Services**
**Date of initial referral to CPSE:**  /  /
**Date initial consent for evaluation received:**  /  /
**Date of IEP meeting to determine initial eligibility:**  /  /

**Date of Committee on Preschool Special education (CPSE) Meeting:**  /  /
**Type of Meeting:**

☐ **Initial**               ☐ **Requested Review**
☐ **Annual Review**         ☐ **Reevaluation**
☐ _____

**Date IEP is to be Implemented:**  /  /
**Projected Date of Next Review:**  /  /

**Projected Date of Reevaluation Meeting:**  /  /

---

*(Continued)*

## PRESENT LEVELS OF ACADEMIC ACHIEVEMENT, FUNCTIONAL PERFORMANCE, AND INDIVIDUAL NEEDS

**Current functioning and individual needs in consideration of**

- the results of the initial or most recent evaluation, the student's strengths, and the concerns of the parents;
- the student's needs related to communication, behavior, use of Braille, assistive technology, limited English proficiency; and
- how the student's disability affects participation in appropriate activities.

**Academic Achievement, Functional Performance, and Learning Characteristics:**

Current levels of knowledge and development in subject and skill areas, including activities of daily living, level of intellectual functioning, adaptive behavior, expected rate of progress in acquiring skills and information, and learning style.

**Social Development:**

The degree and quality of the student's relationships with peers and adults, feelings about self, and social adjustment to school and community environments.

**Physical Development:**

The degree or quality of the student's motor and sensory development, health, vitality, and physical skills or limitations that pertain to the learning process.

**Management Needs:**

The nature of and degree to which environmental modifications and human or material resources are required to enable the student to benefit from instruction. Management needs are determined in accordance with the factors identified in the areas of academic achievement, functional performance and learning characteristics, social development and physical development.

## MEASURABLE ANNUAL GOALS AND SHORT-TERM INSTRUCTIONAL OBJECTIVES/BENCHMARKS

| **Annual Goal:** | |
|---|---|
| **Evaluative Criteria:** | |
| **Procedures to Evaluate Goal:** | |
| **Evaluation Schedule:** | |
| **Instructional Objectives or Benchmarks:** | |
| | |
| | |
| | |

| **Annual Goal:** | |
|---|---|
| **Evaluative Criteria:** | |
| **Procedures to Evaluate Goal:** | |
| **Evaluation Schedule:** | |
| **Instructional Objectives or Benchmarks:** | |
| | |
| | |
| | |

### Recommended Special Education Programs And Services

| **Special Education Program/Services** | | | | |
|---|---|---|---|---|
| | **Frequency** | **Duration** | **Location** | **Initiation Date** |
| | | | | / / |
| | | | | / / |
| | | | | / / |

| **Related Services** | | | | |
|---|---|---|---|---|
| | **Frequency** | **Duration** | **Location** | **Initiation Date** |
| | | | | / / |
| | | | | / / |
| | | | | / / |

*(Continued)*

**FORM 4.1**   (Continued)

### Program Modifications/Accommodations/Supplementary Aids and Services

|  | Frequency | Duration | Location | Initiation Date |
|---|---|---|---|---|
|  |  |  |  | /  / |
|  |  |  |  | /  / |
|  |  |  |  | /  / |

### Assistive Technology Devices/Services

|  | Frequency | Duration | Location | Initiation Date |
|---|---|---|---|---|
|  |  |  |  | /  / |
|  |  |  |  | /  / |
|  |  |  |  | /  / |

### Supports for School Personnel on Behalf of Student

|  | Frequency | Duration | Location | Initiation Date |
|---|---|---|---|---|
|  |  |  |  | /  / |
|  |  |  |  | /  / |
|  |  |  |  | /  / |

### Special Transportation Needs:

☐ None
☐ Student has special transportation needs as recommended below:
☐ Special seating - Specify:
☐ Vehicle and/or equipment needs - Specify:
☐ Adult supervision - Specify:
☐ Type of transportation - Specify:
☐ Other accommodations - Specify:
☐ Other preschool transportation needs:

### Testing Accommodations

The following individual appropriate accommodations are necessary to measure the academic achievement and functional performance of the student on state and districtwide assessments. Recommended testing accommodations will be used consistently in the student's education program:

• in the administration of districtwide assessments of student achievement, consistent with school district policy; and

• in the administration of state assessments of student achievement, consistent with State Education Department policy.

| Testing Accommodation | Conditions | Specifications |
|---|---|---|
|  |  |  |
|  |  |  |
|  |  |  |

### Participation in State and Districtwide Assessments

The student will participate in the same state and districtwide assessments that are administered to general education students.

The student will participate in the following alternate assessments for state and districtwide assessments:

Explain why the state and districtwide alternate assessments selected are appropriate for the student:

### Participation With Age-Appropriate Peers

Provision of special education services in a setting with no regular contact with age-appropriate peers without disabilities should only be considered when the nature or severity of the child's disability is such that education in a less restrictive environment with the use of supplementary aids and services cannot be satisfactorily achieved.

Explanation of the extent, if any, to which the student will not participate in appropriate activities with age-appropriate nondisabled peers:

Will the preschool student receive services in a setting with no regular contact with age-appropriate peers without disabilities? Yes  No

## REPORTING PROGRESS TO PARENTS

Identify when periodic reports on the progress the student is making toward meeting the annual goals will be provided to the student's parents:

## PLACEMENT RECOMMENDATION

| 10 Month Placement:<br>**Approved Preschool Program Provider:** |  |
|---|---|
| Extended School Year Eligible: Yes ☐   No ☐<br>If yes:  Reason:<br>Projected dates of services:   /  /   to   /  / |  |
| Provider: | Site: |

*(Continued)*

**FORM 4.1**   (Continued)

| PARENT INFORMATION | |
|---|---|
| **Student's Name:** | |
| **Mother's/Guardian's Name:** | **Telephone:** |
| **Street:** | **County of Residence:** |
| **City:** | **Native Language of Parent/ Guardian:** |
| **Zip:** | **Interpreter Needed for Meeting:** Yes ☐  No ☐ |
| **Father's/Guardian's Name:** | **Telephone:** |
| **Street:** | **County of Residence:** |
| **City:** | **Native Language of Parent/ Guardian:** |
| **Zip:** | **Interpreter Needed for Meeting:** Yes ☐    No ☐ |
| ☐ **Surrogate Parent Needed** | |
| **Surrogate Parent's Name :** | **Date Appointed:**   /  / |
| **Street:** | **Telephone:** |
| **City:** | **Native Language of Surrogate Parent:** |
| **Zip:** | **Interpreter Needed for Meeting:** Yes ☐    No ☐ |

**CPSE Participants**

| Name | Professional Title | CPSE Member Role[1] |
|---|---|---|
| | | |
| | | |
| | | |
| | | |
| | | |
| | | |

## CPSE Timeline and Process

Be sure to check your local State Education Agency for timeline requirements.

**Figure 4.2**    CPSE Referral Timeline

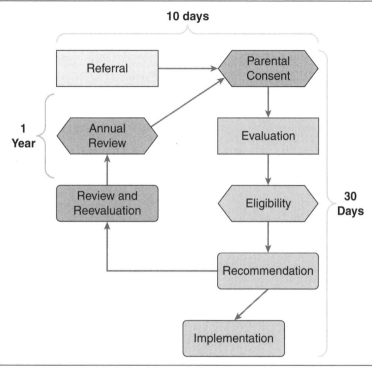

Note: Adapted from Erie I BOCES conference.

### Activity

Develop a counseling plan, based on the case of Joseph. Use the following Web site to include pertinent resources: http://www.montgomeryschoolsmd.org/curriculum/pep/research.html

## Definitions Related to Eligibility Under
## Part C of the IDEA Amendments of 2004

Under Part C of IDEA, states must provide services to any child needing EI services because the child

- Experiencing developmental delays in one or more areas of cognitive development, physical development, communication development, social or emotional development, and adaptive development.
- Has a diagnosed physical or mental condition, which has a high probability of resulting in developmental delay.

## Questions for Reflection

1. How is the CPSE different from the CSE?
2. What role does early intervention play?
3. Who are the members of the CPSE?
4. What laws guide the CPSE process?

# Process and Services

## School Age

**A** school counselor is an important member of the CSE team. Counselors are called on to provide emotional support, behavior management training, and assist students in making social connections. Often, counselors have fostered a strong relationship with parents and are able to provide support and advocacy at these meetings. Although school counselors are not mandated members, every effort should be made to attend as many CSE meetings as possible. School counselors need to have the knowledge and ability to advocate to the district's special education department and building administrators to be invited to meetings as their input is valuable and their support is essential. School counselors have a responsibility to provide a comprehensive program that encompasses the needs of all students. That is why membership and attendance is imperative.

## COMMITTEE ON SPECIAL EDUCATION (CSE)

The individuals who need to be involved with the decision-making process and service provision for school-aged children and youth may vary somewhat dependent on the outcome of the decisions that are discussed in the student's IEP as well as across school districts. Study teams, which were defined in Chapter 3, and committees on special education (CSE) are the two primary groups of professionals and lay personnel involved. A committee on special education is a multidisciplinary team established in accordance with the provisions of section 4402 of the Education Law found in the following Web site: http://www.vesid.nysed.gov/specialed/publications/lawsandregs/part200.htm. Check your local state education agency for laws specific to your state.

The committee meets to establish classification, placement, programming, appropriate services, testing modifications, and most importantly to write the IEP.

Each CSE must include, but is not limited to:

- the parents or persons in parental relationship to the student;
- at least one general education teacher of the student whenever the student is or may be participating in the general education environment;
- one special education teacher of the student, or, if appropriate, a special education provider of the student;
- a school psychologist;
- a representative of the school district who is qualified to provide or supervise special education and who is knowledgeable about the general curriculum and the availability of resources of the school district, provided that an individual who meets these qualifications may also be the same individual appointed as the special education teacher or the special education provider of the student or the school psychologist;
- an individual who can interpret the instructional implications of evaluation results. Such individual may also be the individual appointed as the general education teacher, the special education teacher or special education provider, the school psychologist, the representative of the school district or a person having knowledge or special expertise regarding the student when such member is determined by the school district to have the knowledge and expertise to fulfill this role on the committee;
- a school physician, if specifically requested in writing by the parent of the student or by a member of the school at least 72 hours prior to the meeting;
- an additional parent member of a student with a disability residing in the school district or a neighboring school district, except when the parents of the student request that the additional parent member not participate in the meeting;
- other persons having knowledge or special expertise regarding the student, including related services personnel as appropriate, as the school district or the parent(s) shall designate; and
- if appropriate, the student. Beginning at age 14, the student must be invited if the purpose of the meeting is to consider the need for transition services.

## SUBCOMMITTEE ON SPECIAL EDUCATION[1]

The membership of each Subcommittee on Special Education must include, but is not limited to:

- the parents of the student;
- one general education teacher of the student whenever the student is or may be participating in the general education environment;
- the student's special education teacher or, if appropriate, a special education provider of the student;
- a representative of the school district who is qualified to provide, administer, or supervise special education and who is knowledgeable about the general curriculum and who is knowledgeable about the availability of resources of the school district, who may also fulfill the requirement of the special education teacher or the school psychologist;
- a school psychologist, whenever a new psychological evaluation is reviewed or a change to a program option with a more intensive staff/student ratio, as set forth in section 200.6(g)(4) of the Regulations of the Commissioner, is considered;
- an individual who can interpret the instructional implications of evaluation results, who may be a member appointed as the general education teacher, special education teacher, school district representative, school psychologist, or other persons having knowledge or special expertise regarding the student;
- such other persons having knowledge or special expertise regarding the student, including related services personnel as appropriate, as the committee or the parent shall designate; and

- the student, if appropriate. Beginning at age 14, the student must be invited if the purpose of the meeting is to consider the need for transition services.

A Subcommittee on Special Education may perform the functions of the CSE, *except* when a student is considered for placement for the *first time* in:

- a special class; or
- a special class outside of the student's school of attendance (i.e., outside the school the student would normally attend if not disabled); or
- a school primarily serving students with disabilities or a school outside of the student's district.

If a recommendation of a subcommittee is not acceptable to the student's parent(s), the parent may submit a written request to refer to the recommendation to the CSE for its review. Upon receipt of such written request by the parent, the CSE must meet and review the recommendation of the Subcommittee.

Each subcommittee must report annually the status of each student with a disability within its jurisdiction to the CSE.

---

[1] Does not apply to CPSE

# CONTINUUM OF SERVICES (LEAST RESTRICTIVE ENVIRONMENT)

Part B of IDEA requires that the Least Restrictive Environment (LRE) must be selected in order that students with disabilities be educated alongside their nondisabled peers to the maximum extent appropriate. Children and youth also have a right to a free appropriate public education (FAPE). Ultimately, many decisions regarding placements for students with disabilities depend on the severity of the disability and what resources exist in the school/community. As indicated before, decisions should not be made on what is available and convenient, rather on what best meets the needs of the students with disabilities. The continuum of alternative placement options, from least to most restrictive environments, includes home/hospital, separate school, separate class, resource room, to a regular class (Sciarri, 2004). Table 5.1 further details education and placement options (Hallahan & Kauffman, 2006).

There continues to be much controversy over placing all students with disabilities in their neighborhood schools in general education classrooms for the full day, otherwise known as *full inclusion* (Hallahan & Kaufmann, 2006). On the positive side, students with disabilities are exposed to positive peer role models, may be more challenged to learn, and seen as receiving more quality, effective education. They are seen as labeled less and more of a minority group than people who are educationally inadequate due to inherent disability issues. Arguments against full inclusion include general educators not being skilled or ready to teach students with disabilities, satisfaction with alternative placement options, the misnomer that people with disabilities are a minority, and the possible negative educational and social impact on nondisabled peers. It is important to differentiate *first-generation inclusion,* whereby services were added on to general education versus *second-generation inclusion,* which involves systemic change and teaching for diversity as the norm (Ferguson, 1995; Turnbull, Turnbull, Shank, & Leal, 1999). If the fundamental principles of accurately and comprehensively assessing the needs of students with disabilities, and providing appropriate services, the controversy around the inclusion issue may for many be a moot issue.

**Table 5.1**    School-age Continuum of Services

| Educational Option | Description |
|---|---|
| **Regular Classroom** | Teacher can meet needs of students with disabilities in terms of skills and resources |
| **Regular Teacher with Consultation** | *Indirect:* Special educator instructs teacher, refers teacher to resources, or demonstrates methods and materials<br><br>*Direct:* Special educator provides accommodations, modifications, and supports directly to the student in a general education setting. |
| **Itinerant Services** | Special educator travels to schools, providing services to teacher, or instructs students individually or in small groups |
| **Resource Teacher** | Works in one school; provides students with disabilities in a room outside of the regular classroom; assesses students' needs and consults with teachers |
| **Self-Contained Classroom** | Usually involves 15 or fewer students with disabilities, may be of various categories, typically instructed by special educator; usually separated from non disabled peers most of the day, except for classes such as gym. |
| **Special Day Schools** | All day placement typically organized around a specific disability category; equipped to meet educational needs of that disability |
| **Hospital or Homebound Instruction** | Typically for students with physical disabilities; or for emotional, behavioral disorders if alternative placements not available; student confined to home/hospital; homebound teacher keeps in contact with regular teacher |
| **Residential School** | Highest level of specialization; students remain in institution for education and other daily living help; may return home on weekends |

## Student Experiencing Academic Failure is Referred to the School's Student Support Team (SST), Child Study Team (CST), etc.

### Section 100.2 (ee) of the Regulations of the Commissioner of Education and January 2000 New York State Education Department Guidelines for Implementing Academic Intervention Services (AIS)

- Did the school consider AIS for student prior to referral?
- Does the child meet the district criteria for AIS?
- Are the specific AIS services delineated in a written plan?
- Were the AIS services evaluated and/or modified prior to referral?
- Was information/training on the specific characteristics and needs of the child provided to the AIS providers?

## Referral

### A Committee on Special Education (CSE) referral may be made by:

- Teachers
- Professional staff members of the school district in which the child resides or in the public or private school the child legally attends
- Parents/Guardians
- Physicians
- Judicial officers
- The commissioner or designee of a public agency with responsibility for the welfare, health, or education of children
- An individual on his or her own behalf if he or she is 18 years of age or an emancipated minor

**Figure 5.1** CSE Process

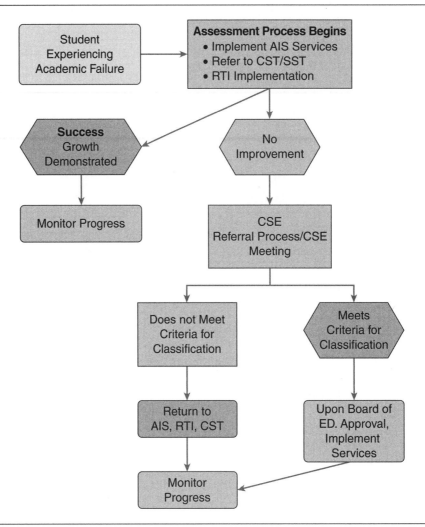

---

*Included in a referral:*

- The reason for believing that an educational disability exists
- Any test results, records, or reports to show attempts to remediate the student's performance prior to the referral
- A description of the extent of parental contact or involvement prior to the referral

*Sections 200.4 (a) and 200.5 (a) of the*
*Regulations of the Commissioner of Education*

- A copy of the referral forwarded to the building administrator
- Describe previous attempts to remediate the student's performance
- Describe the purpose of the evaluation and uses for the information

# PARENTAL CONSENT

An evaluation cannot begin until the parent has given written permission to do so.

## Request consent from the parent for an evaluative information

- Provide notice to the parent in their native language or mode of communication used by parent
- Include a description of the proposed evaluation

**Figure 5.2** CSE Timeline

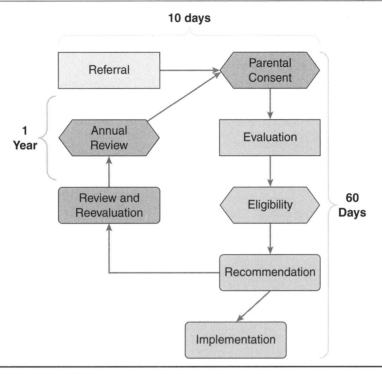

Be sure to check your Local Education Agency for the timeline requirements.

*Adapted from Erie I BOCES

- Include a consent form
- Include state-required parental guidelines
- Provide community supports
- State reason for the referral

## Indicate that the parent may submit evaluative information to be considered by the CSE

After parental consent is received in written form, the district has 60 calendar days to conduct a CSE meeting

- best practice is to leave room for delays, parental conflicts/cancellations, so that the meeting may be rescheduled within the 60-calendar day period

All evaluations must be completed within this period.

## EVALUATION

### Federal Regulations Section 300.345 (a–f)

*Evaluations should include the following information:*

- Review of any existing evaluations
- A current physical exam
- Individual psychological evaluation
- Social history
- Observations of student in current educational setting
- Functional Behavioral Assessment if behavior is impeding the student's learning or that of others
- Administer any evaluations in the student's native language

- Assess the student in all areas related to the suspected disability
- Information from the parent
- Strengths of the student
- Guidance for determining specific strategies for teachers
- Provide information to determine that general education without support services cannot meet the student's needs
- Provide functional information relevant to IEP development

# CSE MEETING

## Must be held within 60 calendar days of the written parental consent

### *Federal Regulations Section 300.345 (a–f)*

Notify parents:

- In their native language or other mode of communication
- Provide notice to parents within ten days of meeting
- Describe purpose of meeting
- Invite parents to review evaluation results
- Indicate that parents are equal partners participating in the development of a recommendation regarding eligibility for special education and the development of the IEP, if appropriate
- Include date, time, and location
- Identify persons expected to attend meeting by name and title
- State that parents have the right to bring others to the meeting who have knowledge of, or special expertise of, the child or the disability
- Include a statement indicating that if the parent is unable to attend, they may reschedule and/or arrange for participation via phone conference
- Ask parents if there is a need for reasonable accommodations such as a translator, reader, interpreter, access to an elevator, etc.
- Parents may request the participation of the physician with at least 72 hours prior to meeting
- State that the parent has the right to decline, in writing, a parent member
- Include procedural safeguards notice
- Invite the student, if appropriate

## CSE Committee Members

### *200.3 (a)(1)(i–x) of the Regulations of the Commissioner*

- Parents or persons in parental relationship to the student
- Not less than one regular education teacher of the student
- Not less than one special education teacher of the student
- A school psychologist
- A representative of the school district who is qualified to provide or supervise special education and who is knowledgeable about the general education curriculum and the availability of resources of the school district
- An individual who can interpret the instructional implications of evaluation results
- A school physician, if specifically requested in writing by the parent or member of the school at least 72 hours prior to the meeting
- An additional parent member of a student with a disability residing in the school district or a neighboring school district
- Other persons having knowledge or special expertise regarding the student, including related services personnel as appropriate
- If appropriate, the student

## CSE meetings determine the following:

- Classification, if a student meets the criteria for one of the thirteen disabilities
- Strengths and weaknesses of a child's academic and behavioral functioning
- Annual goals relating to the academic, social, physical, and management needs of the student
- Related services (OT, PT, Speech, Counseling) including the frequency, duration, and location of each service
- The least restrictive environment in which the student will access the general education curriculum (The Continuum of Services, 200.6 of the Regulations of the Commissioner)

    Consultant teacher services
    Resource room
    Special size classes
    Home and hospital instruction
    In-state or out-of-state private schools
    12-month special service and/or program

- Transition services (for students over the age of 15)
- Adaptive equipment
- Test modifications
- Classroom accommodations (e.g., preferential seating, modified curriculum, etc.)

## Initiation of Services

After the CSE meeting at which it is determined that a student will receive special education services, Board of Education approval must be made AND initiation of services must begin within 30 school days of the CSE meeting.

## Reevaluation/Triennial

The reevaluation will help determine an individual student's continuing eligibility and need for special education. A reevaluation occurs every three years to provide current assessment information on students in special education.

- After the multidisciplinary team meets and reviews the student's program for the previous year, their recommendations will be made to the CSE Chairperson.
- Parental consent MUST be obtained as it is only valid for 30 days.
- Within a letter for consent for reevaluation, the service providers, including the school psychologist, MUST state, in detail, the assessments, tests, and/or instruments used to evaluate the child.

## Annual Review

Annual review meetings may be conducted by the CSE Subcommittee. Participants include:

- The parents of the student
- Not less than one regular education teacher of the student
- Not less than one special education teacher of the student
- A representative of the school district who is qualified to provide, administer, or supervise special education and who is knowledgeable about the general education curriculum
- A school psychologist whenever a new psychological evaluation is reviewed
- An individual who can interpret the instructional implications of the evaluation results
- Such other persons having knowledge or special expertise regarding the student
- The student, if appropriate

The full CSE committee must meet for the following cases:

- Initial evaluations
- Student is recommended for placement in a more restrictive setting
- Parental request
- Any cases requiring the presence of the school physician

# IEP COMPONENTS

Since the changes to IDEA in 2004 (see Chapter 2 for recent updates) to the assessments required by NCLB, the IEP does not have to include short-term objectives (Hallahan & Kauffman, 2006). However, preschool goals still require measurable and observable objectives. While there is no standard IEP format across schools, the essential components must be included. Although understandable from a practical standpoint, IEPs should not be written based on available services and placements. IEPs should be completed after evaluation is done and identification of the disability has occurred, but prior to placements decision have been made.

As Bateman and Linden (1998) have indicated, IEPs sometimes are written at the wrong time and for the wrong reasons. The U.S. Department of Education, Office of Special Education and Rehabilitative Services publishes a comprehensive "Guide to the Individualized Education Program" found at http://www.ed.gov/offices/OSERS/OSEP/Products/IEP_Guide/#IEP%20Guide.

In addition, samples of the components of IEPs, as well as IEP templates and completed IEPs are presented on the following pages.

# COMPONENTS OF THE IEP

## Present Levels of Educational Performance

This information usually comes from the evaluation results such as classroom tests and assignments, individual tests given to decide eligibility for services or during reevaluation, and observations made by parents, teachers, related service providers, and other school staff. The statement about "current performance" includes how the child's disability affects his or her involvement and progress in the general curriculum (Sample PLEP, Resource D)

## Annual goals

These are goals that the child can reasonably accomplish in a year. Goals may be academic, address social or behavioral needs, relate to physical needs, or address other educational needs. The goals must be measurable-meaning that it must be possible to measure whether the student has achieved the goals. (Sample Goals, Resource E)

## Special Education and Related Services

The IEP must list the special education and related services to be provided to the child or on behalf of the child. This includes supplementary aids and services that the child needs. It also includes modifications (changes) to the program or supports for school personnel—such as training or professional development—that will be provided to assist the child.

A child may require any of the following related services in order to benefit from special education. Related services, as listed under IDEA, include (but are not limited to):

- Audiology services
- Counseling services
- Early identification and assessment of disabilities in children
- Medical services
- Occupational therapy
- Orientation and mobility services

- Parent counseling and training
- Physical therapy
- Psychological services
- Recreation
- Rehabilitation counseling services
- School health services
- Social work services in schools
- Speech-language pathology services
- Transportation

## Participation with Nondisabled Children

The IEP must explain the extent (if any) to which the child will not participate with nondisabled children in the regular class and other school activities.

## Participation in State and Districtwide Tests

Most states and districts give achievement tests to children in certain grades or age groups. The IEP must state what modifications in the administration of these tests the child will need. If a test is not appropriate for the child, the IEP must state why the test is not appropriate and how the child will be tested instead.

## Testing and Program Modifications

(Sample Testing Accommodations, Table 5.2; Table 5.3)

(Sample Program Modifications, Table 5.4)

## Dates and Places

The IEP must state when services will begin, how often they will be provided, where they will be provided, and how long they will last.

## Transition Service Needs

Transition planning, for students beginning at age 15 (and sometimes younger) involves helping the student plan his or her courses of study (such as advanced placement or vocational education) so that the classes the student takes will lead to his or her postschool goals.

Transition services, for students beginning at age 15 (and sometimes younger) involves providing the student with a coordinated set of services to help the student move from school to adult life. Services focus on the student's needs or interest in such areas as higher education or training, employment, adult services, independent living, or taking part in the community

## Measuring Progress

The IEP must state how the child's progress will be measured and how parents will be informed of that program.

For Sample PLEP Statements, see Resource D

# WRITING ANNUAL GOALS

Measuring mastery for improved spelling is simple and quantitative. The student will spell eighteen words correctly in a weekly spelling test of twenty words, four out of five weeks. It is easily measurable and observable. However, consider the more subjective areas in need of improvement that counselors may need to measure. The student will improve his/her self-esteem in a weekly test given four out of five weeks? Not so easily measured or observed. This is where a more qualitative and descriptive nature of writing goals becomes necessary. When writing goals of a behavioral or social/emotional nature, remember one simple phrase . . . WHAT DOES IT LOOK LIKE?

**Table 5.2**    Testing Accommodations

| Accommodation Name | Possible Testing Accommodations | Examples of Acceptable Conditions | Example of Acceptable Specifications |
|---|---|---|---|
| Flexible Schedule/ Timing | Extended time | For tests longer than 40 minutes in length | 1.5 × 2 × |
| | Provide breaks during testing | On all tests over 30 minutes | Specify length of break (i.e., 5 min per 30 minutes of testing) |
| Flexible Setting | Separate setting | For all tests | 5 or 10 minutes break every 30 or 40 minutes |
| | Individual setting | For tests requiring extended writing (essay) responses | Small group (specify # of students in group, i.e., 3–5) |
| Method of Presentation | Directions read | With the exception of math testing that measures basic calculation skills | Specify # of additional times |
| | Oral reading of passages (not listening sections), multiple choice questions, and/or extended response items | With the exception of tests that measure spelling and grammar skills | Specify the # of additional times |
| | Clarify directions | For all extended writing tests | Specify # of times |
| | Provide additional examples of directions | On all tests | Specify # of examples |
| | Simplify language in directions | On all tests | Specify # of times explained |
| | Large print | On all tests | |
| Method of Response | Use of a spell checker or grammar checker device | With the exception of tests that measure spelling and grammar | |
| | Deletion of spelling, paragraphing, and/or punctuation requirements | With the exception of tests that measure written mechanics | |
| | Dictate or answer questions using a tape recorder | On all tests requiring extended writing answers | |

| | Provide computer or word processor | On all tests requiring extended writing answers | |
| --- | --- | --- | --- |
| | Scribe | On all tests requiring written responses | |
| Other | Use of a calculator, arithmetic table, or abacus | Mathematics tests that do not assess proficiencies involving basic calculations | With the exception of tests that measure written mechanics |
| | Papers secured to work area with tape or magnets | On all tests | |
| Braille | Any that speak to this | | |

**Table 5.3**    Testing Accommodation Examples

| Examples of Acceptable Duration | Examples of Acceptable Frequency | Examples of acceptable Location |
| --- | --- | --- |
| Duration of writing assignments | Daily | All academic classes |
| Duration of structured activities | Weekly | Hallway |
| During class period | Every 2 hours, etc. | Cafeteria |
| During new lessons and units | 1 × per week | Specify a class (i.e., math, ELA, etc.) |
| Duration of transitions between classes | 4 × per year | Nurse's office |
| Specify # of minutes (i.e., 5 min, 20 min, etc.) | 2 × per month | |

*Accommodations may be altered to best meet the needs of the students. Be sure to clearly specify on the IEP.

## Goal Writing Formula

1. Who (student)

2. Will do what (observable behavior in functional terms)

3. To what degree (criterion for mastery; anticipated level)

4. Under what conditions (circumstances or givens)

**Table 5.4**    Sample Program Modifications

| Program Modification | Examples of Disability or Student Characteristics |
| --- | --- |
| Extended time for writing assignments | LD; poor attention; difficulty remaining on task |
| Allow oral responses | LD; severe deficits in written mechanics; poor physical/motor coordination affecting writing |
| Provide books on tape and/or audio texts | LD; severe deficits in reading; visual impairments |
| Provide specially designed reading instruction | LD; severe deficits in reading |
| Provide a question guideline for structuring reading comprehension activities | LD; deficits in reading; difficulty remaining on task |
| Provide chart of basic math facts or calculator | LD in math; difficulty with math processing/computations; unable to memorize basic math facts |
| Allow student to speak aloud as they solve problems | LD in math; difficulty with math processing computations |
| Allow provision for practice/repetition of newly acquired skills | LD; deficits in math |
| Permit the use of tape recorders, calculators, and computers | LD; deficits in reading, math; poor physical/motor coordination |
| Modify curriculum for below average reading skills | LD; deficits in reading |
| Use of graphic organizers | LD; poor attention; difficulty remaining on task |
| Teacher provided notes or outlines of unit information | LD; poor attention, difficulty remaining on task; writing tasks completed at a slow rate |
| Allow student to read text aloud rather than silently | LD; processing difficulties |
| Presentation of curriculum content into organized smaller parts | LD; processes information at a slower rate; difficulty remaining on task |
| Present information and new concepts at a slow rate and allow adequate time for auditory and visual processing | LD; processes information at a slower rate: CAPD |
| Allow student sufficient time to consider and answer questions | LD; processes information at a slower rate: CAPD |
| Provide instructional materials in alternative formats | LD; poor attention; difficulty remaining on task |
| Seating close to adult/teacher | LD; visual impairments; hearing impairments; difficulty remaining on tasks |
| Schedule rest periods for fatigue | Health impairments; emotional/mental health impairments when administered medication may affect stamina |

| | |
|---|---|
| Provide study outlines of key concepts | LD; poor attention; difficulty remaining on task; writing tasks completed at a slower rate |
| Use of a study corral for independent work | Difficulty remaining on task |
| Use adaptive or special furniture (i.e., study corral, bean bag chairs, etc.) | Difficulty remaining on task; health impairments |
| Use visual cues | Difficulty remaining on task |
| Shorten tasks | Difficulty remaining on task |
| Increase line spacing between questions on assignments | Visual–perceptual difficulties |
| Use verbal prompts and hand signals | Difficulty remaining on task |
| Begin with a review task, then move into more difficult or new tasks | LD; difficulty with auditory processing; poor attention; poor memory |
| Allow previews and reviews of content material | LD; difficulty with auditory processing; poor attention; poor memory |
| Provide two minutes warnings before transitions | LD; poor attention; distractibility; autism |
| Use generalization strategies in instruction and relate material to real life situations | LD; ED; difficulty remaining on task |
| Provide hands-on or direct experiences whenever possible | LD; ED; difficulty remaining on task |
| Use pictures and concrete objects to support learning | LD; ED; difficulty remaining on task |
| Work in small group settings to enable individualized attention/instruction | LD; ED; difficulty remaining on task |
| Supplement written instructions with oral instructions and vice versa | LD; difficulty remaining on task; difficulty following/understanding directions; CAPD; hearing impairments |
| Repeat instructions more than once | LD; difficulty remaining on task; difficulty following/understanding directions; CAPD; hearing impairments |
| Redefine important vocabulary words and terminology | LD; CAPD; poor attention |
| Accompany homework assignments with written instructions and examples of how to complete tasks | LD; difficulty remaining on task; difficulty following/understanding directions; CAPD; hearing impairments |
| Incorporate the student into activity groups | LD; ED; difficulty remaining on task |
| Design alternative worksheets or tests that allow student to respond in their preferred mode (i.e., MC; T/F) | LD; difficulty remaining on task; difficulty following/understanding directions; CAPD; hearing impairments |
| Allow student extra time to go between classes | Health impairments |

*(Continued)*

**Table 5.4** (Continued)

| | |
|---|---|
| Allow student to listen to music while working independently on assignments | Difficulty remaining on task |
| Use various learning strategies (i.e., mnemonics, pictorial representations of abstract concepts, etc.) | LD; ED; difficulty remaining on task |
| Develop systematic methods for maintaining organization and following classroom routine | ED; difficulty remaining on task |
| Structure classroom environment to accommodate specialized needs for reduced visual and auditory distractions or mobility | LD; ED; visual or hearing impairments; health impairments; ADD/ADHD |
| Develop independence by having student self-monitor their performance through charting, self-instruction and self-talk | ED |
| Adjust lighting and acoustics | Visual and hearing impairments |
| Stimulus reduction (i.e., soundproof walls, carpeting, opaque windows, enclosed bookcases, study corral, etc.) | Visual and hearing impairments; autism; MR; CAPD; health impairments; ADD/ADHD |
| Incentive/reward system | LD; ED; difficulty remaining on task |
| Assignment of a paraprofessional staff | LD; ED |
| Behavior Intervention Plan | LD; ED; autism; MR |
| Family Intervention Programs | Any applicable student |

*This list is not exhaustive. Accommodations may be changed or combined to meet the needs of the individual student.

## Problem-Solving Goal

The student will identify and utilize steps in the decision-making process reflected in his personal decisions and choices by using the eight problem-solving steps of:

- identifying the purpose of the decision
- gathering information
- identifying the principles to judge the alternatives
- brainstorming and listing different possible choices
- evaluating each choice in terms of its consequences
- determining the best alternative
- putting the decision into action
- evaluating the outcome of the decision and action steps

when encountering a choice.

For more sample goals, see Resource E

# PROGRAM AND TEST MODIFICATIONS AND ACCOMMODATIONS WITH RATIONALE

## Specific Deficits that Compromise Test Performance

All definitions taken from DSM-IV-TR except where specified

## ADHD (Attention Deficit/Hyperactivity Disorder)

Six or more of the following symptoms that have persisted for at least six months to a degree that is maladaptive and inconsistent with developmental level:

### Hyperactivity

- often fidgets with hands or feet or squirms in seat
- often leaves seat in classroom or in other situation in which remaining seated is expected
- often runs about or climbs excessively in situations in which it is inappropriate (in adolescents or adults, may be limited to subjective feelings of restlessness)
- often has difficulty playing or engaging in leisure activities quietly
- is often "on the go" or acts as if "driven by a motor"
- often talks excessively

### Impulsivity

- often blurts out answers before questions have been completed
- often has difficulty awaiting turn
- often interrupts or intrudes on others (butts into conversation or games)

## CAPD (Central Auditory Processing Disorder)

*Diagnosis of CAPD requires specialized testing by audiologists*

The inability of the brain to process incoming auditory signals (the brain identifies sounds by analyzing physical characterizes of sounds: frequency, intensity, temporal features)

Once we analyze or process the sound, then we construct meaning.

### Types of processing difficulties:

- figure-ground discrimination—listening for meaning in the presence of background noise
- auditory memory—remembering what you hear
- paying attention to what you hear
- auditory discrimination problems—hearing the incorrect sound ("hat" for "that")

### Those with CAPD:

- have difficulty following directions, this may be situation specific
- have difficulty remembering information presented auditorally
- have difficulty remaining attentive
- may be overly sensitive to noises or noisy environments

### Communication Strategies:

- Gain attention through the use of cues
- Monitor comprehension
- Allow extra processing time
- Modify instructions—brevity, rephrasing, multisensory
- Allow for breaks
- Develop language skills

## Feelings of Anxiety (Generalized Anxiety Disorder)

excessive anxiety and worry occurring more days than not for at least six months about a number of events or activity

person finds it difficult to control the worry

anxiety and worry are associated with three or more of the following symptoms (only one is required for children)

- restlessness or feelings keyed up or on edge
- being easily fatigued
- difficulty concentrating or mind going blank
- irritability
- muscle tension
- sleep disturbance

the anxiety is not about having a panic attack, being embarrassed in public, being contaminated, being away from home or close relatives, serious illness, having multiple complaints, PTSD, or other diagnoses of anxiety

anxiety, worry, or physical symptoms cause clinically significant distress or impairment in social, occupational, or other important areas of functioning

disturbance is not a direct effect of a substance or medication and does not occur exclusively during a mood disorder

## Feelings of Depression—Major Depressive Episode

Five or more of the following symptoms have been present during the same two-week period and represent a change from previous functioning; at least one of the symptoms is either 1) depressed mood; or 2) loss of interest or pleasure

- depressed mood most of the day, nearly every day
- markedly diminished interest or pleasure in all, or almost all, activities most of the day, nearly every day
- significant weight loss when not dieting or weight gain, or decrease or increase in appetite nearly every day
- insomnia or hypersomnia nearly every day
- psychomotor agitation or retardation nearly every day
- fatigue or loss of energy nearly every day
- feelings of worthlessness or excessive or inappropriate guilt
- diminished ability to think or concentrate or indecisiveness, nearly every day
- recurrent thoughts of death, recurrent suicidal ideation without a specific plan, or a suicide attempt or specific plan for committing suicide

## Learning Disability

Part 300: Specific Learning Disability is defined as follows:

(i) *General.* The term means a disorder in one or more of the basic psychological processes involved in understanding or in using language, spoken or written, which manifests itself in an imperfect ability to listen, think, speak, read, write, spell, or do mathematical calculations, including conditions such as perceptual disabilities, brain injury, minimal brain dysfunction, dyslexia, and developmental aphasia.

(ii) *Disorders not included.* The term does not include learning problems that are primarily the result of visual, hearing, or motor disabilities, of mental retardation, of emotional disturbance, or of environmental, cultural, or economic disadvantage.

### Characteristics of Learning Disabilities

**Reading:**

- problems related to deficit language skills
- phonological skills: the ability to understand, words and how the various letters make certain sounds

## Written Language:

- problems in handwriting, spelling, or composition

## Spoken Language:

- mechanical and spoken uses of language
- trouble with syntax (how words are linked to make meaningful sentences)
- trouble with semantics (word meaning)

## Math

- trouble computing facts and/or solving problems
- difficulty with word problems

## Perceptual, Perceptual–Motor, and Coordination

- visual/auditory problems resulting in seeing or hearing things wrong
- fine and gross motor skill problems

## Memory, Cognitive, Metacognitive

- short-term memory: recalling information after they have learned it
- working memory: ability to keep information in mind while working on another task
- cognition: ability to solve problems and use strategies
- metacognition: awareness of what skills, strategies, and resources are needed to perform a task effectively and the ability to use self-regulatory mechanisms to ensure the successful completion of a task
- comprehension monitoring: abilities employed while one reads and attempts to comprehend textual material

**Table 5.5**    Suggestions for Modifications Before a Test

| Modification | Rationalization |
|---|---|
| Provide study guide | Addresses feelings of anxiety increase when in an unfamiliar situation; a study guide will provide students with the information they need to know, reducing anxiety |
| Simplify language of text directions | Addresses poor comprehension and word attack skills; using simpler language of the directions will give students a clear understanding of the task |
| Simplify language of test questions | Addresses poor comprehension and word attack skills; using simpler language of the test questions will allow students to convey content knowledge without the disability hindering |
| Revise format and contest of classroom test | Addresses poor perceptual organization; a clearly organized test will be easier for students to read and understand |
| Teach test-taking skills | Addresses comprehension deficits as well as feelings of anxiety during test. Teaching students the steps in taking a multiple choice test will better able them to complete the test with success while reducing anxiety |

**Table 5.6**     Suggested Test Modifications—Multiple Choice

### Multiple Choice

| | Recommended Changes | Rationale |
|---|---|---|
| **Content** | Relate to instructional objectives | This will allow the student to accomplish the goals outlined in his/her IEP |
| | Frequent testing vs. fewer tests | To address poor short-term memory, frequent testing will be more effective in attaining what the student knows about a particular subject |
| **Readability** | Eliminate unnecessary words | Poor comprehension skills and poor word attack skills can impair the student's ability to relay his knowledge of any particular topic |
| | Use vocabulary terms the student knows | |
| | Decrease the use of complex language | |
| | Use short sentences | Using shorter sentences will allow the student to keep focused on the question and accommodate for poor short-term memory. |
| **Format** | Clear & dark print on a solid, nondistracting background | Address visual organizational difficulties in a clear, well-space test to allow the student to better organize his or her thoughts reduce distractibility |
| | Proper spacing & sequencing of items | |
| | Boldface verbs and directive words | To better allow the student to understand the directions, boldface them to give a visual clue as to exactly what is expected |
| | Avoid tricky items | To compensate for problems with comprehension, avoid using confusing or tricky questions that might inhibit the student in correctly conveying his or her knowledge. |
| **Appearance** | Entire test typed | To address difficulties with visual organization, a clearly typed test will not distract a student's sense of visual perception allowing him or her to relay his knowledge about a particular subject |
| | Adequate spacing to respond to items | Giving the test proper spaces in which to respond to question will allow the student to remain visually organized. |

**Table 5.7**    Suggested Test Modifications—Essay

Essay

|  | *Recommended Changes* | *Rationale* |
|---|---|---|
| **Content** | Relate to instructional objectives | This will allow the student to accomplish the goals outlined in his/her IEP. |
|  | Frequent testing vs. fewer tests | To address poor short-tem memory, frequent testing will be more effective in attaining what the student knows about a particular subject. |
| **Readability** | Use clear language in directions | Poor comprehension skills and poor word attack skills can impair the student's ability to relay his knowledge of any particular topic. |
|  | Provide specific criteria of necessary responses |  |
| **Format** | Give writing prompt in clear, outlined manner | Poor visual perception can impair the student's ability to organize information that is presented in a block paragraph form |
|  | **Boldface**, <u>underline</u>, or *italicize* any specific or necessary instruction | Important words or directions will stand out allowing a student with poor visual perception or comprehension to understand clearly the writing task |
| **Appearance** | Provide outline | Poor perception and comprehension limits a student to clearly relay his or her knowledge of a particular subject—outlines help the student organize his or her thoughts |
|  | Provide lined paper | Allow for a student with poor visual perception to keep thoughts organized |

**Table 5.8**    Suggested Test Modifications—True or False

True or False

|  | *Recommended Changes* | *Rationale* |
|---|---|---|
| **Content** | Relate to instructional objectives | This will allow the student to accomplish the goals outlined in his/her IEP. |
|  | Frequent testing vs. fewer tests | To address poor short-term memory, frequent testing will be more effective in attaining what the student knows about a particular subject. |
| **Readability** | Eliminate double negatives | Confusing language can inhibit the student's ability to relay his or her knowledge |
|  | Eliminate backward-sounding questions |  |
|  | Each true–false item should target only one fact at a time and should restrict statements to a single idea | Multi-facet questions can confuse the student as to exactly what is being asked |

*(Continued)*

**Table 5.8** Continued)

|  | *Recommended Changes* | *Rationale* |
|---|---|---|
|  | When designing true–false items, avoid absolute words (such as all, always, never) and indefinite adjectives, generalizations, and qualifying terms (such as usually, generally, sometimes). | Language can be subjective and therefore the student becomes more focused on hypothesizing what the teacher meant as opposed to the content knowledge |
| **Format** | Type words "true" and "false" and have student circle or underline | Provides a clear method of response and avoids confusing an illegible "T" with an "F" |
| **Appearance** | Entire test typed | To address difficulties with visual organization, a clearly typed test will not distract a student's sense of visual perception allowing him or her to relay his knowledge about a particular subject. |
|  | Adequate spacing to respond to items | Giving the test proper spaces in which to respond to questions will allow the student to remain visually organized. |

## Possible Test Modifications for Specific Learners

| | |
|---|---|
| Large-type editions of tests | For students with **visual** difficulties/deficits |
| Increased spacing between test items | For students with **motor** difficulties/deficits |
| Reduce number of test items per page | For students with **visual perception** difficulties |
| Multiple-choice items in vertical format with answer bubble to right of response choices | For students with **visual perception** difficulties |
| Reading passages with one complete sentence per line | For students with **visual perception** and **comprehension** difficulties |
| Increase size of answer blocks/bubble | For students with **vision** and/or **motor** difficulties |

## Revised Test Directions

| | |
|---|---|
| Directions read to student | Provides clear understanding of tasks |
| Directions reread for each page of questions | Keep student focused and accommodate for difficulties with comprehension |
| Language in directions simplified | For students with comprehension difficulties and/or limited vocabulary |
| Verbs in directions underlined or highlighted | Clear and constant reminders of task |
| Cues (e.g., arrows and stop sign) on answer form | For students with visual perception difficulties and short attention spans |
| Additional examples provided | Clear understanding of tasks and expectation |

## Use of Aids/Assistive Technology

- Audiotape
- Tape recorder
- Amanuensis (Scribe)
- Calculator

- Abacus
- Arithmetic tables
- Spell-check device
- Grammar-check device
- Computer (including talking word processor)
- Listening section repeated more than the standard number of times
- Listening section signed more than the standard number of times
- Masks or markers to maintain place
- Papers secured to work area with tape/magnets
- Test passages, questions, items, and multiple-choice responses read to student
- Test passages, questions, items, and multiple-choice responses signed to student

## Method of Response

- Allow marking of answers in booklet rather than answer sheet
- Use of additional paper for math calculations

## Other

- On-task focusing prompts
- Waiving spelling requirements
- Waiving paragraphing requirements
- Waiving punctuation requirements

# EXAMPLES OF QUESTIONS TO ASK TO DETERMINE IF ACCOMMODATIONS ARE NEEDED:

- Are instructional materials used in the classroom provided in a revised format (e.g., nonstandard print or spacing)?
- Does the student have difficulty maintaining his or her place in a standard examination booklet?
- Does the student have a visual, perceptual, or motor impairment that requires large-type or Braille materials?
- Is the student able to read and understand directions?
- Is this accommodation provided to the student in the classroom?
- Can the student follow oral directions from an adult or audiotape?
- Does the student need directions repeated frequently?
- What aids are used for classroom instruction?
- What assistive technology devices are indicated on the student's IEP?
- Has the student been identified as having a reading disability?
- Does the student have low/poor reading skills that may require the reading of tests or sections of tests that do not measure reading comprehension in order for the student to demonstrate knowledge of subject areas?
- Does the student have difficulty tracking from one paper to another and maintaining his or her place?
- Does the student have a disability that affects the ability to record his or her responses in the standard manner?
- Can the student use a pencil or writing instrument?
- What aids are used in the classroom and for homework assignments (e.g., word processor, adaptive writing instruments or dictating to a tape recorder or scribe)?
- Is the student identified as having a disability that affects the ability to spell?
- Has the student been identified as having a disability that affects his/her ability to compute or memorize basic math facts?
- Does the student have a visual or motor disability that affects the ability to use paper and pencil to perform computations?
- Does the student have difficulty staying on task?

# MODIFICATION OF ASSIGNMENTS & CURRICULUM

- Provide student with samples and models of work that are "at standard."
- Provide student with rubric detailing your expectations and upon which specific criteria they will be evaluated.
- Simplify complex directions.
- Divide tasks into parts; assign one part at a time.
- Extend or adjust time for task completion.
- Give frequent short quizzes and fewer long tests.
- Monitor closely as student begins assignments to ensure understanding.
- Shorten assignments, adjust the length.
- Structure assignment so that it is broken down into smaller segments.
- Check assignment midway through (or sooner) for corrective feedback.
- Reduce paper/pencil tasks.
- Have student dictate work while someone else records/transcribes.
- Allow different ways to answer other than in writing.
- Adjust the reading level of the assignment.
- Modify the length of the task.
- Increase the novelty of the task (i.e., turn into game format or provide other materials for student use—such as dry erase boards/colored markers rather than paper/pencil).
- Reduce the amount of required copying from the board.
- Reduce the amount of required copying from a book.
- Increase personal assistance (e.g., peer tutor, teacher, paraprofessional).
- Provide handouts that have fewer items on page, and are easy to read.
- Allow use of computer for written tasks.
- Provide choices of projects/assignments that draw on range of student interests and strengths.
- Limit number of choices in tasks, topics, and activities.
- Allow demonstration of mastery by alternative methods (i.e., oral tests).
- Assist student in determining the amount of time the assignment should take to complete.
- Reduce the number of problems on the page.
- Enlarge the print size and spacing on the page.
- Allow student to print rather than write in cursive if easier and faster.
- Provide in-class assistance on homework assignments.
- Modify homework as needed—being responsive to parent feedback.

## Instructional Interventions and Accommodations

- Preview/review major concepts.
- Contextualize lessons (gestures, props, visuals, demonstrations).
- Use cooperative learning structures (particularly use of partners/pairs).
- Explicitly teach study skills/learning strategies (e.g., note taking, active reading strategies, proofreading, use of dictionary, outlining, skimming).
- Extensive use of graphic organizers
- Increased teacher modeling and use of visual aids during instruction
- Provision of student models (work samples showing standards of acceptable and exemplary student)
- Guided practice (i.e., use of partial outlines, do first few items together)
- Provide study guides, advanced organizers, notes
- Use of technology and games for skill practice
- Extensive use of concrete manipulatives and hands-on approaches
- Use of calculators, manipulatives, tables/charts during math
- Use of tape recorders (for directions, prewriting, books on tape)
- Allow extra time for written responses
- Additional time for work completion

- Allow choice in ways to demonstrate knowledge/mastery
- Provide highlighted texts that indicate key concepts and information
- Set up consistent routines and efficient procedures for beginning lessons, transitioning between lessons, getting and putting away materials
- Introduce or preview new vocabulary before beginning new lesson
- Use varied questioning strategies to elicit active participation of all students (i.e., use of response cards, unison responses)
- Increase the frequency/amount of direct feedback
- Increase the amount of practice and review
- Write key concepts on board, summarize
- Allow extra "wait time" or "think time" (at least five seconds).
- Give multisensory instructions/directions (not just verbal or written).
- Ensure student has understood directions (i.e., be able to tell them back to you or partner, demonstrate understanding of directions before being asked to do seat work/independent work)
- Limit distractions in work area (e.g., use of privacy board)
- Increase use of direct and indirect signals, prompts, cues
- Organization/study skills interventions
- Utilize a program that specifically instructs students in organization and study skills
- By the 3rd or 4th grade, teach and require use of a binder/notebook to organize assignments
- Require use of a backpack or book bag to carry to and from school daily
- Teach and require use of assignment calendar or daily/weekly assignment sheet with monitoring and expectation of daily usage
- Model recording of assignments for each subject area
- Teacher/aide or student buddy to assist with recording of assignments
- Have an end-of-day check by teacher for expected books and materials to take home
- Provide students with handouts that are already three-hole punched
- Color code books, notebooks, and materials to help distinguish different subject areas and make location quicker and easier
- Place a "things to do" list taped to desk.
- Arrange for easy access to supplies and materials
- Break down long assignments into smaller increments
- Monitor progress on long-term assignments with frequent feedback along the way
- Limit the amount of materials/clutter on the student's desk
- Post a schedule of the daily activities. Use a master calendar that shows when assignments are due
- Use a standard procedure for turning in homework and assignments
- Use a contract for assignments that need to be completed in class or at home
- Provide time and assistance for cleaning out/sorting students' messy desks, backpacks, notebooks, and lockers
- Record all assignments in a consistent place in the room (e.g., corner of the board)
- Provide models of well-organized papers, projects, science boards, etc.
- Increase rewards and incentives for being organized
- Explicitly teach study skills (e.g., note taking, test taking strategies, RCRC (read/cover/recite/check)
- Provide direct assistance getting started on homework assignments and projects at school

## Academic Strategies and Interventions

- Teach prerequisite skills needed to do grade level/classroom work
- Structure seat work to include activities to reinforce learning that can be done successfully at student's independent level and grade level activities with a peer partner
- More time daily engaged in reading at instructional level
- More time daily engaged in reading at independent level

- Direct, systematic instruction to build skills in area(s) of identified weakness
- Consult with special education teacher/other staff for strategies and suggestions in how to teach concepts/skills in a different way
- Increase use of visuals, charts, models, and exemplars for easy student reference
- Use of multisensory techniques to present information, cue students, and aid in learning of all content areas
- Supplement instruction using alternative approaches to teaching the concept/skill
- Increase student use of manipulatives and tools of technology to learn skills and concepts and reinforce learning
- Utilize books on tape—student listens and follows along in text
- Teach active reading strategies (i.e., SQ3R), summarizing, identifying main ideas, story, grammar skills
- Allow use of calculators, graph paper to align numbers, charts, manipulatives, and other aides for math
- Teach math facts using mnemonics to make rhymes
- Set math facts to music and practice at regular intervals
- Provide several process examples in math
- Increase instruction to explicitly teach: the writing process, prewriting strategies, handwriting, coherent and expanded sentence/paragraph writing, written organization, mechanics, editing
- Modify written work requirements (e.g., shorten assignment, allow student to dictate responses, allow to print rather than write in cursive)
- Testing modifications and adaptations (for nonstandardized, teacher/classroom tests)
- Eliminate unnecessary words and confusing language on the test
- Underline or color highlight directions or key words in direction.
- Read test to student with poor reading skills (in class or other location)
- Tape record the test questions so student can listen to tape while reading it and replay to work at his/her own pace
- Allow student to tape record his/her answers to essay questions or dictate to a scribe
- Read, paraphrase, and clarify all test questions to students as needed
- Provide copies that are easy to read (typed, well-spaced, and formatted)
- For math tests, allow use of graph paper or other paper that can be attached to test
- Divide test into parts, administering on different days or periods during the day, rather than rushing to complete in one sitting
- Test in a different location—one that has fewer distractions
- Give partial credit for what is done correctly
- Score tests for number correct/total number assigned per student (which can be shortened for individual students)
- Collaborate with special educators to rewrite the tests for students with special needs (i.e., shorter sentences, simplified vocabulary, easier to read format such as enlarging print, reducing # of items on page)
- Eliminate need to first copy questions from board or book onto paper, and allow to write directly on test or in test booklet, if needed
- Lower the readability level of the questions—revise the wording to ask the same question with easier to understand vocabulary if necessary
- Avoid negatively stated questions
- Prior to test, review, review, review!
- Administer frequent short quizzes (not necessarily graded) throughout the teaching unit, reviewing the next day, so students have feedback on their understanding of the material
- Use a variety of modes or types of questions (i.e., multiple choice, matching, fill in the blank, true or false, short answer)

- Place multiple choice items vertically rather than horizontally
- Allow extended time for completing the test
- Point out careless errors and allow chance to correct before grading
- Take written test again orally, and average the two grades

## Attention and Memory Accommodations

- Provide preferential seating [e.g., closer to teacher, near positive role model(s)]
- Stand near student when giving directions or presenting lessons
- Reduce/minimize distractions (visual, auditory, spatial, movement)
- Provide study carrel/office area for seat work
- Provide privacy boards/other partitions for seat work/test taking
- Use visual/graphic depictions of routines, procedures, steps
- Reduce auditory distractions through use of tools (i.e., earphones)
- Reduce noise level in room
- Reduce clutter in environment—especially in direct visual field
- Seat away from high traffic areas, windows and doors
- Add color to increase focus on work (e.g., colored poster board under student's work on desk, highlighting key words)
- Use eye contact and voice modulation to maintain attention
- Avoid interruptions in classroom routine
- Establish a calm, predictable environment
- Increase use of signals to increase attention to and alert students of approaching transitions, changes of routine, etc.
- Vary the method of lesson presentation
- Increase use of partner/buddy throughout the day to help focus attention to task, check understanding of directions, assist with recording of assignments on assignment calendar, practice/review spelling words, times tables, etc.
- Provide tasks/tests in segments so student turns in one segment before receiving the next part
- Label, highlight, underline, and add color to important parts of tasks
- Provide memory aids such as number lines, pictures, tables/charts, formulas
- Have student repeat directions, restate in his/her own words
- Give both oral and visual instructions for assignments
- Increase incentive (e.g., earn points/rewards) for on-task behavior
- Require student to record assignments and monitor on daily basis
- Use mnemonics and association strategies to aid with memory
- Use melody and rhythm to help with memory of information
- Significantly increase opportunities for review and practice

## Behavioral Accommodations and Supports

- Establish a calm, structured, predictable environment
- Increase the monitoring and supervision
- Use discreet private signals with the student
- Place student near tolerant peer/good role model
- Increase distance between desks
- Allow student to reverse and straddle chair (for wider base of support)
- Plan student seating (bus, classroom, cafeteria, auditorium)
- Provide student with cooling off options (time and space to regroup)
- Provide student with two-seat option (e.g., desk a or desk b) and different options for doing work in various locations/positions
- Define child's work space and boundaries (e.g., colored masking tape)
- Utilize class and/or individual behavior plans

- Allow student to move to another location in room to regain control (student initiated)
- Increase communication with parent—more frequent conferences and planning meetings trying to build a partnership on behalf of student
- Increase phone contact with parents remembering to share positive observations as well as concerns
- Establish a home/school communication form or system for behavior monitoring
- Buddy up with another teacher (e.g., time away in other classroom)
- Identify what will be most motivating as incentives for that student (e.g., leadership roles, responsibilities, tangible rewards, working to earn tangible or activity reinforcers individually or for the group)
- Increase opportunity for positive reinforcement when displaying appropriate behavior and increase immediacy of reward schedule
- Significantly increase positive attention and encouragement
- Let student know you are interested in helping him/her, dialogue with student about his/her needs, encourage open communication
- Give student choices (a or b), and involve in own problem solving
- Notify and conference with other school personnel (e.g., counselor, assistant principal, other teachers)
- Discuss inappropriate behavior with student in private
- Write a contract for student behavior (e.g., goal to work on/reward)
- Use role play with student to practice appropriate behavior
- Increase the immediacy of rewards
- Look for small steps to success and positively reinforce those steps

## Social/Emotional/Coping Strategies and Supports

- Try various seating arrangements to provide a situation in which student feels comfortable
- Assign classroom/school responsibilities to the student
- Try to identify what is causing the student stress and frustration
- Reduce number of assignments or modify to enable greater student success rate
- Reduce paper/pencil tasks and allow other means of output
- Extend time for assignment completion
- Use short, one-concept commands and directions, accompanied by demonstrations or a visual example
- Use a timer to determine the amount of time to be spent for a particular task
- Provide activities at which student can be successful (academically and socially)
- Involve student in peer tutoring activities with younger children
- Arrange for student to carry messages to other classrooms or to the office
- Discover student's interests and provide activities that match those interests
- Attempt to involve student in extracurricular activities
- Call attention to the student's strengths and display his/her talents
- Give student responsibility of being teacher's assistant, peer tutor, model, group leader, etc.
- Consult with other teachers, support personnel (e.g., guidance counselor, nurse, assistant principal)
- Increase communication with parents
- Increase 1:1 opportunities to meet with student, conference, and establish a supportive relationship
- Assign a peer buddy who will be supportive and tolerant
- Teach appropriate social skills, coping strategies, and problem solving
- Positively reinforcement student's use/application of appropriate social skills and coping strategies
- Pair student with an upper grade tutor, staff member, or "special friend."
- Significantly increase positive interactions, frequency of encouragement and feedback

## Assistive Technology

The American School Counselor Association recommends that school counselors promote technological applications that are appropriate for students' individual needs. Students in the 21st Century are surrounded by technological advancements, with children starting computer use as early as kindergarten The National Telecommunications Information Administration & Economics and Statistics Administration (2002) indicated that ninety percent or 48 million children and youth between the ages of 5 and 17 now use computers http://www.ncrel.org/engauge/skills/divide.htm. Therefore, technological assistance may be important to students with special needs in helping them perform to the best of their abilities, as well as in keeping pace with the educational environment.

As defined in IDEA, an assistive technology *device* means any item, piece of equipment, or product system, whether acquired commercially off the shelf, modified, or customized, that is used to increase, maintain, or improve the functional capabilities of a child with a disability. (34 CFR 300.5) An assistive technology *service* means any service that directly assists a child with a disability in the selection, acquisition, or use of an assistive technology device. (34 CFR 300.6) http://www.isbe.net/SPEC-ED/html/assist_tech.htm

In addition, the Assistive Technology Act of 2004 sought to increase access to assistive technology in order that individuals with disabilities have greater control over their lives and better function in their environments, such as school http://www.ed.gov/about/offices/list/osers/policy.html. Note, the Center for Applied Special Technology (2004) does not limit technological options to expensive or "high-tech" devices, but emphasizes equipment that assists students to better function in a given environment. There have been several clarifications from the Office of Special Education and Rehabilitative Services (OSERS) on the use of AT by students with disabilities. These include the following:

- AT must be provided by the school district at no cost to the family.
- AT must be determined on a case-by-case basis; it is required if needed to ensure access to free and appropriate public education (FAPE).
- If the IEP team determines that AT is needed for home use to ensure FAPE, it must be provided.
- The student's IEP must reflect the nature of the AT and amount of supportive AT services required.
- A parent is accorded an extensive set of procedural safeguards, including the provision of AT to the child. http://atto.buffalo.edu/registered/ATBasics/Foundation/intro/introATidea.php

It is crucial, therefore, that school counselors be cognizant of the existence of a gamut of assistive technology devices, and how they can enhance the academic performance of the needs of their individual students with special needs.

Please refer to the comprehensive list of resources *on Assistive Technology and Special Needs* provided by Internet4Classrooms http://www.internet4classrooms.com/assistive_tech.htm, *Technology's Role in the Special Education Classroom http://home.swbell.net/jraneri/technology.html,* as well as catalogs such as the *Enabling Devices Product Catalog* http://enablingdevices.com/catalog and those produced by *Rehabtool* (rehabtool.com)

### Activity

Develop an Assistive Technology Plan for a school district. Review model programs such as the *Illinois Assistive Technology Program* http://www.iltech.org/publications.asp#Resources and the University of Texas at Austin Lab http://www.edb.utexas.edu/ATLab/learnmore.php. Consult with your with your school district technology experts, and online articles, such as *Assistive Technology for students with mild disabilities http://www.kidsource.com/kidsource/content2/assistive_technology.html* will also assist in the development of such a list.

**FORM 5.1**    Recommended Changes to the Classroom Test

To be consistent with documentation, use this form or one similar to track accommodations and rationale for reporting purposes.

Student: _____ Date: _____

Subject: _____ Teacher: _____

Type of Test: _____

| Type of Test Change | Recommended Changes | Rationale |
|---|---|---|
| Content | | |
| Readability | | |
| Format | | |
| Appearance | | |

Copyright © 2009 by Corwin Press. All rights reserved. Reprinted from *The School Counselor's Guide to Special Education* by Barbara C. Trolley, Heather S. Haas, and Danielle Campese Patti. Thousand Oaks, CA: Corwin Press, www.corwinpress.com. Reproduction authorized only for the local school site or nonprofit organization that has purchased this book.

**FORM 5.2**  Adaptation/ Modification Worksheet

*To be consistent with documentation, use this form or one similar to track accommodations and rationale for reporting purposes.*

Student: _____ Date: _____

Subject: _____ Teacher: _____

Type of Test: _____

| Specific Deficits That Compromise Test Performance |
| --- |
| |

| | Adaptation/Modification | Rationale |
| --- | --- | --- |
| Before the test | | |
| During the test | | |

Copyright © 2009 by Corwin Press. All rights reserved. Reprinted from *The School Counselor's Guide to Special Education* by Barbara C. Trolley, Heather S. Haas, and Danielle Campese Patti. Thousand Oaks, CA: Corwin Press, www.corwinpress.com. Reproduction authorized only for the local school site or nonprofit organization that has purchased this book.

**FORM 5.3**   Sample School-Age IEP

*Check with your district , local education agency, or state education department for laws and regulations regarding IEP documents to use.*

**School District Name**

**Street Address**

**City, State, and Zip Code**

**Telephone Number**

| Student Name: | Date of Birth:  /  / | Age: |
|---|---|---|

Disability Classification: Choose one

| | |
|---|---|
| Street: | Telephone: |
| City: | County of Residence: |
| Zip: | Male [ ] Female [ ] |
| Student ID#: | Native Language of Student: |
| Current Instructional Grade/Grade Equivalent: | Interpreter for Student Needed: |
| Racial/Ethnic Group of Student: Choose One | Yes [ ] No [ ] |
| Medical Alerts: | If yes, specify language: |
| | Surrogate Parent Needed: Yes [ ] No [ ] |

Other Information:

Date of initial referral:  /  /

Date initial consent for evaluation received:  /  /

Date of IEP meeting to determine initial eligibility:  /  /

Date of Committee on Special Education (CSE) Meeting to Develop this IEP:  /  /

Type of Meeting:

[ ] Initial [ ] Requested Review [ ] Annual Review [ ] Reevaluation

[ ] _____

Date IEP is to be Implemented:  /  /

Projected Date of Next Review:  /  /

Projected Date of Reevaluation Meeting:  /  /

- the student's needs related to communication, behavior, use of Braille, assistive technology, limited English proficiency;

- how the student's disability affects involvement and progress in the general curriculum; and

- the student's needs as they relate to transition from school to postschool activities for students beginning with the first IEP to be in effect when the student turns age 15 (and younger if deemed appropriate).

| Transcript Information—Secondary Students Only | |
|---|---|
| Diploma Credits Earned: | Expected Date of High School Completion:   /   / <br> Projected # years to graduate: |
| Commencement-level State Tests Passed: | Expected Diploma: |

**Academic Achievement, Functional Performance, and Learning Characteristics:**

Current levels of knowledge and development in subject and skill areas, including activities of daily living, level of intellectual functioning, adaptive behavior, expected rate of progress in acquiring skills and information, and learning style.

**Social Development:**

The degree and quality of the student's relationships with peers and adults, feelings about self and social adjustment to school and community environments.

**Physical Development:**

The degree or quality of the student's motor and sensory development, health, vitality, and physical skills or limitations that pertain to the learning process.

**Management Needs:**

The nature of and degree to which environmental modifications and human or material resources are required to enable the student to benefit from instruction. Management needs are determined in accordance with the factors identified in the areas of academic achievement, functional performance and learning characteristics, social development, and physical development.

*(Continued)*

**FORM 5.3** (Continued)

### Measurable Postsecondary Goals (Ages 15 and older)

For students beginning with the first IEP to be in effect when the student turns age 15 (and younger if deemed appropriate), identify the appropriate measurable postsecondary goals based on age-appropriate transition assessments relating to training, education, employment, and, when appropriate, independent living skills.

Training:

Education:

Employment:

Independent Living Skills (when appropriate):

*Transition Plan age requirements vary from state to state.

### Measurable Annual Goals

* For students with severe disabilities who would meet the eligibility criteria to take the New York State Alternate Assessment, the IEP must also include short-term instructional objectives and benchmarks for each annual goal.

- **Annual Goal:** What the student will be expected to be able to do by the end of the year in which the IEP is in effect.
- **Evaluative Criteria:** How well and over what period of time the student must demonstrate performance in order to consider the annual goal to have been met..
- **Procedures to Evaluate Goal:** The method that will be used to measure progress and determine if the student has met the annual goal.
- **Evaluation Schedule:** The dates or intervals of time by which evaluation procedures will be used to measure the student's progress.

| | |
|---|---|
| **Annual Goal** | |
| **Evaluative Criteria** | |
| **Procedures to Evaluate Goal** | |
| **Evaluation Schedule** | |

(Add additional annual goals as appropriate)

### Recommended Special Education Programs and Services

| Special Education Program/Services | | | | |
|---|---|---|---|---|
| | **Frequency** | **Duration** | **Location** | **Initiation Date** |
| . | . | . | . | /  / |
| . | . | . | . | /  / |

| Special Education Program/Services | | | | |
|---|---|---|---|---|
| | **Frequency** | **Duration** | **Location** | **Initiation Date** |
| . | . | . | . | / / |
| . | . | . | . | / / |

| Related Services | | | | |
|---|---|---|---|---|
| | **Frequency** | **Duration** | **Location** | **Initiation Date** |
| . | . | . | . | / / |
| . | . | . | . | / / |

| Program Modifications/Accommodations/Supplementary Aids and Services | | | | |
|---|---|---|---|---|
| | **Frequency** | **Duration** | **Location** | **Initiation Date** |
| . | . | . | . | / / |
| . | . | . | . | / / |

| Assistive Technology Devices/Services | | | | |
|---|---|---|---|---|
| | **Frequency** | **Duration** | **Location** | **Initiation Date** |
| . | . | . | . | / / |
| . | . | . | . | / / |

| Supports for School Personnel on Behalf of Student | | | | |
|---|---|---|---|---|
| | **Frequency** | **Duration** | **Location** | **Initiation Date** |
| . | . | . | . | / / |
| . | . | . | . | / / |

**Special Transportation Needs:**

[ ] None

[ ] Student has special transportation needs as recommended below:

[ ] Special seating—Specify:

[ ] Vehicle and/or equipment needs—Specify:

[ ] Adult supervision—Specify:

[ ] Type of transportation— Specify:

[ ] Other accommodations—Specify:

*(Continued)*

**Other:**

**Testing Accommodations:**

The following individual appropriate accommodations are necessary to measure the academic achievement and functional performance of the student on state and districtwide assessments. Recommended testing accommodations will be used consistently:

- in the student's education program,

- in the administration of districtwide assessments of student achievement, consistent with school district policy, and

- in the administration of state assessments of student achievement, consistent with state education department policy.

| Testing Accommodation | Conditions | Specifications |
|---|---|---|
| . | . | . |
| . | . | . |
| . | . | . |

**Participation in State Assessments**

[ ] The student will participate in the same state assessments that are administered to general education students.

   [ ] Graded: The student will take the state assessment with his/her grade level peers.

   [ ] Ungraded: The student will take the state assessment based on chronological age because his/her instructional levels in English and mathematics are three or more years below the grade-level coursework of the student's nondisabled peers.

[ ] The student will participate in the New York State Alternate Assessment (NYSAA) for Students with Severe Disabilities.

   Explain why the state assessment(s) administered to general education students is not appropriate for the student and why the alternate assessment selected is appropriate for the student: _____

**Participation in Districtwide Assessments**

[ ] The student will participate in the same districtwide assessments that are administered to general education students.

[ ] The student will participate in the following alternate assessment for districtwide assessments:

   Explain why the districtwide assessment(s) administered to general education students is not appropriate for the student and why the alternate assessment selected is appropriate for the student:

**Removal from the general educational environment occurs only when the nature or severity of the disability is such that, even with the use of supplementary aids and services, education cannot be satisfactorily achieved.**

[ ] Explanation of the extent, if any, to which the student will not participate in general education programs, including extracurricular and other nonacademic activities:

[ ] The student will not participate in the general education physical education program, but will participate in specially designed or adapted physical education.

**Language other than English exemption**

[ ] No

[ ] Yes, the student's disability adversely affects the ability to learn a language, and the student is excused from the language other than English requirement.

---

**Coordinated Set of Transition Activities (School to Postschool)**

For students beginning with the first IEP to be in effect when the student turns age 16 (and younger if deemed appropriate) needed transition services/activities to facilitate the student's movement from school to postschool activities.

| Coordinated Set of Transition Activities | Activity | School District/ Agency Responsible | Date |
|---|---|---|---|
| Instruction | . | . | |
| Related Services | . | . | |
| Development of Employment/Other Postschool Adult Living Objectives | . | . | |
| Community Experience | . | . | |
| Acquisition of Daily Living Skills | . | . | |
| Functional Vocational Assessment | . | . | |

*Transition Plan age requirements vary from state to state.

---

**Placement Recommendation**

Ten-Month Placement:

---

| **Extended School Year Eligible:** | |
|---|---|
| [ ] Yes [ ] No | Projected dates of services:  /  /  to  /  / |
| If yes: Provider: | Site: |

## Reporting Progress to Parents

Identify when periodic reports on the progress the student is making toward meeting the annual goals will be provided to the student's parents:

## Recommendations Upon Declassification

Date Declassified:     /     /

IEP recommendations to continue upon declassification:

| Testing Accommodations | Conditions | Specifications |
|---|---|---|
|  |  |  |
|  |  |  |
|  |  |  |

Continued Eligibility for Local Diploma ("Safety Net"): [ ] Yes [ ] No
Continued "Language Other Than English" Exemption: [ ] Yes [ ] No

**Declassification Support Services to be provided during the first year that a student moves from a special education program to a full-time general education program.**

| Service | Initiation Date | Frequency | Duration | Ending Date |
|---|---|---|---|---|
| . | / / | . | . | / / |
| . | / / | . | . | / / |
| . | / / | . | . | / / |

## Parent Information

Student's Name:

| Mother's/Guardian's Name: | Telephone: |
|---|---|
| Street: | County of Residence: |
| City: | Native Language of Parent/Guardian: |
| Zip: | Interpreter Needed for Meeting: Yes [ ] No [ ] |
| Father's/Guardian's Name: | Telephone: |
| Street: | County of Residence: |
| City: | Native Language of Parent/Guardian: |
| Zip: | Interpreter Needed for Meeting: Yes [ ] No [ ] |

| [ ] Surrogate Parent Needed | Date Appointed:     /     / |
|---|---|
| Surrogate Parent's Name: | Telephone: |
| Street: | Native Language of Surrogate Parent: |
| City: | Interpreter Needed for Meeting:<br>     Yes [ ] No [ ] |
| Zip: | |

**Committee Participants**

[ ] CSE

[ ] Subcommittee

| Name | Professional Title | Committee Member Role[1] |
|---|---|---|
| . | . | |
| . | . | . |
| . | . | . |
| . | . | . |
| . | . | . |

1. If the parent or another CSE member participated (with parent and school district agreement) through alternative means, indicate the manner in which he or she participated (e.g., video or telephone conference calls).

Copyright © 2009 by Corwin Press. All rights reserved. Reprinted from *The School Counselor's Guide to Special Education* by Barbara C. Trolley, Heather S. Haas, and Danielle Campese Patti. Thousand Oaks, CA: Corwin Press, www.corwinpress.com. Reproduction authorized only for the local school site or nonprofit organization that has purchased this book.

**FORM 5.4** A Quick Look at the IEP

The following document can be helpful for teachers and service providers to reference a one-page summary of the student's pertinent information. This completed form must be kept in a secure place as all information is, of course, confidential.

NOTE: This cannot fulfill the regulations that all the educators, related service providers, and support personnel of a student receive a copy of the student's IEP. It is simply meant to provide educators and service providers with a user-friendly and quick reference to the students' abilities, needs, and services.

Name: _____ Grade: _____

Disability: _____ D.O.B. _____

CSE Date: _____ Teacher: _____

| Special Alerts/Medical Concerns | |
| --- | --- |

| Program/Related Services | |
| --- | --- |

| Program Modifications, Conditions, and Specifications | |
| --- | --- |

| Test Modifications, Conditions, and Specifications | |
| --- | --- |

**Present Levels of Performance Summary**

| Domain | Strengths | Needs/Difficulties |
| --- | --- | --- |
| Academic | | |
| Social | | |
| Physical | | |
| Management | | |

| Goals: | |
| --- | --- |
| 1. | 2. |
| 3. | 4. |

Copyright © 2009 by Corwin Press. All rights reserved. Reprinted from *The School Counselor's Guide to Special Education* by Barbara C. Trolley, Heather S. Haas, and Danielle Campese Patti. Thousand Oaks, CA: Corwin Press, www.corwinpress.com. Reproduction authorized only for the local school site or nonprofit organization that has purchased this book.

*For a sample completed IEP, see Resource F*

Students who do not meet eligibility for receiving special education programming or services may be eligible for an accommodation plan under Section 504 of the American with Disabilities Act. Following is an example of a 504 Accommodation Plan. Section 504 is a GENERAL EDUCATION initiative and should NOT be reviewed by a CSE, but rather by a 504 Committee. It is not intended to be a safety net for special education services, but rather an accommodation plan to provide classroom and/or testing modifications and accommodations. Best practice would be to evaluate the student for a 504 Accommodation Plan separately from the Committee on Special Education.

## Questions for Reflection

1.  What is the special education process at your school? In your district?

2.  How is this process documented and communicated?

3.  What percentage of students in your school has been evaluated? In your district?

4.  What is the percentage of students who have IEPs? 504 Plans?

5.  How behaviorally written are the goals? Are they individualized?

6.  What tools are used to assess progress towards goals?

7.  What community resources exist to assist students with special needs in your school and district?

8.  What is the school counselor role in regard to CSE meetings? Development of IEPs? Development of 504 Plans?

9.  Who are the professionals on your CSE? How frequently do they meet?

Sample 504 Accommodation Plan

| Date 504 Meeting: | Purpose of Meeting: | |
|---|---|---|
| Student Name: | Date of Birth: | |
| Age: | Telephone: | |
| Address: | Student ID #: | |
| Male _____ Female _____ | Current Grade: | |
| Dominant Language of Student: | Interpreter Needed: | |
| Initial Date of Eligibility: | Date of Initiation of Services: Projected Date of Review: | |
| Medical Alerts: | | |
| Parent/Guardian's Name and Address: | | |
| Telephone: | County of Residence: | |
| Second Parent/Guardian's Name and Address: | | |
| Telephone | County of Residence: | |
| Dominant Language of Parent/Guardian: | Interpreter Needed: | |

## PRESENT LEVELS OF PERFORMANCE

**1. Academic/Educational Achievement and Learning Characteristics**: Address current levels of knowledge and development in subject and skill areas, including activities of daily living, level of intellectual functioning, adaptive behavior, expected rate of progress in acquiring skills and information, and learning style.

| **Present Levels:** | |
|---|---|
| **Abilities:** | |
| **Needs:** | |

**2. Social Development:** Describe the quality of the student's relationships with peers and adults, feelings about self, social adjustment to school and community environment, and behaviors that may impede learning.

| **Present Levels:** | |
|---|---|
| **Abilities:** | |
| **Needs:** | |

**3. Physical Development:** Describe the student's motor and sensory development, health, vitality, and physical skills or limitations that pertain to the learning process.

| Present Levels: | |
|---|---|
| Abilities: | |
| Needs: | |

**4. Management Needs:** Describe the nature and degree to which environmental modifications and human or material resources are required to address academic, social, and physical needs.

**A functional behavioral assessment** should be completed for any student who demonstrates behaviors that impede learning. A functional behavioral assessment becomes the basis for positive behavioral interventions, strategies, and supports for the student.

| Present Levels: | |
|---|---|
| Abilities: | |

## II. LONG-TERM ADULT OUTCOMES

**Long-Term Adult Outcomes:** Beginning at age 14 or younger if appropriate, state long-term adult outcomes reflecting students' needs, preferences, and interests in:

| Postsecondary Education/Training: | |
|---|---|
| Employment: | |
| Community Living: | |

## III. MEASURABLE ANNUAL GOALS

The student will ambulate throughout the school setting, avoiding obstacles within a given amount of time in four out of five trials.
    Criteria:
    Procedure:
    Responsibility:
    Schedule:

## IV. ELIGIBILITY DETERMINATION AND ACCOMMODATIONS

Students eligible for 504 assistance are those who have any physical or mental impairment that substantially limits one or more major life activities.

*(Continued)*

**FORM 5.5** (Continued)

| Describe the student's impairment: | |
|---|---|
| What is the major life activity affected by the impairment? | |

**B. Extended School Year Services Yes No**

| B. Special Education Programs/Related Services | Initiation Date | Frequency | Size | Location |
|---|---|---|---|---|
| | | | | |

| C. Supplementary Aids & Services and/or Program Modification or Supports for the Student | Initiation Date | Frequency | Duration | Location |
|---|---|---|---|---|
| | | | | |

| D. Describe any assistive technology devices or services needed: | |
|---|---|
| E. Describe the program modifications or supports for school personnel that will be provided on behalf of the student to address the annual goals and participation in general education curriculum and activities: | |

**F. Assessment**

| 1. Individual Testing Modification(s): | | |
|---|---|---|
| **Accommodation Name** | **Accommodation** | **Specifications/ Conditions** |
| | | |

| 2. State why the student will not participate in a state or district wide assessment: | |
|---|---|
| 3. Explain how the student will be assessed: | |

## V. ACADEMIC COURSES

| | |
|---|---|
| | |

## VI. PARTICIPATING AGENCIES FOR STUDENTS WHO REQUIRE TRANSITION SERVICES

Participating Agencies which have agreed to provide transition services/supports (before the students leave the secondary school program):

| | |
|---|---|
| Agency Name: | |
| Telephone Number: | |
| Service: | |
| Implementation date if different from IEP implementation date: | |

## VII. COORDINATED SET OF ACTIVITIES LEARNING TO LONG-TERM ADULT OUTCOMES

If any of the following areas are *not* addressed, explain why:

| Coordinate Set of Activities | Activity | School District/ Agency Responsible | Date |
|---|---|---|---|
| **Instruction:** | | | |
| **Related Services:** | | | |
| **Employment/ Postsecondary Education:** | | | |
| **Community Experience: (if appropriate)** | | | |
| **Activities of Daily Living:** | | | |
| **Functional Vocational Assessment:** | | | |

## VIII. GRADUATION INFORMATION FOR SECONDARY STUDENTS

| | |
|---|---|
| **Credential/Diploma Sought:** | |
| **Expected Date of High School Completion:** | |
| **Credits Earned to Date:** | |

*(Continued)*

**FORM 5.5** (Continued)

## IX. SUMMARY OF SELECTED RECOMMENDATIONS

| | |
|---|---|
| **Accommodation Plan:** | |
| **Recommended Placement Sept.–June:** | |
| **Extended School Year (ESY) Services:** | |
| **Recommended Placement July and August:** | |
| **Transportation Needs:** | |

## X. REPORTING PROGRESS TO PARENTS

| | |
|---|---|
| **State manner and frequency in which progress will be reported:** | |

## XI. COMMITTEE PARTICIPANTS

The list of names or signatures above indicates attendance/participation at the committee meeting and not necessarily agreement with the Section 504 recommendations developed at the meeting.

| Name | Professional Title | Committee Member Role |
|---|---|---|
| | | |
| | | |
| | | |
| | | |
| | | |
| | | |

Copyright © 2009 by Corwin Press. All rights reserved. Reprinted from *The School Counselor's Guide to Special Education* by Barbara C. Trolley, Heather S. Haas, and Danielle Campese Patti. Thousand Oaks, CA: Corwin Press, www.corwinpress.com. Reproduction authorized only for the local school site or nonprofit organization that has purchased this book.

# 6

# Process and Services

## *College*

Transition is defined as the "process of preparing students to meet the challenges of adulthood, including those involved in postsecondary education, vocational pursuits, and home and community" (Lewis & Doorlag, 2003, p. 446). Many professionals should be involved in collaboration and communication with regard to transition planning:

**Principals/Administrators:** Provide leadership, guidance, support; impact on service quality and data collection.

**General Education Teachers, Career Vocational Teachers, Special Education Teachers:** Build academic and social skills, self-determination and self-advocacy abilities, and community connections.

**Transition Coordinator or Service Coordinator:** Assist with postsecondary planning and links families and students with community resources. In addition to helping students with disabilities identify preferences, establish goals, and build postsecondary skills; collaborating with general educators regarding course of study; connecting with adult services for people with disabilities; and following up with students post graduation, these specialists also complete many broad transition functions. These tasks include: increasing transition services to target groups; affecting service priorities and service distribution; enhancing communication across agencies and disciplines; providing quality assurance and monitoring; conducting interagency problem solving; and monitoring service costs.

**School Counselors:** Implement counseling programs and provide support through classroom guidance, helping with postsecondary planning and college applications, and counseling to understand self.

**School Psychologists:** Conducts psychoeducational assessments, educational planning consultation, and makes instructional recommendations.

**Occupational Therapists, Physical Therapists, Speech and Language Therapists, and Nurses:** Provide schools, future employers, and other postsecondary professionals, where appropriate, education as to students with disabilities, medical conditions, health care needs, communication issues.

**School Assistance Counselors and Resources Officers (SROs):** (Former) Provides prevention/intervention services for children and youth at risk for substance abuse or behavioral problems; assists with identification of students at risk; communicates with families. (Latter) Provides police presence and assists with ensuring safe school environment; proactive in detecting potentially unsafe situations.

**Vocational Rehabilitation Counselor:** Provides information to IEP team about vocational services and student eligibility; writes Individual Plan for Employment (IPE) for eligible students; support; coordination of services. (Kochhar-Bryant, 2003, pp. 41–44).

**Community Services:** Support transition students and consult with IEP teams. Examples include: developmental disabilities, vocational rehabilitation services; community rehabilitation or community public or mental health services; residential and respite services; one-stop employment centers; postsecondary institutions; social work services; adult agencies and advocacy organizations; dropout prevention programs; business-education partnerships; assistive technology organizations; alcohol and substance abuse, correctional education and juvenile services; employers and employment specialists; recreation and leisure programs; adult education programs; parent training and information centers; and transportation offices (Kochhar-Bryant, 2004, p. 57).

**Job Coach:** A person who assists adult workers with disabilities, . . . providing vocational assessment, instruction, overall planning, and interaction assistance with employers, family, and related government and service agencies (Hallahan & Kauffman, 2006, p. 71).

# COLLEGE, EMPLOYMENT, AND DAILY LIVING

Just as with the general population of students in high school, students with disabilities need to think about and plan for the future. The overall transition pathways include academic, career-technical training, employment and supported setting (Greene & Kochhar-Bryant, 2004). While the rate of students with disabilities graduating from high school is increasing, only 25.5% graduated with a standard high school diploma in 1997–1998 (Sciarri, 2004). Further detailed statistics involving conditions for youth with disabilities post high school are outlined by Kochhar-Bryant (2004).

## College

There are many college options for students with disabilities, which include:

**Career & Technical Colleges:** Colleges which offer many options such as associate degree certificates, preparing students for technical occupations, and work apprenticeships, preparing graduates for jobs in industrial or service trades.

**Community Colleges:** Public, two-year colleges, typically in the community, offering technical and continuing education courses, leading to a license, certificate, or Associate of Arts or Science degree.

**Four-year Colleges & Universities:** Wide variety of courses, offering undergraduate Bachelor of Arts and Science degrees, and graduate study. (Kochhar-Bryant, 2004, pp. 25–26)

## Employment

For students looking at employment post–high school, offering vocational opportunities within the high school curriculum, building social, job searching and retention skills, networking with local educational agencies (LEAs), and promoting positive public relations with and education to perspective employers are important areas to address.

All of the above training will benefit students with disabilities who are looking at post–high school employment, whether the focus is the military, competitive workplaces, or other settings.

**Military:** Military service can provide students with disabilities a job, training, and life skills. However, military branches are not required to provide people with disabilities with accommodations (Brown, 2000; HEATH Resource Center, 2006).

**Competitive Employment :** A workplace that provides employment that pays at least minimum wage and in which most workers are nondisabled (Hallahan & Kauffman, 2006, p. 162).

Some graduates with disabilities cannot independently function in a competitive work environment, and may need supported employment.

**Supported Employment:** A method of integrating people with disabilities who cannot work independently into competitive employment; includes use of an employment specialist, or job coach, who helps the person function on the job (Hallahan & Kauffman, 2006, p. 71).

For students with more severely handicapping disabilities, sheltered workshops or day activity/treatment programs may be required.

**Sheltered Workshop:** A facility that provides a structured environment for persons with disabilities in which they can learn skills can be either a transitional placement or a permanent arrangement (Hallahan & Kauffman, 2006, p. 161).

**Day Activity Programs:** Programs that teach daily living skills, social skills, recreational opportunities, and general education such as that pertaining to medication.

## Daily Living

Students preparing to graduate from high school may need assistance in learning daily living skills, such as how to keep a house, cook, shop, balance a checkbook, and pay bills. While many graduates may continue to live at home while pursuing postsecondary training or employment, some will choose to move to a college dorm, an apartment shared with other students, or a group home.

**Community Residential Facility (CRF):** A place, usually a group home, in an urban or residential neighborhood where about three to ten adults with mental retardation live under the supervision of house parents; transitional placement to learn skills that will assist in more independent living or a permanent placement (Hallahan & Kauffman, 2006, p. 161). **Supported Living**: An approach to living arrangements for those with mental retardation that stresses living in natural settings rather than in institutions, big or small. (Hallahan & Kauffman, 2006, p. 161).

In addition to daily living skills, graduates with disabilities must become empowered, engaging in self-advocacy efforts with employers, college disability coordinators, or peers. In addition, they need to become comfortable with community participation and learn how to develop and engage in appropriate leisure activities (Kochhar-Bryant, 2004). It is also important to note that transition planning in IEPs is compatible with standards-based education (Kochhar-Bryant & Bassett, 2003).

# TRANSITION PLANS

As an IDEA 2004 requirement, IEPs need to contain a transition service plan by, if not before, the age of 16 for students with disabilities. This IEP, which must include linkages and responsibilities of participating agencies before students leave high school, needs to be annually reviewed. Specific transition-related content in the IEP should include:

- Postsecondary goal statements
- Present level of performance
- Goals and objectives
- Related and community based services
- Coordinated set of activities

(Kochhar-Bryant, 2004, p. 47)

As indicated above in the last component, this plan should include more than employment or college plans, such as adjustment to life after high school areas. HK2 (Halpern, 1993) identifies three quality of life areas that should be considered: adult role performance, physical and material well-being, and personal fulfillment. In addition, it is important that this plan go beyond the "letter of the law" and be of practical value. All plans should be student centered, such as individualized education plans.

**SAMPLE 6.1**

# LEVEL 1 CAREER ASSESSMENT

## Mandated Elements

*Student Interview:*

A one-to-one direct conversation with the student to determine the student's perception of what they expect as a result of participating in the schooling process

*Parent Interview:*

May be performed as a fact-to-face interview or in the form of a mail home questionnaire

*Educational Staff Reports:*

Checklist completed by two educational staff members per year who have regular contact with the student over a two-year period (four checklists completed by four educators over two years)

*Career Interest Information*

Expressed interest: determines student interest based on what the student says he/she is interested in

Manifest interest: determines student interest by observing student and determining what types of activities a student chooses to do when allowed to select (information may also be obtained from the educational staff report and parent interview)

Interest inventories: series of questions that ask the student to choose between different types of activities appropriate for students with abstract reasoning abilities and students who have had a variety of work/career-related experiences

*(Text continued on page 113)*

**FORM 6.1**  Annual Summary Sheet

| Action | | Suggested Age Range |
|---|---|---|
| _____ | Administer initial vocational assessment | 12 |
| _____ | Discuss the following curriculum areas at IEP meetings:<br>• Academic<br>• Social<br>• Language/communication<br>• Occupational<br>• Self-help skills<br>• Self-advocacy skills | 12–15 |
| _____ | Develop and implement strategies to increase responsibilities and independence at home | 12–15 |
| _____ | Complete periodic vocational evaluations | 12–21 |
| _____ | Introduce & discuss transition services | 14 |
| _____ | Notify parents that transition services will be incorporated into the IEP beginning at age 15 | 14 |
| _____ | Assure that copies of work-related documents are available:<br>• Social security card<br>• Birth certificate<br>• Obtain working papers (if appropriate) | 14–16 |
| _____ | Obtain parental consent so that the appropriate adult agency representative can be involved | 14–16 |
| _____ | Develop transition component of IEP and annually thereafter | 15+ |
| _____ | Discuss adult transition with CSE | 15–21 |
| _____ | Consider summer employment/ volunteer experience | 15–20 |
| _____ | Explore community leisure activities | 15–21 |
| _____ | Consider the need for residential opportunities, including completing applications, as appropriate | 15–21 |
| _____ | Obtain personal ID card | 16–18 |
| _____ | Obtain driver's training & license | 16–18 |

*(Continued)*

**FORM 6.1** (Continued)

| Action | Suggested Age Range |
|---|---|
| **Action** | |
| _____ Develop Transportation/Mobility Strategies: | 16–21 |
| • Independent travel skills training | |
| • Public or para-transit transportation | |
| • Needs for travel attendant | |
| _____ Investigate SSDI/SSI/Medicaid programs | 16–18 |
| _____ Consider guardianship or emancipation | 16–18 |
| _____ Develop & update employment plans | 16–21 |
| _____ Involve VESID/CBVH, as appropriate, within 2 years of school exit | 16–21 |
| _____ Research possible adult living situations | 16–18 |
| _____ Investigate postschool opportunities (further educational vocational training, college, military, etc.) | 16–18 |
| _____ Seek legal guardianship | 18 |
| _____ Apply for postschool college & other training programs | 17–21 |
| _____ Male students register for the draft. (No exceptions) | 18 |
| _____ Register to vote | 18 |
| _____ Review health insurance coverage: inform insurance company of son/daughter disability & investigate rider of continued eligibility | 18 |
| _____ Complete transition to employment, further education or training, and community living, affirming arrangements are in place for the following | 18–21 |
| • Postsecondary/Continuing education | |
| • Employment | |
| • Legal/advocacy | |
| • Personal independence/Residential | |
| • Recreation/Leisure | |
| • Medical/Health | |
| • Counseling | |
| • Financial/Income | |
| • Transportation/Independent travel skills | |
| • Other: | |

Copyright © 2009 by Corwin Press. All rights reserved. Reprinted from *The School Counselor's Guide to Special Education* by Barbara C. Trolley, Heather S. Haas, and Danielle Campese Patti. Thousand Oaks, CA: Corwin Press, www.corwinpress.com. Reproduction authorized only for the local school site or nonprofit organization that has purchased this book.

**LETTER 6.1**

## SAMPLE PARENT/GUARDIAN ORIENTATION LETTER

Dear (parent/guardian)

During the Individualized Education Program (IEP) meeting this year we will be discussing long-term planning with you and your child. We will look at where your child is going when completing school, what skills need to be developed in order to get there, and what linkages to other agencies may be necessary. The goal is to work together to ensure that your child has the opportunity to gain employability, academic, social, and living skills important to making the transition from school to work or further education and community living. We will also provide you with information about adult services that may be necessary to support your child's transition from high school to adult life.

Because the focus of this year's meeting is somewhat different, the following are some changes you might encounter:

1. Some skills that are important to develop are best taught at home by the parent; therefore, you and your child may be responsible for helping reach some of the goals listed on the IEP.

2. At the high school level, there will be a shift to skills that are important to employment, further education, and community living. The high school program will also relate to your child's needs and long-term goals for further education, employment, and community living.

3. As a parent/guardian, you know your child better than anyone and we need input from you. Enclosed is the Transition Questionnaire that we ask you to fill out and bring with you to the IEP meeting. This form asks you to identify the skills you see as important for us to work on with your child during the next year.

4. Since transition planning will be a part of your child's CSE meeting, individuals representing adult service agencies may be invited to participate at the IEP meeting. Through this opportunity to hear about available services, program eligibility requirements, and resources, you will be better able to decide with your child what agencies and services can benefit him/her after school.

5. Because this is long-term planning and is directly related to a student's goals for further education, living, and working, it is important that your child and you be present at IEP meetings.

We feel that by teaching the skills needed to live, learn, and work in the community and by providing you with additional information about adult services and programs, we can better meet the goal for which we are all striving—the successful participation of your child in adult life.

We look forward to working together toward this goal at the IEP meeting.

Sincerely,

(CSE Chairperson)

Transition Services, January 1993. Adapted from O'Leary and Paulson (1991)

Copyright © 2009 by Corwin Press. All rights reserved. Reprinted from *The School Counselor's Guide to Special Education* by Barbara C. Trolley, Heather S. Haas, and Danielle Campese Patti. Thousand Oaks, CA: Corwin Press, www.corwinpress.com. Reproduction authorized only for the local school site or nonprofit organization that has purchased this book.

**LETTER 6.2**

## STUDENT ORIENTATION LETTER

Dear (student)

You are invited to come to the next meeting with the Committee on Special Education, which is being held on <insert date> at <time> at <location>. We would like to talk with you about how you are doing in school, what you want to do in the future, and what activities your individualized educational program should include.

These activities are added to your program to help you prepare for your future and to learn the skills that you will need as an adult to be successful in living, learning, and working after you leave school. Activities may be in the classroom, in the community, or at worksites, for example. Transition services will be provided by the school district from the time you are age 15 until you leave school.

Before the meeting, please think about what you want to do after leaving school, what you can do now, and what skills you still need to learn. We would like you to come to the meeting ready to share your ideas, such as:

- What kind of job do you want to have?
- Where will you live—on your own or with others?
- What type of college or job training interests you?
- What will you do in your free time?
- How much money can you earn, and how will you pay bills?
- How you will get around—by car or by riding the bus or subway?

At the meeting, you will also receive information to help you make choices. The following people have been invited to come to the meeting to help plan your program: <insert names or identities>. Some people know you and have suggestions to make, or they know about different programs for you to consider.

Remember this is the beginning step. You will have time during the next few years to try different ideas. The school district will work with you all along the way, to help you explore and decide what you want to do in the future, and to help you prepare for it.

I look forward to seeing you at the meeting, and to having your help to plan a good program for your future success.

Sincerely,

CSE Chairperson

Copyright © 2009 by Corwin Press. All rights reserved. Reprinted from *The School Counselor's Guide to Special Education* by Barbara C. Trolley, Heather S. Haas, and Danielle Campese Patti. Thousand Oaks, CA: Corwin Press, www.corwinpress.com. Reproduction authorized only for the local school site or nonprofit organization that has purchased this book.

*Annual Summary Sheet:*

The only part of the Level 1 career assessment process that is included with the IEP. As the student, family, school, and other agencies begin working together to prepare the transition student to enter the world of work, further education, and community living, the following information will guide the process. It may help for the student and other family members to complete the questionnaire separately, and then compare ideas and discuss them prior to coming to the IEP meeting. Sharing the completed questionnaire with the other committee members at the meeting is one way to help them better understand the student's plans and ideas for the future.

These forms should be used in meetings with students over the age of 15 to assess transition readiness and to identify needs.

# EXIT SUMMARIES

Exit summaries are designed to identify students' abilities, skills, needs, limitations, and recommendations, in order to facilitate the students' transition from high school to postsecondary education or employment. Education regarding the students' disabilities and needed accommodations may be included in this written report, which needs to be completed and given to the student before the end of high school. This summary is completed within a team process, managed by the LEAs, and should include the following members:

- Special education teacher
- General education teacher
- School Psychologist
- Nondistrict program; Adult agency personnel where appropriate (http://www.vesid.nysed.gov/specialed/idea/studentexit.htm)

The following information should be considered when preparing the Student Exit Summary:

- Employability Profile;
- Career and Technical Education Skills Achievement Profile;
- Career Plan;
- Transcripts;
- Functional Behavior Assessments;
- Adaptive Behavior Assessments;
- Psychological Assessments;
- Strength-Based Assessments;
- Information from the student and family, pertinent school staff and agency personnel regarding student abilities, strengths, skills, needs, and limitations;
- Supports, accommodations, environmental modifications, and compensatory strategies that have been beneficial in supporting student success;
- Assistive technology devices and assistive services that have been helpful to the student. Include both low-tech (e.g., Velcro, laminated communication boards) and high-tech items (e.g., commercial communication systems; speech recognition software) from which the student has benefited;
- Individual student needs/functional limitations (eligibility for adult services, supports, and benefits is often based on deficiencies rather than strengths);
- Individual student strengths/skills so an employer or postsecondary institution has a clear understanding as to what the student can offer;
- Challenges the student might encounter in postsecondary school, employment or independent living; and
- Community agencies and adult service providers to whom the student may already be connected noting the status of those connections (e.g., application completed, eligibility established, acceptance into a program, etc.). (http://www.vesid.nysed.gov/specialed/idea/studentexit.htm)

**FORM 6.2** Transition Plan Questionnaire

As the student, family, school, and other agencies begin working together to prepare the transition student to enter the world of work, further education, and community living, the following information will guide the process. It may help for the student and other family members to complete the questionnaire separately, and then compare ideas and discuss them prior to coming to the IEP meeting. Sharing the completed questionnaire with the other committee members at the meeting is one way to help them better understand the student's plans and ideas for the future.

Student Name _____ Date _____

Social Security Number _____ Birthdate _____

Current Address _____

_____

Current Telephone Number _____ _____

Expected Date of Graduation/School Completion _____

Parent's Name _____

### I.  Vocational Needs

1.  After graduation from school, what career path would you like the student to follow?

_____Competitive Part-Time Employment        _____Adult/Continuing Education Program

_____Competitive Full-Time Employment        _____Two-Year College

_____Supported Employment                    _____Four-Year College

_____Sheltered Employment                    _____Military

_____Vocational School/Training              _____Other:_____

2.  What kind of jobs seem most interesting to the student?

3.  What kinds of jobs does he or she most dislike?

4.  What vocational training programs do *you* prefer for the student?

5.  What are the jobs that you do not want the student to do?

6.  What medical concerns do you have about the student's vocational placement, if any?

7.  What skills does the student need to develop to reach career goals?

8.  What vocational education classes would you like the student to enroll in?

9.  What job do you foresee the student doing after school is completed?

### II.  Further education

Please answer the following if the student is considering the idea of attending college, business, or trade school; if not, skip to section III.

1. What further education beyond high school would you like your son or daughter to obtain?

    _____ Adult and Continuing Education       _____ Two-year College Study

    _____ Business School                       _____ Four-year College Study

    _____ Trade School                          _____ Graduate Study

    _____ Apprenticeship

2. What career(s) would further education prepare the student to enter, or would the student need assistance to decide on a specific career?

3. What does the student like best about doing school assignments?

4. What does the student like least about doing school assignments?

5. What skills does the student need to develop in order to be a good student?

6. What living arrangements do you foresee for the student while going on to further education or training—living at home and commuting or living away from home in a dormitory or other living arrangement?

7. What concerns do you have about the student's ability to commute to classes or to live in a dormitory?

8. What kinds of help on campus will the student need to get the most out of classes?

9. What kinds of financial aid will you need to be able to pay for the training?

## III. Personal Management/Living Arrangements

1. What chores or responsibilities does the student presently have at home?

2. What other tasks would you like the student to be able to do at home?

3. After graduation from school, what do you think the student's living situation will be?

    _____ At home                  _____ Apartment with support

    _____ Foster home              _____ Independent apartment

    _____ Group home               _____ Other: _____

4. In which of the following independent living areas does the student need instruction?

    _____ Clothing care               _____ Parenting/child development

    _____ Sex education               _____ Community awareness

    _____ Meal preparation & nutrition _____ Measurement

    _____ Household management        _____ Time management/organization

    _____ Hygiene/grooming            _____ Safety

    _____ Health/first aid            _____ Self-advocacy

    _____ Transportation/Mobility skills _____ Interpersonal Skills

    _____ Consumer skills             _____ Other:_____

*(Continued)*

## IV. Leisure & Recreation Needs

1. In what leisure or recreational activities does the student participate alone?


2. In what leisure or recreational activities does the student participate with your family?


3. In what leisure or recreational activities does the student participate with friends?


4. In what other leisure or recreational activities would you like to see the student participate?


5. In what leisure or recreational activities do you not want the student to participate?


6. What classes or activities do you recommend for the student's participation in order to develop more leisure interests and skills?


## V. Financial

1. As an adult, what financial support will the student have (check all that apply)?

   _____earned income                    _____trust/will

   _____unearned income                 _____supplemental security income

   _____insurance                        _____Medicaid

   _____general public assistance       _____other support _____

   _____food stamps

2. What are the financial needs you think the student will have as an adult?


## VI. General

1. When transitions have been made in the past, such as from one school to another, were problems encountered, and if so, what were they?


2. What are other agencies that currently provide services for the student or are expected to do so after graduation?


3. What would you like the school district to do to assist you in planning for your son or daughter's living, working, and educational needs after completing high school?


Transition Planning, January 1993. Adapted from O'Leary & Paulson (1991).

Copyright © 2009 by Corwin Press. All rights reserved. Reprinted from *The School Counselor's Guide to Special Education* by Barbara C. Trolley, Heather S. Haas, and Danielle Campese Patti. Thousand Oaks, CA: Corwin Press, www.corwinpress.com. Reproduction authorized only for the local school site or nonprofit organization that has purchased this book.

**FORM 6.3**  Transition Planning Inventory

The form below may be helpful for recording action steps discussed at the IEP planning meeting when transition services are discussed.

| | No Needs | Explore Needs | Immediate Needs | Comments |
|---|---|---|---|---|
| **Education**<br>Vocational assessment | | | | |
| Vocational training | | | | |
| Appropriate curriculum to meet transition needs | | | | |
| Academic skills | | | | |
| **Legal/Advocacy**<br>Advocacy needs/ understanding rights | | | | |
| Wills | | | | |
| Trusts | | | | |
| Military service | | | | |
| Voter registration | | | | |
| Guardianship | | | | |
| **Personal Independence/ Residential**<br>Personal care | | | | |
| Shopping | | | | |
| Managing time | | | | |
| Meal preparation | | | | |
| Household chores | | | | |
| Apartment seeking | | | | |
| Human sexuality | | | | |
| Telephone skills | | | | |
| Identification of living options | | | | |
| Decision-making skills | | | | |
| **Recreation/Leisure**<br>Community recreational activities | | | | |
| Special interest areas | | | | |
| Leisure time activities | | | | |

*(Continued)*

**FORM 6.3** (Continued)

| | No Needs | Explore Needs | Immediate Needs | Comments |
|---|---|---|---|---|
| **Financial/Income** <br> Supplemental security income (SSI) | | | | |
| Money management/ budgeting | | | | |
| Salary considerations | | | | |
| Banking skills | | | | |
| **Medical/Health** <br> Medication | | | | |
| Insurance (dental and medical) | | | | |
| Need for ongoing medical care | | | | |
| Disability/Medicaid | | | | |
| Managing Medical Care | | | | |
| **Employment** <br> Employment options (competitive, supported, sheltered work) | | | | |
| Work behaviors | | | | |
| Job-seeking skills | | | | |
| On-the-job training | | | | |
| Experience to date | | | | |
| **Transportation** <br> Use of public transportation | | | | |
| Mobility issues | | | | |
| Transportation to and from work | | | | |
| Transportation to and from community activities | | | | |
| **Postsecondary/ Continuing education** <br> Application assistance | | | | |
| Transportation | | | | |

| | No Needs | Explore Needs | Immediate Needs | Comments |
|---|---|---|---|---|
| Financial aid | | | | |
| Contact/coordinate with campus disabled student services office | | | | |
| Study skills | | | | |
| College/program selection | | | | |
| Transfer of evaluation information | | | | |
| Parent training | | | | |
| Orientation program | | | | |
| College fairs | | | | |
| On-campus support (reader, note taker, sign interpreter, tutor, personal care attendant, other) | | | | |
| **Other Support Needs** Counseling | | | | |
| Social behaviors | | | | |
| Respite | | | | |
| Other | | | | |

\* Adapted from Erie I BOCES

Copyright © 2009 by Corwin Press. All rights reserved. Reprinted from *The School Counselor's Guide to Special Education* by Barbara C. Trolley, Heather S. Haas, and Danielle Campese Patti. Thousand Oaks, CA: Corwin Press, www.corwinpress.com. Reproduction authorized only for the local school site or nonprofit organization that has purchased this book.

**FORM 6.4**   Level I Vocational Assessment

Date:

Student DOB:

Building:

Participants' Signatures: *Student, Special Education Rep, Parent, Guidance Rep*

Definition of Long Term Vocational Goal:

Student (What do you plan to be doing two years after completing your secondary level educational program?):

Parent (What would you like to see the student doing two years after completion of his/her secondary educational program?):

Areas of immediate need:

Current hobbies/interests/vocationally related activities:

*Adapted from Erie I BOCES

Copyright © 2009 by Corwin Press. All rights reserved. Reprinted from *The School Counselor's Guide to Special Education* by Barbara C. Trolley, Heather S. Haas, and Danielle Campese Patti. Thousand Oaks, CA: Corwin Press, www.corwinpress.com. Reproduction authorized only for the local school site or nonprofit organization that has purchased this book.

**FORM 6.5**  Student Exit Summary

Student Name: _____ Date of Birth: _____

Date of Graduation/Exit:

Type of Diploma:

_____Regents with Advanced Designation

_____Regents

_____Local

_____IEP

_____H.S. Equivalency

Contact Person:

Date Completed:

## PART I: SUMMARY OF ACADEMIC ACHIEVEMENT AND FUNCTIONAL PERFORMANCE

| AREA | Present Level of Performance (upon school exit) | Needs (essential accommodations, assistive technology, environmental or material resources or modifications needed) |
|---|---|---|
| Academic Achievement/Functional Performance/Learning Characteristics | | |
| Social Development | | |
| Physical Development | | |

## PART II: POSTSECONDARY GOALS

| Postsecondary Goal | Recommendations to Assist Student to Meet Postsecondary Goals |
|---|---|
| Education and Training: | |
| Employment: | |
| Independent Living (if appropriate): | |

Copyright © 2009 by Corwin Press. All rights reserved. Reprinted from *The School Counselor's Guide to Special Education* by Barbara C. Trolley, Heather S. Haas, and Danielle Campese Patti. Thousand Oaks, CA: Corwin Press, www.corwinpress.com. Reproduction authorized only for the local school site or nonprofit organization that has purchased this book.

## Questions for Reflection

1. Who is responsible for the transition plans and exit summaries at your school? In your district?

2. What community resources exist for postsecondary students?

3. What are the major skills students with disabilities need in transitioning out of high school?

4. How are parents of students with disabilities involved in this transition process?

5. What are the major stumbling blocks for students and their families in transitioning out of high school?

# 7

# Legal and Ethical Issues in Special Education

**M**uch attention has been given to special education in the legal arena since the Rehabilitation Act of 1973 and the Education for All Handicapped Children Act (PL94-142) were passed in the mid-1970s. The 1990s welcomed both the Individuals with Disabilities Education Act (IDEA), allowing children and youth to have a free and appropriate public education (IDEA was recently amended in 2004) and the American with Disabilities Act (ADA), ensuring that people with disabilities would receive nondiscriminatory treatment. In 2001, the No Child Left Behind Act (NCLB) was signed into law, ensuring educational accountability, emphasizing maximized learning for all children, and putting into place a future plan for highly qualified teachers. Essentially, the two types of federal laws to which school counselors need attend are education and civil rights laws. The fundamental principle underlying all of these laws is that students with disabilities have their needs identified and met. Finn, Rotherham, and Hokanson (2001) argue that current federal legislation is not adequate and that new laws are needed, while some say that the instruction needs to be right for students with special needs in order for them to be educated well (Kauffman, 2002; Kauffman & Hallahan, 2005; Zigmond, 2003). Some of the inherent difficulties include delineating what is the "right" instruction, utilizing the "one size fits all model" (i.e., all students with disabilities receiving the same rather than individualized educational services), laws being open to different interpretation, conflicts among and ambiguity in federal and state education laws, and school district policy. Living in a litigious society has also impacted on special education. Parents may sue because they believe their children and youth are not getting enough services or could be stigmatized by receiving services. Other less sophisticated parents may not be aware of their rights, and school counselors are left in the middle between the family and the school. Clearly it is important that school counselors have basic knowledge of key special education–related laws. Due to the enormous tasks school counselors are addressing, their minimal time and large caseloads, and their lack of legal training, it is important that they have access to summaries of key special education legislation and to resources such as books and school legal consultants to turn to when legal questions arise. Many Web sites also now exist, such as:

http://www.ncea.org/publicpolicy/federalprograms/idea.asp,
http://www.schoolcounselor.org/files/7-1-52%20Guillot-Miller.pdf,
http://www.nls.org/specedat.htm,

These Web sites can be helpful resources to school counselors in addressing special education legal topics.

# TIMELINE OF SPECIAL EDUCATION IN THE UNITED STATES

1798:   The Fifth Congress passed the first federal law concerned with the care of persons with disabilities (Braddock, 1987). This law authorized a Maine hospital to provide medical services for sick and disabled sailors.

1820s and 1870s:   Special, segregated schools created for the mentally ill, blind, and deaf individuals.

1933:   Parents began forming special education advocacy groups to improve educational opportunities for their children.

1954:   *Brown v. Board of Education* decision On May 17, 1954, the Supreme Court unanimously declared that "separate educational facilities are inherently unequal" and, as such, violated the 14th Amendment to the United States Constitution, which guarantees all citizens "equal protection of the laws."

1964:   Civil Rights Act passed.

1965:   Head Start Economic Opportunities Act passed.

1965:   Elementary and Secondary Education Act passed.

1966:   Title VI added to the Elementary and Secondary Education Act which established the Bureau of Education for the Handicapped to provide leadership in special education programming.

1970s:   Title VI repealed, and the Education of the Handicapped Act (EHA) passed.

1971:   *PARC vs. Pennsylvania* decision determined that schools may not exclude students who have been classified with mental retardation. Also, the court mandated that all students must be provided with a free public education.

1972:   *Mills vs. Board of Education* decision. In *Mills v. Board of Education*, the court adopted "a presumption that among the alternative programs of education, placement in a regular public school class with appropriate ancillary services is preferable to placement in a special school class."

1973:   Section 504 of the Rehabilitation Act passed. - "No otherwise qualified individual with disabilities in the United States . . . .shall solely by reason of his disabilities, be excluded from participation in, be denied the benefits of, or be subjected to discrimination under any program, or activity receiving Federal financial assistance . . ."

1974:   Amendments to the Elementary and Secondary Education Act.

1975:   Congress passed the Education for All Handicapped Children Act, PL 94-142. This federal law, also known as EHA, required states to provide "a free, appropriate public education for every child between the ages of 3 and 21 (unless state law does not provide free, public education to children 3 to 5 or 18 to 21 years of age) regardless of how, or how seriously, he may be handicapped."

1986:   PL 99-372 passed, referred to as the Handicap Children's Protection Act. This act allows parents or guardians to be reimbursed for reasonable legal costs if they win a hearing or court action.

1986:    PL 99-457 passed, the Early Childhood Acts Parts H and B. Calls for IFSPs (Individual Family Services Plan) and interagency coordinating.

1988:    PL 100-407 Technology-Related Assistance for Individuals with Disabilities Act. This act recognizes that students with disabilities need assistive technology to perform better and more independently.  The act also authorizes funding to allow states to create statewide systems of technological assistance to meet those needs.

1990:    PL 101-392 The Carl D. Perkins Vocational and Applied Technology Act. This law requires that vocational education for students with disabilities be provided, be in the least restrictive environment, and when appropriate, be a part of the individualized education program. PL 101-392 also requires that individuals with disabilities (who are not members of special populations) be provided equal access to vocational programs.

1990:    PL 101-476 IDEA, Individuals with Disabilities Education Acts, goes into effect. This act, which is also known as the Education of the Handicapped Act Amendments of 1990, renamed the earlier EHA laws and their amendments.  An important part of this act is that the word "handicapped" was replaced with the word "disabled."

1990:    PL 101-336 ADA: Americans with Disabilities Act. This act extends Section 504 of PL 93-112 by requiring the rights of equal access and reasonable accommodations in employment and services provided by both private and public sectors.

1997:    IDEA reauthorized.

2004:    On November 17, 2004, President George W. Bush signed into law H.R.1350, legislation to reauthorize the Individuals with Disabilities Education Act (IDEA) through the year 2011. On December 3, 2004, the President signed the reauthorized Individuals with Disabilities Education Act of 2004 (IDEA 2004) into law.

Implied in this legal discussion are questions pertaining to ethics, such as professionals "serving two masters," feeling accountable to students' families and administration, and to laws (Crockett & Kauffman, 1999; Howe & Miramontes, 1992). What is legal isn't always ethical, and school counselors must ultimately rely on their professional codes of ethics. Consultation with senior colleagues may also help to dispel ethical concerns, assuming the consultant is objective and professional. Looking inward into one's own professional conscience is also part of the ethical problem-solving process. Numerous special education issues exist that evoke ethical questions. These issues include such queries as: "How are services to students with special needs balanced with those required by regular education students? What is the impact of inclusion on students with and without disabilities educationally and socially? Are labels identifying students with disabilities needs or are they stereotyping them? What is the school counselors' role if educational services required by law are not being offered to the students, parents are unaware of these requirements, and the school is not offering them? Are service providers appropriately credentialed?" The most fundamental area to explore is that of school counselors of students without disabilities, and needing to empower, not give sympathy to, students with disabilities (Sciarri, 2004). The essence of the legal and ethical issues tied to special education is that students' needs must be appropriately and thoroughly evaluated, and met.

# INDIVIDUALS WITH DISABILITIES EDUCATION ACT (IDEA)

IDEA is our nation's special education law.  IDEA was originally enacted by Congress in 1975 to make sure that children with disabilities had the opportunity to receive a free appropriate public education, just like other children. The law has been revised many times over the years.

The reauthorization of IDEA was signed into law on December 3, 2004 by President George W. Bush.  Provisions became effective on July 1, 2005, with the exception of some elements of the definition of "highly qualified teacher" that took effect upon the signing of the act. The most notable changes in IDEA 2004 are as follows: (for a complete copy of the law, visit www.ed.gov/about/offices/list/osers/index.html.)

1. 614(a)(1)(D)(iii)
   a. IDEA 2004 adds a provision for parental consent for initial evaluation for children who are wards of the state. The LEA must make reasonable efforts to obtain informed consent from the parent unless: the parent's whereabouts are unknown; parental rights have been terminated; parental rights have been appointed to another individual by a judge.

2. 614(a)(1)(C)(i)and (ii)
   a. IDEA 2004 adds a 60-day timeline to complete an initial evaluation, unless an individual state has established a timeline.

3. 614(A)(1)(D)(ii)(l)
   a. IDEA 2004 provides for the absence of consent for an initial evaluation if the parent of a child does not provide consent or the parent fails to respond to a request to provide consent. The LEA may use the due process hearing procedures to obtain authority for evaluation, except to the extent inconsistent with state law relating to such parental consent.

4. 614(b)(6)
   a. IDEA 2004 outlines procedures for evaluating a child suspected of having a specific learning disability. The LEA is not required to consider a severe discrepancy between achievement and intellectual ability and may use a process that determines if the child responds to scientific, research-based intervention as part of the evaluation process.

5. 614(a)(2)
   a. IDEA 2004 outlines procedures for reevaluations.
      i. The LEA determines that the educational or related services needs, including improved academic achievement and functional performance, of the child warrant a reevaluation; or
      ii. The child's parents or teacher requests a reevaluation
   b. A reevaluation shall occur no more frequently than once a year, unless the parent and the LEA agree otherwise; and at least once every three years, unless the parent and the LEA agree that a reevaluation is unnecessary.

6. 614(c)(5)(B)
   a. IDEA 2004 provides exception to requirements for evaluation before a change in eligibility. An evaluation is not required before the termination of a child's eligibility if the termination of eligibility is due to graduation or due to the child exceeding the age of eligibility.

7. 614(c)(1)(B)(i)and (ii)
   a. IDEA 2004 adds a requirement to evaluate the child's present levels of academic achievement and the related developmental needs of the child.

The major purposes of the IDEA are:

- to ensure that all children with disabilities have available to them a "free appropriate public education" that emphasizes special education and related services designed to meet their unique needs and prepare them for employment and independent living;
- to ensure that the rights of children and youth with disabilities and their parents are protected;
- to assist states, localities, educational service agencies, and federal agencies to provide for the education of all children with disabilities; and
- to assess and ensure the effectiveness of efforts to educate children with disabilities. (Section 300.1)

The regulations for IDEA define a "child with a disability" as including a child (a) who has been evaluated according to IDEA's evaluation requirements (specified at Sections 300.530–300.536); (b) who has been determined, through this evaluation, to have one or more of the disabilities listed below; and (c) who, because of the disability, needs special education and related services. The disabilities listed by IDEA are:

- mental retardation;
- a hearing impairment, including deafness;
- a speech or language impairment;
- a visual impairment, including blindness;
- serious emotional disturbance (hereafter referred to as emotional disturbance);
- an orthopedic impairment;
- autism;
- traumatic brain injury;
- other health impairment;
- a specific learning disability;
- deaf-blindness; or
- multiple disabilities. [Section 300.7 (a)(1)]

## Some Procedural Safeguards Under the IDEA

- the right of parents to inspect and review their child's educational records
- the right of parents to obtain an independent educational evaluation (IEE)
- the right of parents to be given prior written notice on matters regarding the identification, evaluation, or educational placement of their child, or the provision of FAPE to their child
- the right of parents or public agencies to request mediation and an impartial due process hearing on these matters (at a minimum, mediation must be available whenever an impartial due process hearing is requested)
- the right of parents to be given a full explanation of all of the procedural safeguards available under IDEA and the State complaint procedures
- the right of parents or public agencies to appeal the initial hearing decision to the State Education Agency (SEA) if the SEA did not conduct the hearing
- the right of the child to remain in his or her present educational placement, unless the parent and the public agency agree otherwise, while administrative or judicial proceedings are pending
- the right of parents or public agencies to bring a civil action in an appropriate state or federal court to appeal a final hearing decision
- the right of parents to request reasonable attorney's fees from a court for actions or proceedings brought under the IDEA under the circumstances described in Section 300.513
- the right of parents to give or refuse consent before their child is evaluated or reevaluated
- the right of parents to give or refuse consent before their child is provided with special education and related services for the first time
- discipline procedures for students with disabilities

## IDEA's Definition of a "Child with a Disability"

The IDEA provides a definition of a "child with a disability," which is presented in its entirety below. The law also lists 13 separate categories of disability under which children may be eligible for special education and related services. These definitions are also presented verbatim, as found in Section 300.7(c)(1)-(13).

### *Section 300.7 Child with a disability*

"(a) General. (1) As used in this part, the term child with a disability means a child evaluated in accordance with Sections 300.530–300.536 as having mental retardation, a hearing impairment including deafness, a speech or language impairment, a visual impairment including blindness, serious emotional disturbance (hereafter referred to as emotional disturbance), an orthopedic impairment, autism, traumatic brain injury, any other health impairment, a specific learning disability, deaf-blindness, or multiple disabilities, and who, by reason thereof, needs special education and related services.

"(2)(i) Subject to paragraph (a)(2)(ii) of this section, if it is determined, through an appropriate evaluation under Sections 300.530-300.536, that a child has one of the disabilities identified in paragraph (a)(1) of this section, but only needs a related service and not special education, the child is not a child with a disability under this part.

"(ii) If, consistent with Section 300.26(a)(2), the related service required by the child is considered special education rather than a related service under State standards, the child would be determined to be a child with a disability under paragraph (a)(1) of this section.

"(b) Children aged 3 through 9 experiencing developmental delays. The term child with a disability for children aged 3 through 9 may, at the discretion of the State and LEA and in accordance with Section 300.313, include a child—

"(1) Who is experiencing developmental delays, as defined by the State and as measured by appropriate diagnostic instruments and procedures, in one or more of the following areas: physical development, cognitive development, communication development, social or emotional development, or adaptive development; and

"(2) Who, by reason thereof, needs special education and related services.

"(c) Definitions of disability terms. These terms are defined in Chapter 2, Table 2.2.

## REQUIREMENTS UNDER SECTION 504 OF THE REHABILITATION ACT OF 1973

Section 504 of the Rehabilitation Act of 1973 protects the rights of individuals with disabilities in programs and activities that receive federal funds. Section 504 provides that: "No otherwise qualified individual with a disability in the United States . . . shall, solely by reason of her or his disability, be excluded from the participation in, be denied the benefits of, or be subjected to discrimination under any program or activity receiving Federal financial assistance . . ."

The U.S. Department of Education (ED) enforces Section 504 in programs and activities that receive funds from ED. Recipients of these funds include public school districts, institutions of higher education, and other state and local education agencies. ED has published a regulation implementing Section 504 (34 C.F.R. Part 104), and maintains an Office for Civil Rights (OCR), with 12 enforcement offices and a headquarters office in Washington, D.C., to enforce Section 504 and other civil rights laws that pertain to recipients of funds.

## FREE APPROPRIATE PUBLIC EDUCATION (FAPE)

The Section 504 regulation requires a school district to provide a "free appropriate public education" (FAPE) to each qualified person with a disability who is in the school district's jurisdiction, regardless of the nature or severity of the person's disability.

Under the law, a free appropriate public education (FAPE) means special education and related services that:

- are provided to children and youth with disabilities at public expense, under public supervision and direction, and without charge;
- meet the standards of the State Education Agency (SEA), including the requirements of the IDEA;
- include preschool, elementary school, or secondary school education in the State involved; and
- are provided in keeping with an individualized education program (IEP) that meets the requirements of law, as specified in Sections 300.340–300.350. (Section 300.13)

# AMERICANS WITH DISABILITIES ACT (ADA)

Over 54 million Americans with physical or mental impairments that substantially limit daily activities are protected under the ADA. These activities include working, walking, talking, seeing, hearing, or caring for oneself. People who have a record of such an impairment and those regarded as having an impairment are also protected. The Americans with Disabilities Act (ADA) gives civil rights protection to individuals with disabilities that is like that provided to individuals on the basis of race, sex, national origin, and religion. It guarantees equal opportunity for individuals with disabilities in employment, public accommodations, transportation, state and local government services, and telecommunications.

# ELEMENTARY AND SECONDARY EDUCATION ACT (ESEA)

ESEA, which was first enacted in 1965, is the principal federal law affecting K–12 education. The No Child Left Behind Act is the most recent reauthorization of the ESEA.

# NO CHILD LEFT BEHIND AT (NCLB)

The No Child Left Behind Act of 2001 (No Child Left Behind) is a landmark in education reform designed to improve student achievement and change the culture of America's schools. President George W. Bush describes this law as the "cornerstone of my administration."

With passage of No Child Left Behind, Congress reauthorized the Elementary and Secondary Education Act (ESEA)—the principal federal law affecting education from kindergarten through high school. In amending ESEA, the new law represents a sweeping overhaul of federal efforts to support elementary and secondary education in the United States. It is built on four commonsense pillars: accountability for results; an emphasis on doing what works based on scientific research; expanded parental options; and expanded local control and flexibility.

# FAMILY EDUCATIONAL RIGHTS AND PRIVACY ACT (FERPA)

The Family Educational Rights and Privacy Act (FERPA; 20 U.S.C. § 1232g; 34 CFR Part 99) is a Federal law that protects the privacy of student education records. The law applies to all schools that receive funds under an applicable program of the U.S. Department of Education.

FERPA gives parents certain rights with respect to their children's education records. These rights transfer to the student when he or she reaches the age of 18 or attends a school beyond the high school level. Students to whom the rights have transferred are "eligible students."

Parents or eligible students have the right to inspect and review the student's education records maintained by the school. Schools are not required to provide copies of records unless, for reasons such as great distance, it is impossible for parents or eligible students to review the records. Schools may charge a fee for copies.

1.   Parents or eligible students have the right to request that a school correct records that they believe to be inaccurate or misleading. If the school decides not to amend the record, the parent or eligible student then has the right to a formal hearing. After the hearing, if the school still decides not to amend the record, the parent or eligible student has the right to place a statement with the record setting forth his or her view about the contested information.

2.   Generally, schools must have written permission from the parent or eligible student in order to release any information from a student's education record. However,

FERPA allows schools to disclose those records, without consent, to the following parties or under the following conditions (34 CFR § 99.31):

- School officials with legitimate educational interest;
- Other schools to which a student is transferring;
- Specified officials for audit or evaluation purposes;
- Appropriate parties in connection with financial aid to a student;
- Organizations conducting certain studies for or on behalf of the school;
- Accrediting organizations;
- To comply with a judicial order or lawfully issued subpoena;
- Appropriate officials in cases of health and safety emergencies; and
- State and local authorities, within a juvenile justice system, pursuant to specific state law.

Schools may disclose, without consent, "directory" information such as a student's name, address, telephone number, date and place of birth, honors and awards, and dates of attendance. However, schools must tell parents and eligible students about directory information and allow parents and eligible students a reasonable amount of time to request that the school not disclose directory information about them. Schools must notify parents and eligible students annually of their rights under FERPA. The actual means of notification (special letter, inclusion in a PTA bulletin, student handbook, or newspaper article) is left to the discretion of each school.

## Confidentiality and School Records

There are provisions under the IDEA (and other Federal laws as well) that protect the confidentiality of a child's education records. These safeguards address three issues: (a) the use of personally identifiable information; (b) who may have access to a child's records; and (c) the parents' right to request that their child's records be amended.

*Personally identifiable information* means information that includes: (a) the name of the child, parent, or other family member; (b) the address of the child; (c) a personal identifier number (such as the child's social security number or student number); or (d) a list of personal characteristics or other information that would make it possible to identify the child with reasonable certainty [Section 300.500 (b)(3)]. With a number of exceptions, you must give your consent before any personally identifiable information can be disclosed by the school system (Section 300.571). These exceptions are specified by your state or other participating agency's policy in keeping with Section 99.31 of the regulations for the Family Educational Rights and Privacy Act (FERPA), P.L. 93-380. (Regulations for the entire FERPA can be found in 34 CFR Section 99.1 through Section 99.67. IDEA's regulations on confidentiality—Section 300.560 through Section 300.577—contain several references to FERPA.) You have the right to know the policies and procedures that participating agencies in your state must follow regarding the gathering, storage, disclosure to third parties, retention, and destruction of personally identifiable information (Section 300.561). You can obtain this information through your district's special education director or through the state's Office of Special Education.

*Access to a child's education records* is frequently a concern of parents. The IDEA guarantees you as parents the right to inspect and review all education records relating to your child that the public agency collects, maintains, or uses regarding the identification, evaluation, and educational placement of your child and the provision of FAPE to your child (Sections 300.501 and 300.562). Should you ask to review your child's records, the public agency must respond to the request without unnecessary delay and before any meeting regarding an IEP or a due process hearing involving your child, and in no case later than 45 days after the request has been made [Section 300.562(a)]. You also have the right to receive a response to your reasonable requests for explanations and interpretations of the records. You may ask the agency to provide you with a copy of your child's records, and the school may charge you a reasonable fee for making the copies, as long as this fee does not effectively prevent you from exercising your right to inspect and review the records. Schools may not charge you for searching for or retrieving the records [Section 300.566

(b)]. You also have the right to have a representative inspect and review the records. Furthermore, you have the right to obtain from the school district or other participating agency a list of the types of education records that are collected, maintained, or used by the agency, and where these records are kept (Section 300.565).

In keeping with the requirements of the FERPA, only certain individuals besides you, as parents, may have access to your child's records. These individuals may include, for example, teachers or officials of the school or state who have a legitimate educational interest in the records. The school or other participating agency is required by law to maintain a record of all parties who obtain access to a child's educational records collected, maintained, or used under Part B of IDEA (with the exception of parents and authorized employees of the agency). This record should include the name of the person who accessed the records, the date, and the purpose for which the person was authorized to use the records (Section 300.563).

The *right to request that records be amended* is also given to parents under the law. If you believe the information in your child's records is inaccurate or misleading or that information in the records violates your child's right to privacy or other rights, you may request that the agency that maintains this information amend it [Section 300.567 (a)]. The agency must then decide, within a reasonable period of time, whether to amend the information in accordance with your request [Section 300.567(b)]. If the agency decides to refuse to amend the information as requested, it must inform you of this decision, as well as advise you of your right to a hearing [Section 300.567(c)].

If you decide to challenge the school district's or other participating agency's refusal through a hearing, you have the right to present evidence showing why you feel the information in your child's records should be amended (Section 99.22 of FERPA). You may also, at your own expense, be assisted or represented by one or more individuals of your choice, including an attorney. The hearing must be conducted by an individual who does not have a direct interest in its outcome, and the educational agency or institution must make its decision in writing within a reasonable amount of time after the hearing (Section 300.570 of IDEA refers readers to Section 99.22 of FERPA). The decision must be based solely on the evidence presented at the hearing and must include a summary of the evidence and the reasons for the decision.

Should the result of the hearing be in your favor, the district or other participating agency must amend the information in your child's records accordingly and inform you in writing that it has done so [Section 300.569(a)]. If, however, the result of the hearing is that the information about your child is not inaccurate, misleading, or otherwise in violation of his or her privacy or other rights, then the agency must inform you that, as parents, you have the right to place in your child's records a statement commenting on the information or setting forth any reasons you have for disagreeing with the decision [Section 300.569(b)]. The district must then place your statement in the records and keep it there as long as the record or contested portion is maintained by the agency. If the record of your child (or the contested portion) is disclosed by the agency to any party, the explanation must also be disclosed to that party [Section 300.569(c)].

IDEA '97 adds an additional provision regarding educational records and the inclusion of disciplinary information in those records. A state may now require that a public agency include in the records of a child with a disability a statement of any current or previous disciplinary action taken against the child. This statement would be transmitted to the same extent that the disciplinary information is included in, and transmitted with, the student records of nondisabled children [Section 300.576(a)]. This statement may include:

- a description of any behavior engaged in by the child that required disciplinary action,
- a description of the disciplinary action taken, and
- any other information that is relevant to the safety of the child and other individuals involved with the child. [Section 300.576(b)]

If the State adopts such a policy and the child transfers from one school to another, the transmission of any of the child's records must include both the child's current IEP and any statement of current or previous disciplinary action taken against the child [Section 300.576(c)].

## Excerpts From Federal Regulations Regarding Evaluations and Reevaluations

### §300.7 Child with a disability

(a) General. (1) As used in this part, the term child with a disability means a child evaluated in accordance with §§300.530-300.536 as having mental retardation, a hearing impairment including deafness, a speech or language impairment, a visual impairment including blindness, serious emotional disturbance (hereafter referred to as emotional disturbance), an orthopedic impairment, autism, traumatic brain injury, any other health impairment, a specific learning disability, deaf-blindness, or multiple disabilities, and who, by reason thereof, needs special education and related services.

(2)(i) Subject to paragraph (a)(2)(ii) of this section, if it is determined, through an appropriate evaluation under §§300.530-300.536, that a child has one of the disabilities identified in paragraph (a)(1) of this section, but only needs a related service and not special education, the child is not a child with a disability under this part.

(ii) If, consistent with §300.26(a)(2), the related service required by the child is considered special education rather than a related service under State standards, the child would be determined to be a child with a disability under paragraph (a)(1) of this section.

(b) Children aged 3 through 9 experiencing developmental delays. The term child with a disability for children aged 3 through 9 may, at the discretion of the State and LEA and in accordance with §300.313, include a child—

(1) Who is experiencing developmental delays, as defined by the State and as measured by appropriate diagnostic instruments and procedures, in one or more of the following areas: physical development, cognitive development, communication development, social or emotional development, or adaptive development; and

(2) Who, by reason thereof, needs special education and related services.

### §300.532 Evaluation procedures

Each public agency shall ensure, at a minimum, that the following requirements are met:

(a) (1) Tests and other evaluation materials used to assess a child under Part B of the Act –

(i) Are selected and administered so as not to be discriminatory on a racial or cultural basis; and

(ii) Are provided and administered in the child's native language or other mode of communication, unless it is clearly not feasible to do so; and

(2) Materials and procedures used to assess a child with limited English proficiency are selected and administered to ensure that they measure the extent to which the child has a disability and needs special education, rather than measuring the child's English language skills.

(b) A variety of assessment tools and strategies are used to gather relevant functional and developmental information about the child, and information related to enabling the child to be involved in and progress in the general curriculum (or for a preschool child, to participate in appropriate activities), that may assist in determining –

(1) Whether the child is a child with a disability under §300.7; and

(2) The content of the child's IEP.

(c) (1) Any standardized tests that are given to a child –

(i) Have been validated for the specific purpose for which they are used; and

(ii) Are administered by trained and knowledgeable personnel in accordance with any instructions provided by the producer of the tests.

(*Disability Categories: State Terminology, Definitions and Eligibility Criteria*, February 2004, Project FORUM at NASDSE, p. 82)

(2) If an assessment is not conducted under standard conditions, a description of the extent to which it varied from standard conditions (e.g., the qualifications of the person administering the test, or the method of test administration) must be included in the evaluation report.

(d) Tests and other evaluation materials include those tailored to assess specific areas of educational need and not merely those that are designed to provide a single general intelligence quotient.

(e) Tests are selected and administered so as best to ensure that if a test is administered to a child with impaired sensory, manual, or speaking skills, the test results accurately reflect the child's aptitude or achievement level or whatever other factors the test purports to measure, rather than reflecting the child's impaired sensory, manual, or speaking skills (unless those skills are the factors that the test purports to measure).

(f) No single procedure is used as the sole criterion for determining whether a child is a child with a disability and for determining an appropriate educational program for the child.

(g) The child is assessed in all areas related to the suspected disability, including, if appropriate, health, vision, hearing, social and emotional status, general intelligence, academic performance, communicative status, and motor abilities.

(h) In evaluating each child with a disability under §§300.531–300.536, the evaluation is sufficiently comprehensive to identify all of the child's special education and related service needs, whether or not commonly linked to the disability category in which the child has been classified.

(i) The public agency uses technically sound instruments that may assess the relative contribution of cognitive and behavioral factors, in addition to physical and developmental factors.

(j) The public agency uses assessment tools and strategies that provide relevant information that directly assists persons in determining the educational needs of the child.

## §300.533 Determination of needed evaluation data

(a) Review of existing evaluation data. As part of an initial evaluation (if appropriate) and as part of any reevaluation under Part B of the Act, a group that includes the individuals described in §300.344, and other qualified professionals, as appropriate, shall –

(1) Review existing evaluation data on the child, including –

(i) Evaluations and information provided by the parents of the child;

(ii) Current classroom-based assessments and observations; and

(iii) Observations by teachers and related service providers; and

(2) On the basis of that review, and input from the child's parents, identify what additional data, if any, are needed to determine –

(i) Whether the child has a particular category of disability, as described in §300.7, or, in case of a reevaluation of a child, whether the child continues to have such a disability;

(ii) The present levels of performance and educational needs of the child;

(iii) Whether the child needs special education and related services, or in the case of a reevaluation of a child, whether the child continues to need special education and related services; and

(iv) Whether any additions or modifications to the special education and related services are needed to enable the child to meet the measurable annual goals set out in the IEP of the child and to participate, as appropriate, in the general curriculum.

(*Disability Categories: State Terminology, Definitions and Eligibility Criteria*, February 2004, Project FORUM at NASDSE, p. 83).

(b) Conduct of review. The group described in paragraph (a) of this section may conduct its review without a meeting.

(c) Need for additional data. The public agency shall administer tests and other evaluation materials as may be needed to produce the data identified under paragraph (a) of this section.

(d) Requirements if additional data are not needed. (1) If the determination under paragraph (a) of this section is that no additional data are needed to determine whether the child continues to be a child with a disability, the public agency shall notify the child's parents –

(i) Of that determination and the reasons for it; and

(ii) Of the right of the parents to request an assessment to determine whether, for purposes of services under this part, the child continues to be a child with a disability.

(2) The public agency is not required to conduct the assessment described in paragraph (d)(1)(ii) of this section unless requested to do so by the child's parents.

### §300.534 Determination of eligibility

(a) Upon completing the administration of tests and other evaluation materials –

(1) A group of qualified professionals and the parent must determine whether the child is a child with a disability as defined in §300.7; and

(2) The public agency must provide a copy of the evaluation report and the documentation of determination of eligibility to the parent.

(b) A child may not be determined to be eligible under this part if –

(1) The determinant factor for that eligibility determination is –

(i) Lack of instruction in reading or math; or

(ii) Limited English proficiency; and

(2) The child does not otherwise meet the eligibility criteria under §300.7(a).

(c)(1) A public agency must evaluate a child with a disability in accordance with §§300.532 and 300.533 before determining that the child is no longer a child with a disability.

(2) The evaluation described in paragraph (c)(1) of this section is not required before the termination of a student's eligibility under Part B of the Act due to graduation with a regular high school diploma, or exceeding the age eligibility for FAPE under State law.

### §300.535 Procedures for determining eligibility and placement

(a) In interpreting evaluation data for the purpose of determining if a child is a child with a disability under §300.7, and the educational needs of the child, each public agency shall –

(1) Draw upon information from a variety of sources, including aptitude and achievement tests, parent input, teacher recommendations, physical condition, social or cultural background, and adaptive behavior; and

(2) Ensure that information obtained from all these sources is documented and carefully considered.

(b) If a determination is made that a child has a disability and needs special education and related services, an IEP must be developed for the child in accordance with §§300.340-300.350.

(*Disability Categories: State Terminology, Definitions and Eligibility Criteria*, February 2004, Project FORUM at NASDSE, p. 84)

## Questions for Reflection

1. Identify the specific impact of each of the laws on the school counselor's role in working with students with special needs.

2. Explore any special education litigations that have taken place in your district, your locale, and your state. Examine reasons for complaints, issues raised, and outcome.

3. What steps should school counselors take to resolve being caught between the school's administration and the families of students with special needs?

4. What types of advocacy should be undertaken for students with special needs, and to what extent?

5. Examine your own response to controversial issues in the field and the impact of your reactions on your ability to work with students with special needs. How do you fundamentally feel about providing school counseling services for these students?

# Resource A

## MENTAL RETARDATION

### Definition

*Part 300*: Mental retardations means significantly subaverage general intellectual functioning, existing concurrently with deficits in adaptive behavior and manifested during the developmental period, which adversely affects a student's educational performance

### Prevalence

As many as 3 out of every 100 people in the country have mental retardation (The Arc, 2004). Nearly 613,000 children ages 6 to 21 have some level of mental retardation and need special education in school (*Twenty-fourth Annual Report to Congress*, U.S. Department of Education, 2002). In fact, one out of every ten children who need special education has some form of mental retardation.

### Assessment

To diagnose mental retardation, professionals look at the person's mental abilities (IQ) and his or her adaptive skills. Both of these are highlighted in the definition of mental retardation.

- People scoring below 70 on a standardized cognitive test (IQ)

To measure adaptive behavior, professionals look at what a child can do in comparison to other children of his or her age. Certain skills are important to adaptive behavior. These are:

- daily living skills, such as getting dressed, going to the bathroom, and feeding oneself;
- communication skills, such as understanding what is said and being able to answer;
- social skills with peers, family members, adults, and others.

### Etiology

Doctors have found many causes of mental retardation. The most common are:

- Genetic conditions. Sometimes mental retardation is caused by abnormal genes inherited from parents, errors when genes combine, or other reasons. Examples of genetic conditions are Down syndrome, fragile X syndrome, and phenylketonuria (PKU).
- Problems during pregnancy. Mental retardation can result when the baby does not develop inside the mother properly. For example, there may be a problem with the way the baby's cells divide as it grows. A woman who drinks alcohol or gets an infection like rubella during pregnancy may also have a baby with mental retardation.

- Problems at birth. If a baby has problems during labor and birth, such as not getting enough oxygen, he or she may have mental retardation.

- Health problems. Diseases like whooping cough, the measles, or meningitis can cause mental retardation. Mental retardation can also be caused by extreme malnutrition (not eating right), not getting enough medical care, or by being exposed to poisons like lead or mercury.

## Characteristics

There are many signs of mental retardation. For example, children with mental retardation may:

- sit up, crawl, or walk later than other children
- learn to talk later, or have trouble speaking
- find it hard to remember things
- not understand how to pay for things
- have trouble understanding social rules
- have trouble seeing the consequences of their actions
- have trouble solving problems, and/or
- have trouble thinking logically

About 87% of people with mental retardation will only be a little slower than average in learning new information and skills. When they are children, their limitations may not be obvious. They may not even be diagnosed as having mental retardation until they get to school. As they become adults, many people with mild retardation can live independently.

The remaining 13% of people with mental retardation score below 50 on IQ tests. These people will have more difficulty in school, at home, and in the community. A person with more severe retardation will need more intensive support his or her entire life. Every child with mental retardation is able to learn, develop, and grow. With help, all children with mental retardation can live a satisfying life.

## Teaching Tips

- Learn as much as you can about mental retardation.

- Recognize that you can make an enormous difference in this student's life. Find out what the student's strengths and interests are, and emphasize them. Create opportunities for success.

- If you are not part of the student's Committee on Special Education (CSE) team, ask for a copy of his or her Individualized Education Plan (IEP). The student's educational goals will be listed there, as well as the services and classroom accommodations he or she is to receive. Talk to specialists in your school (e.g., special educators) as necessary. They can help you identify effective methods of teaching this student, ways to adapt the curriculum, and how to address the student's IEP goals in the classroom.

- Be as concrete as possible. Demonstrate what you mean rather than just giving verbal directions. Rather than just relating new information verbally, show a picture. And rather than just showing a picture, provide the student with hands-on materials and experiences and the opportunity to try things out.

- Break longer, new tasks into small steps. Demonstrate the steps. Have the student do the steps, one at a time. Provide assistance, as necessary.

- Give the student immediate feedback.

- Teach the student life skills such as daily living, social skills, and occupational awareness and exploration, as appropriate. Involve the student in group activities or clubs.

- Work together with the student's parents and other school personnel to create and implement an educational plan tailored to meet the student's needs. Regularly share information about how the student is doing at school and at home.

## Tips for Parents

- Learn about mental retardation. The more you know, the more you can help yourself and your child.

- Encourage independence in your child. For example, help your child learn daily care skills, such as dressing, feeding him or herself, using the bathroom, and grooming.

- Give your child chores. Keep her age, attention span, and abilities in mind. Break down jobs into smaller steps. For example, if your child's job is to set the table, first ask her to get the right number of napkins. Then have her put one at each family member's place at the table. Do the same with the utensils, going one at a time. Tell her what to do, step by step, until the job is done. Demonstrate how to do the job. Help her when she needs assistance.  Give your child frequent feedback. Praise your child when he or she does well. Build your child's abilities.

- Find out what skills your child is learning at school. Find ways for your child to apply those skills at home. For example, if the teacher is going over a lesson about money, take your child to the supermarket with you. Help him count out the money to pay for your groceries. Help him count the change.

- Find opportunities in your community for social activities, such as scouts, recreation center activities, sports, and so on. These will help your child build social skills as well as to have fun.

- Talk to other parents whose children have mental retardation. Parents can share practical advice and emotional support. Call NICHCY (1.800.695.0285) and ask how to find a parent group near you.

- Meet with the school and develop an educational plan to address your child's needs. Keep in touch with your child's teachers. Offer support. Find out how you can support your child's school learning at home.

# LEARNING DISABILITIES

## Definition

Part 300:  Specific Learning Disability is defined as follows:

(i) *General.* The term means a disorder in one or more of the basic psychological processes involved in understanding or in using language, spoken or written, which manifests itself in an imperfect ability to listen, think, speak, read, write, spell, or do mathematical calculations, including conditions such as perceptual disabilities, brain injury, minimal brain dysfunction, dyslexia, and developmental aphasia.

(ii) *Disorders not included.* The term does not include learning problems that are primarily the result of visual, hearing or motor disabilities, of mental retardation, of emotional disturbance, or of environmental, cultural, or economic disadvantage.

## Prevalence

As many as one out of every five people in the United States has a learning disability. Almost three million children (ages 6 through 21) have some form of a learning disability and receive special education in school. In fact, over half of all children who receive special education have a learning disability (*Twenty-fourth Annual Report to Congress*, U.S. Department of Education, 2002).

## Assessment

### Discrepancy Model

- Uses standardized tests that compare the child's level of ability to what is considered normal development for a person of that age and intelligence.

### Response to Intervention (RTI)

- Based on significant difference in performance compared to peers, low rate of progress even with high-quality interventions, special education need, consideration of LD exclusion factors
- Types of tests used to assess are usually direct measures of specific skills needed for success in the classroom

## Etiology

Today, a leading theory is that learning disabilities stem from subtle disturbances in brain structures and functions. Some scientists believe that, in many cases, the disturbance begins before birth.

- Errors in fetal brain development
- Other factors that affect brain development
- Genetic factors
- Tobacco, alcohol, and other drug use
- Problems during pregnancy or delivery
- Toxins in the child's environment

## Characteristics

- may have trouble learning the alphabet, rhyming words, or connecting letters to their sounds;
- may make many mistakes when reading aloud, and repeat and pause often;
- may not understand what he or she reads;
- may have real trouble with spelling;
- may have very messy handwriting or hold a pencil awkwardly;
- may struggle to express ideas in writing;
- may learn language late and have a limited vocabulary;
- may have trouble remembering the sounds that letters make or hearing slight differences between words;
- may have trouble understanding jokes, comic strips, and sarcasm;
- may have trouble following directions;
- may mispronounce words or use a wrong word that sounds similar;
- may have trouble organizing what he or she wants to say or not be able to think of the word he or she needs for writing or conversation;
- may not follow the social rules of conversation, such as taking turns, and may stand too close to the listener;
- may confuse math symbols and misread numbers;
- may not be able to retell a story in order (sequence)
- may not know where to begin a task or how to go on from there.

## Teaching Tips

- learn as much as you can about the different types of LD
- emphasize what the student's strengths and interests are
- give the student positive feedback and lots of opportunities for practice
- review the student's evaluation records to identify where *specifically* the student has trouble
- talk to specialists in your school (e.g., special education teacher) about methods for teaching this student
- provide instruction and accommodations to address the student's special needs
- break tasks into smaller steps and give directions verbally and in writing
- give the student more time to finish schoolwork or take tests
- let the student with reading problems use textbooks-on-tape (available through Recording for the Blind and Dyslexic)

- let the student with listening difficulties borrow notes from a classmate or use a tape recorder
- let the student with writing difficulties use a computer with specialized software that spell checks, grammar checks, or recognizes speech
- learn about the different testing modifications that can really help a student with LD show what he or she has learned
- teach organizational skills, study skills, and learning strategies (these help all students but are particularly helpful to those with LD)
- work with the student's parents to create an educational plan tailored to meet the student's needs
- establish a positive working relationship with the student's parents—through regular communication, exchange information about the student's progress at school

## Tips for Parents

- learn about LD. The more you know, the more you can help yourself and your child
- praise your child when he or she does well
- find out what your child really enjoys doing, such as dancing, playing soccer, or working with computers and give your child plenty of opportunities to pursue his or her strengths and talents
- find out the ways your child learns best—does he or she learn by hands-on practice, looking, or listening?
- make homework a priority. Read more about how to help your child be a success at homework
- pay attention to your child's mental health (and your own!)
- talk to other parents whose children have learning disabilities. Call NICHCY {1.800.695.0285} and ask how to find parent groups near you
- meet with school personnel and help develop an educational plan to address your child's needs
- establish a positive working relationship with your child's teachers

# EMOTIONAL DISTURBANCE

## Definition

Part 300  Emotional disturbance is defined as follows:

(i)   The term means a condition exhibiting one or more of the following characteristics over a long period of time and to a marked degree that adversely affects a child's educational performance:
   A.  an inability to learn that cannot be explained by intellectual, sensory, or health factors;
   B.  An inability to build or maintain satisfactory interpersonal relationships with peers and teachers;
   C.  Inappropriate types of behavior or feelings under normal circumstances;
   D.  A generally pervasive mood of unhappiness or depression; or
   E.  A tendency to develop physical symptoms or fears associated with personal or school problems.

(ii)  The term includes schizophrenia. The term does not apply to children who are socially maladjusted, unless it is determined that they have an emotional disturbance.

## Prevalence

In the 2000–2001 school year, 473,663 children and youth with an emotional disturbance were provided special education and related services in the public schools (*Twenty-fourth Annual Report to Congress*, U.S. Department of Education, 2002).

## Assessment

Because there is no specific screening technique to determine emotional disturbance, many factors are observed and noted. Interviews and observations of the child should be made by the school psychologist, social work, or school counselor. The following should be observed and reviewed:

- School records: grades, teacher reports, disciplinary actions and referrals
- Teacher interviews
- Family interviews—home visit
- Must exclude LD, ADHD, and neurological disorder
- Physical examination: health records and attendance records
- Observations must be made in all settings in which the student lives, plays, and learns

## Etiology

The causes of emotional disturbance have not been adequately determined. Although various factors such as heredity, brain disorder, diet, stress, and family functioning have been suggested as possible causes, research has not shown any of these factors to be the direct cause of behavior or emotional problems.

## Characteristics

- Hyperactivity (short attention span, impulsiveness);
- Aggression/self-injurious behavior (acting out, fighting);
- Withdrawal (failure to initiate interaction with others; retreat from exchanges of social interaction, excessive fear or anxiety);
- Immaturity (inappropriate crying, temper tantrums, poor coping skills); and
- Learning difficulties (academically performing below grade level).
- Children with the most serious emotional disturbances may exhibit distorted thinking, excessive anxiety, bizarre motor acts, and abnormal mood swings.

## Teaching Tips

- For a child whose behavior impedes learning (including the learning of others), the team developing the child's Individualized Education Program (IEP) needs to consider, if appropriate, strategies to address that behavior, including positive behavioral interventions, strategies, and supports.

- Students eligible for special education services under the category of emotional disturbance may have IEPs that include psychological or counseling services. These are important related services, which are available under law and are to be provided by a qualified social worker, psychologist, guidance counselor, or other qualified personnel.

- Career education (both vocational and academic) is also a major part of secondary education and should be a part of the transition plan included in every adolescent's IEP.

- There is growing recognition that families, as well as their children, need support, respite care, intensive case management, and a collaborative, multiagency approach to services. Many communities are working toward providing these wrap-around services. There are a growing number of agencies and organizations actively involved in establishing support services in the community.

# AUTISM

## Definition

Part 300 (i) Autism means a developmental disability significantly affecting verbal and nonverbal communication and social interaction, generally evident before age 3, that adversely affects a student's educational performance. Other characteristics often associated with autism are engagement in repetitive activities and stereotyped movements, resistance to environmental change or change in daily routines, and unusual responses to sensory experiences. The term does not apply if a child's educational performance is adversely affected primarily because the student has an emotional disturbance defined in paragraph (b)(4) of Part 300.7.

(ii) A child who manifests the characteristics of "autism" after age 3 could be diagnosed as having "autism" if the criteria in paragraph (c)(1)(i) of Part 300.7 are satisfied.

## Prevalence

Autism and Pervasive Developmental Disorder (PDD) occurs in approximately 5 to 15 per 10,000 births. These disorders are four times more common in boys than girls.

## Assessment

A diagnosis of autism is often provided by developmental pediatricians, psychologists, child psychiatrists, or neurologists. At the time of (or prior to) diagnosis, a comprehensive evaluation is typically arranged. Such an evaluation usually includes a neurological examination, tests for biochemical abnormalities, and other assessments designed to rule out physical and diagnostic conditions. A battery of developmental and educational evaluations is also conducted to help develop an appropriate early intervention plan. Family involvement is integral to this entire process.

## Etiology

The causes of autism and PDD are unknown. Currently, researchers are investigating areas such as neurological damage and biochemical imbalance in the brain. These disorders are not caused by psychological factors.

## Characteristics

Some or all of the following characteristics may be observed in mild to severe forms:

- communication problems (e.g., using and understanding language)
- difficulty in relating to people, objects, and events
- unusual play with toys and other objects
- difficulty with changes in routine or familiar surroundings
- repetitive body movements or behavior patterns

Children with autism or PDD vary widely in abilities, intelligence, and behaviors. Some children do not speak; others have limited language that often includes repeated phrases or conversations. People with more advanced language skills tend to use a small range of topics and have difficulty with abstract concepts. Repetitive play skills, a limited range of interests, and impaired social skills are generally evident as well. Unusual responses to sensory information—for example, loud noises, lights, certain textures of food or fabrics—are also common.

## Teaching Tips

The classroom environment should be structured so that the program is consistent and predictable. Students with autism or PDD learn better and are less confused when information is presented visually as well as verbally. Interaction with nondisabled peers is also important, for these students provide models of appropriate language, social, and behavior skills. To overcome frequent problems in generalizing skills learned at school, it is very important to develop programs with parents so that learning activities, experiences, and approaches can be carried over into the home and community.

# TRAUMATIC BRAIN INJURY

## Definition

Part 300: Traumatic brain injury means an acquired injury to the brain caused by an external force, resulting in total or partial functional disability or psychosocial impairment, or both that adversely affect educational performance. The term includes open or closed head injuries or brain injuries from certain medical conditions resulting in mild, moderate, or severe impairments in one or more areas, including cognition, language, memory, attention, reasoning, abstract thinking, judgment, problem solving, sensory, perceptual and motor abilities, psychosocial behavior, physical functions, information processing, and speech. The term does not include injuries that are congenital or caused by birth trauma.

## Prevalence

More than one million children receive brain injuries each year. More than 30,000 of these children have lifelong disabilities as a result of the brain injury.

## Assessment

- The assessment of cognitive and communication problems associated with traumatic brain injury is a continuous, ongoing process involving many professionals. These may include not only physicians, but also speech and language, physical and occupational therapists.

- Immediately after a traumatic brain injury, a neurologist (a doctor specializing in the brain and nervous system) or another doctor may examine the patient's attention, memory, understanding, movement, and speaking.

- Once the assessment of the person's physical condition is concluded, a speech-language pathologist may conduct an assessment of cognitive and communication skills. A neuropsychologist may perform an assessment of other cognitive (thinking) and behavioral abilities.

- Occupational therapists may also conduct an assessment of cognitive skills related to the person's ability to perform "activities of daily living" (ADL) such as getting dressed or preparing meals.

- Hearing should be assessed by an audiologist.

- Throughout the rehabilitation process, all assessments should continue at regular intervals so progress can be documented and treatment plans updated.

- The process of rehabilitation of a person with a traumatic brain injury may last for several months up to a year.

## Etiology

### Open Head Injury

- Results from bullet wounds, etc.
- Penetration of the skull

### Closed Head Injury

- Resulting from falls, motor vehicle crashes, etc.
- Effects tend to be broad (diffuse)
- No penetration to the skull

### Deceleration Injuries (Diffuse Axonal Injury)

- Movement of the skull through space (acceleration) and the rapid discontinuation of this action when the skull meets a stationary object (deceleration) causes the brain to move inside the skull. The differential movement of the skull and the brain

when the head is struck results in direct brain injury, due to diffuse axonal shearing, contusion, and brain swelling.
- *Diffuse axonal shearing:* when the brain is slammed back and forth inside the skull, it is alternately compressed and stretched because of the gelatinous consistency.

## Chemical/Toxic

- Also known as metabolic disorders
- This occurs when harmful chemicals damage the neurons
- Chemicals and toxins can include insecticides, solvents, carbon monoxide poisoning, lead poisoning, etc.

## Hypoxia (Lack of Oxygen)
## Tumors

- Tumors caused by cancer can grow on or over the brain
- Tumors can cause brain injury by invading the spaces of the brain and causing direct damage
- Damage can also result from pressure effects around an enlarged tumor
- Surgical procedures to remove the tumor may also contribute to brain injury

## Infections

- The brain and surrounding membranes are very prone to infections if the special blood-brain protective system is breached
- Viruses and bacteria can cause serious and life-threatening diseases of the brain (encephalitis) and meninges (meningitis)

## Stroke

# Characteristics

The signs of brain injury can be very different depending on where the brain is injured and how severely. Children with TBI may have one or more difficulties, including:

## Physical disabilities:

Individuals with TBI may have problems speaking, seeing, hearing, and using their other senses. They may have headaches and feel tired a lot. They may also have trouble with skills such as writing or drawing. Their muscles may suddenly contract or tighten (this is called spasticity). They may also have seizures. Their balance and walking may also be affected. They may be partly or completely paralyzed on one side of the body, or both sides.

## Difficulties with thinking

Because the brain has been injured, it is common that the person's ability to use the brain changes. For example, children with TBI may have trouble with short-term memory (being able to remember something from one minute to the next, like what the teacher just said). They may also have trouble with their long-term memory (being able to remember information from a while ago, like facts learned last month). Students with TBI may have trouble concentrating and only be able to focus their attention for a short time. They may think slowly. They may have trouble talking and listening to others. They may also have difficulty with reading and writing, planning, understanding the order in which events happen (called sequencing), and judgment.

## Social, behavioral, or emotional problems:

These difficulties may include sudden changes in mood, anxiety, and depression. Children with TBI may have trouble relating to others. They may be restless and may laugh or cry a lot. They may not have much motivation or much control over their emotions.

It's also important to know that, as the child grows and develops, parents and teachers may notice new problems. This is because, as students grow, they are expected to use their brain in new and different ways. The damage to the brain from the earlier injury can make it hard for the student to learn new skills that come with getting older. Sometimes parents and educators may not even realize that the student's difficulty comes from the earlier injury.

## Teaching Tips

When children with TBI return to school, their educational and emotional needs are often very different than before the injury. Their disability has happened suddenly and traumatically. They can often remember how they were before the brain injury. This can bring on many emotional and social changes. The child's family, friends, and teachers also recall what the child was like before the injury. These other people in the child's life may have trouble changing or adjusting their expectations of the child.

Therefore, it is extremely important to plan carefully for the child's return to school. The school will need to evaluate the child thoroughly. This evaluation will let the school and parents know what the student's educational needs are. Find out as much as you can about the child's injury and his or her present needs. Find out more about TBI.

- Give directions one step at a time. For tasks with many steps, it helps to give the student written directions.
- Show the student how to perform new tasks. Give examples to go with new ideas and concepts.
- Have consistent routines. This helps the student know what to expect. If the routine is going to change, let the student know ahead of time.
- Check to make sure that the student has actually learned the new skill. Give the student lots of opportunities to practice the new skill.
- Show the student how to use an assignment book and a daily schedule. This helps the student get organized.
- Realize that the student may get tired quickly. Let the student rest as needed.
- Reduce distractions.
- Keep in touch with the student's parents. Share information about how the student is doing at home and at school.
- Be flexible about expectations. Be patient. Maximize the student's chances for success.
- Give the student more time to finish schoolwork and tests.

## Tips for Parents

- Learn about TBI. The more you know, the more you can help yourself and your child.
- Work with the medical team to understand your child's injury and treatment plan. Don't be shy about asking questions. Tell them what you know or think. Make suggestions.
- Keep track of your child's treatment. A three-ring binder or a box can help you store this history. As your child recovers, you may meet with many doctors, nurses, and others. Write down what they say. Put any paperwork they give you in the notebook or throw it in the box. Also, if you need to share any of this paperwork with someone else, make a copy. Don't give away your original.
- Talk to other parents whose children have TBI. There are parent groups all over the U.S. Parents can share practical advice and emotional support.
- If your child was in school before the injury, plan for his or her return to school. Get in touch with the school. Ask the principal about special education services. Have the medical team share information with the school.
- When your child returns to school, ask the school to test your child as soon as possible to identify his or her special education needs. Meet with the school and help develop an Individualized Education Program (IEP).
- Keep in touch with your child's teacher. Tell the teacher about how your child is doing at home. Ask how your child is doing in school.

# VISUAL IMPAIRMENT

## Definitions

Part 300:  Visual impairment including blindness means an impairment in vision that, even with correction, adversely affects a child's educational performance. The term includes both partial sight and blindness.

Legally blind:  An individual with a visual acuity of 20/200 or less even with correction or has a field loss of 20 degrees or more.

Low Vision:  A person who is still severely impaired after correction, but whom may increase functioning through the use of optical aide, nonoptical aids, environmental modifications and/or techniques.

## Prevalence

The rate at which visual impairments occur in individuals under the age of 18 is 12.2 per 1,000. Severe visual impairments (legally or totally blind) occur at a rate of .06 per 1,000.

## Assessment

A Snellen chart is an eye chart used by eye care professionals and others to measure visual acuity.  An optotype is a standardized symbol for testing vision. Optotypes can be specially shaped letters, numbers, or geometric symbols. For instance, to determine visual acuity, optotypes of different sizes are presented to a person and the smallest size is determined at which the person can reliably identify the optotypes.

## Etiology

There are many possible defects or diseases of the visual system, but, fortunately, many of them appear after the first few years of life. The following selected terms include only a few of the many visual disorders found in young children

- cataracts
- cortical visual impairment
- glaucoma
- infections
- malformations
- ocular-muscle problems: most common is strabismus (one or both eyes out of alignment)
- nystagmus is another ocular-muscle anomaly; manifested by involuntary eye movements, usually noted as "jerky" or "jumpy" eye movement
- ocular trauma: occurs when the eyeball is hit, lacerated, or punctured; always requires medical evaluation and treatment
- optic nerve defects: Optic atrophy occurs when, for a number of possible reasons, the optic nerve does not function properly
- optic nerve hypoplasia (ONH) differs from optic atrophy; in ONH, the optic nerve has regressed in development (usually during the prenatal period, and usually caused by a prenatal insult to the neurological system)
- refractive errors (nearsightedness, farsightedness, astigmatism)
- Retinoblastoma: a tumor behind the eye which, if left untreated, can be both blinding and life-threatening
- Retinopathy of Prematurity (ROP): a condition found primarily (but not exclusively) among premature infants

## Characteristics

The effect of visual problems on a child's development depends on the severity, type of loss, age at which the condition appears, and overall functioning level of the child.

Many children who have multiple disabilities may also have visual impairments resulting in motor, cognitive, and/or social developmental delays.

A young child with visual impairments has little reason to explore interesting objects in the environment and, thus, may miss opportunities to have experiences and to learn. This lack of exploration may continue until learning becomes motivating or until intervention begins.

Because the child cannot see parents or peers, he or she may be unable to imitate social behavior or understand nonverbal cues. Visual handicaps can create obstacles to a growing child's independence.

## Teaching Tips

Children with visual impairments should be assessed early to benefit from early intervention programs, when applicable. Technology in the form of computers and low-vision optical and video aids enable many partially sighted, low vision, and blind children to participate in regular class activities. Large print materials, books on tape, and Braille books are available.

Students with visual impairments may need additional help with special equipment and modifications in the regular curriculum to emphasize listening skills, communication, orientation and mobility, vocation/career options, and daily living skills.

If any of the following is observed, a vision exam is highly recommended.

- Complain of headaches, sore eyes or blurred vision
- Display short attention span when reading or copying
- Must read and reread material several times to comprehend its meaning.
- Have difficulty remembering what was read
- Fail to complete board work on time
- Lose place while reading or use finger to keep place
- Poor handwriting that doesn't improve with practice. Writing up or down hill.
- Squint, blink, or turn head while reading
- Child covers one eye or has poor posture when reading or doing near work.
- Have difficulty judging distance. Trouble hitting a baseball or tennis ball

# HEARING IMPAIRMENT

## Definition

Part 300: Hearing impairment means an impairment in hearing, whether permanent or fluctuating, that adversely affects the child's educational performance but that is not included under the definition of deafness in Section 300.7.

## Prevalence

Hearing loss and deafness affect individuals of all ages and may occur at any time from infancy through old age. The U.S. Department of Education (2002) reports that, during the 2000–2001 school year, 70,767 students aged 6 to 21 (or 1.3% of all students with disabilities) received special education services under the category of "hearing impairment."

About 3-4 in every 1,000 newborns have significant hearing impairment.

## Assessment

With regard to *degree* of hearing loss, the audiologist is looking for quantitative information. Hearing levels are expressed in decibels based on the pure tone average for the frequencies 500 to 4000 Hz and discussed using descriptors related to severity: normal hearing (0–20 dB HL), mild hearing loss (20–40 dB HL), moderate hearing loss (40–60 dB HL), severe (60–80 dB HL) and profound hearing loss (80 dB HL or greater).

With regard to the *type* of hearing loss , the audiologist is looking for information that suggests the point in the auditory system where the loss is occurring. The loss may be *conductive* (a temporary or permanent hearing loss typically due to abnormal conditions of the outer and/or middle ear), *sensorineural* (typically a permanent hearing loss due to disease, trauma, or inherited conditions affecting the nerve cells in the cochlea, the inner ear, or the eighth cranial nerve), *mixed* (a combination of conductive and sensorineural components), or *a central auditory processing disorder* (a condition where the brain has difficulty processing auditory signals that are heard).

## Etiology

After birth, traumas to the head or childhood infections, such as meningitis, measles, or chicken pox, can cause permanent hearing loss. Certain medications, such as the antibiotic streptomycin and related drugs, also can be the cause of the child's hearing problems.

Ear infections like otitis media may cause temporary hearing loss or lead to a permanent hearing impairment if left untreated.

10–20% of hearing loss occurrences are due to postnatal causes.

Hearing loss can be inherited or can be caused by illness or injury.

## Characteristics

There are four types of hearing loss. Conductive hearing losses are caused by diseases or obstructions in the outer or middle ear (the conduction pathways for sound to reach the inner ear). Conductive hearing losses usually affect all frequencies of hearing evenly and do not result in severe losses. A person with a conductive hearing loss usually is able to use a hearing aid well or can be helped medically or surgically.

Sensorineural hearing losses result from damage to the delicate sensory hair cells of the inner ear or the nerves which supply it. These hearing losses can range from mild to profound. They often affect the person's ability to hear certain frequencies more than others. Thus, even with amplification to increase the sound level, a person with a sensorineural hearing loss may perceive distorted sounds, sometimes making the successful use of a hearing aid impossible.

A mixed hearing loss refers to a combination of conductive and sensorineural loss and means that a problem occurs in both the outer or middle and the inner ear. A central hearing loss results from damage or impairment to the nerves or nuclei of the central nervous system, either in the pathways to the brain or in the brain itself.

## Teaching Tips

Hearing loss or deafness does not affect a person's intellectual capacity or ability to learn. However, children who are either hard of hearing or deaf generally require some form of special education services in order to receive an adequate education. Such services may include:

- regular speech, language, and auditory training from a specialist
- amplification systems
- services of an interpreter for those students who use sign language
- favorable seating in the class to facilitate lip reading
- captioned films/videos
- assistance of a note taker, who takes notes for the student with a hearing loss, so that the student can fully attend to instruction
- instruction for the teacher and peers in alternate communication methods, such as sign language
- counseling

Children who are hard of hearing will find it much more difficult than children who have hearing to learn vocabulary, grammar, word order, idiomatic expressions, and other aspects of verbal communication. For children who are deaf or have severe hearing losses, early, consistent, and conscious use of visible communication modes (such as sign language, finger-spelling, and cued speech) and/or amplification and aural/oral training can help reduce this language delay. By age four or five, most children who are deaf are enrolled in school on a full-day basis and do special work on communication and language development. It is important for teachers and audiologists to work together to teach the child to use his or her residual hearing to the maximum extent possible, even if the preferred means of communication is manual. Since the great majority of deaf children (over 90%) are born to hearing parents, programs should provide instruction for parents on implications of deafness within the family.

# DEAFNESS

## Definition

Part 300:  Deafness means a hearing impairment that is so severe that the child is impaired in processing linguistic information through hearing, with or without amplification, that adversely affects a child's educational performance.

## Prevalence

1.3% of all students with disabilities received special education services under the category of "hearing impairment." However, the number of children with hearing loss and deafness is undoubtedly higher, since many of these students may have other disabilities as well and may be served under other categories.

## Assessment

Infants and toddlers (7 months through 2 years) should be screened for hearing loss as needed, requested, mandated, or when conditions place them at risk for hearing disability.

Infants not tested as newborns should be screened before three months of age. Older infants and toddlers who have a greater chance of hearing loss because of certain risk factors should also be screened. These children's hearing should be monitored at least every 6 months until 3 years of age, and at regular intervals thereafter depending on the risk factor.

## Etiology

### Causes before birth (pre-natal causes)

- Many children are born deaf because of a genetic reason.
- Deafness can also be caused by complications during pregnancy. Illnesses such as rubella, cytomegalovirus (CMV), toxoplasmosis, and herpes can cause a child to be born deaf. There is also a range of medicines, known as ototoxic drugs, which can damage the hearing system of a baby before birth.

### Causes in infancy (postnatal causes)

- Being born prematurely can increase the risk of being deaf or of becoming deaf.
- In early childhood, there is a range of things that can be responsible for a child's becoming deaf. Infections like meningitis, measles, and mumps can cause deafness.
- Occasionally deafness is caused by an injury to the head or exposure to loud noise.

## Characteristics

People with hearing loss use oral or manual means of communication or a combination of the two. Oral communication includes speech, lip reading, and the use of residual hearing. Manual communication involves signs and finger-spelling. Total communication, as a method of instruction, is a combination of the oral method plus signing and finger-spelling.

## Teaching Tips

Hearing loss or deafness does not affect a person's intellectual capacity or ability to learn. However, children who are either hard of hearing or deaf generally require some form of special education services in order to receive an adequate education. Such services may include:

- regular speech, language, and auditory training from a specialist
- amplification systems
- services of an interpreter for those students who use sign language
- favorable seating in the class to facilitate lip reading
- captioned films/videos
- assistance of a note taker, who takes notes for the student with a hearing loss
- instruction for the teacher and peers in alternate communication methods, such as sign language

# DEAF-BLINDNESS

## Definition

Part 300: Deaf-blindness means concomitant hearing and visual impairments, the combination of which causes such severe communication and other developmental and educational needs that they cannot be accommodated in special education programs solely for children with deafness or children with blindness.

## Prevalence

As far as it has been possible to count them, there are over 10,000 children (ages birth to 22 years) in the United States who have been classified as deaf-blind (NTAC, 2004). It has been estimated that the adult deaf-blind population numbers 35–40,000 (Watson, 1993).

## Assessment

Districts should have current information that describes the sensory activities (vision and hearing), physical development, orientation and mobility (skills and knowledge), social development, academic abilities, educational achievement, and communicative competence of students who are deaf-blind. This information is best obtained for students who are deaf-blind through a multidisciplinary assessment process.

## Etiology

Major Causes of Deaf-Blindness

### Syndromes

- Down syndrome
- Trisomy 13
- Usher syndrome
- Other

### Multiple Congenital Anomalies

- CHARGE association
- Fetal alcohol syndrome
- Hydrocephaly
- Maternal drug abuse
- Microcephaly
- Other (specify)

*Prematurity as sole known cause*

*Congenital Prenatal Dysfunction*

- AIDS
- Herpes
- Rubella
- Syphilis
- Toxoplasmosis
- Other (specify)

*Postnatal causes*

- Asphyxia
- Encephalitis
- Head injury/trauma
- Miningitis
- Stroke
- Other (specify)

*Other (specify)*

http://www.dblink.org/lib/topics/etiologies.htm#ap

## Characteristics

Challenges for persons with deaf-blindness include:

- inclusion in the family
- transition
- individualized education
- orientation and mobility
- communication

Principal communication systems for persons who are deaf-blind are these:

- touch cues
- gestures
- object symbols
- picture symbols
- sign language
- finger-spelling
- Signed English
- Pidgin Signed English
- Braille writing and reading
- Tadoma method of speech reading
- American Sign Language
- large print writing and reading
- lip-reading speech

## Teaching Tips

- IEPs must be developed consisting of the following:
- communication skills
- social skills
- orientation and mobility skills
- visual skills
- auditory skills

- daily living skills
- academic skills
- specialized skills in reading (e.g., Braille, large print, closed-captioned TV)
- specialized skills in mathematics (e.g., abacus)
- access to technology
- study skills and note-taking strategies
- transition

# SPEECH OR LANGUAGE IMPAIRMENT

## Definition

Part 300: Speech or language impairment means a communication disorder, such as stuttering, impaired articulation, language impairment or voice impairment, that adversely affects a child's educational performance

## Prevalence

More than one million of the students served in the public schools' special education programs in the 2000–2001 school year were categorized as having a speech or language impairment. This estimate does not include children who have speech/language problems secondary to other conditions such as deafness. Language disorders may be related to other disabilities such as mental retardation, autism, or cerebral palsy. It is estimated that communication disorders (including speech, language, and hearing disorders) affect one of every ten people in the United States.

## Assessment

To diagnose speech and language disorders, a speech therapist tests the child's pronunciation, vocabulary, and grammar and compares them to the developmental abilities seen in most children that age. A psychologist tests the child's intelligence. A physician checks for any ear infections, and an audiologist may be consulted to rule out auditory problems. If the problem involves articulation, a doctor examines the child's vocal cords and throat.

## Etiology

Some babies are born with physical conditions, such as cleft lip and cleft palate that make it difficult or impossible to learn to speak. Cleft lip is an incomplete joining of the upper lip. Cleft palate is an abnormal passageway through the roof of the mouth into the airway of the nose. Because these problems are present at birth, they are called congenital.

Following are some other causes of speech impairment:

- brain tumor
- congenital disorders, such as Down syndrome, which also causes mental retardation
- emotional or psychological problems, such as selective mutism
- injuries to the brain, such as head injury
- injury to the muscles needed for speech
- medication side effects
- muscle weakness or paralysis, which may occur in degenerative diseases such as amyotrophic lateral sclerosis or multiple sclerosis
- Parkinson's disease, a degenerative nerve disorder
- profound deafness, or other hearing impairments
- stroke
- surgical removal of the tongue or voice box, known as laryngectomy
- throat cancer or tongue cancer

## Characteristics

A child's communication is considered delayed when the child is noticeably behind his or her peers in the acquisition of speech and/or language skills. Sometimes a child will have greater receptive (understanding) than expressive (speaking) language skills, but this is not always the case.

Speech disorders refer to difficulties producing speech sounds or problems with voice quality. They might be characterized by an interruption in the flow or rhythm of speech, such as stuttering, which is called dysfluency. Speech disorders may be problems with the way sounds are formed, called articulation or phonological disorders, or they may be difficulties with the pitch, volume, or quality of the voice. There may be a combination of several problems. People with speech disorders have trouble using some speech sounds, which can also be a symptom of a delay. They may say "see" when they mean "ski" or they may have trouble using other sounds like "l" or "r." Listeners may have trouble understanding what someone with a speech disorder is trying to say. People with voice disorders may have trouble with the way their voices sound.

A language disorder is an impairment in the ability to understand and/or use words in context, both verbally and nonverbally. Some characteristics of language disorders include improper use of words and their meanings, inability to express ideas, inappropriate grammatical patterns, reduced vocabulary and inability to follow directions. One or a combination of these characteristics may occur in children who are affected by language learning disabilities or developmental language delay. Children may hear or see a word but not be able to understand its meaning. They may have trouble getting others to understand what they are trying to communicate.

## Teaching Tips

- Technology can help children whose physical conditions make communication difficult (e.g., electronic communication systems)
- Allow students sufficient time to consider and answer questions
- Provide a cue for the class, indicating that students must listen
- Speak in brief sentences, omitting unnecessary information and words
- Integrate new vocabulary studied into the context of ongoing information
- Have students rename vocabulary important to the lesson
- Use pictures and concrete objects to support learning
- Ask students to sequence events in a story after they have heard or read the information
- Model good grammar by repeating a sentence correctly when a student makes an error

# OTHER HEALTH IMPAIRMENT

## Definition

Part 300:  Other health impairment means having limited strength, vitality, or alertness, including a heightened alertness to environmental stimuli, that results in limited alertness with respect to the educational environment that
- (i)   is due to chronic or acute health problems such as asthma, attention deficit disorder, or attention deficit hyperactivity disorder, a heart condition, hemophilia, lead poisoning, leukemia, nephritis, rheumatic fever, and sickle cell anemia; and
- (ii)  adversely affects a child's educational performance

## Prevalence

5.3 out of 100 students in the 2001–2002 school year served with special education were classified as Other Heath Impaired.  In 1991–1992, 1.2 out of 100 were classified OHI.

## Assessment

Due to the wide variety of health problems, assessments vary to a degree. Some things to observe include:

- Energy level
- Initiation of contact with others
- Skin tone
- Sores, rashes, cuts not seen before
- Clothing fits differently than usual
- Indications of discomfort or pain
- Side effects from medications or procedures
- Restrictions of activities

## Etiology

- Damage during brain development
- Lack of oxygen, low blood sugar, infections, and physical trauma
- Neurological disorders
- Fetal Alcohol Syndrome
- Accidents
- AIDS
- Children born to substance abusing mothers
- Abuse/neglect

## Characteristics

A child may have a health condition that is not included in any of the listed categories, but which limits his strength and causes problems in learning. Examples of health conditions that may come under the category of other health impaired are:

- Asthma
- Epilepsy
- Diabetes
- Tourette Syndrome
- Fetal Alcohol Syndrome (FAS)
- Attention Deficit Hyperactivity Disorder (ADHD)
- Heart Condition
- Hemophilia

## Teaching Tips

- Prevent paper and objects from slipping by using paper, tape, clipboards, magnets, photo album pages, sticky paper, etc.
- Place a rubber strip on the back of a ruler to draw lines
- Use calculators
- Use felt tip pens and soft lead pencils that require less pressure; use pencil grips
- Allow word processors on written assignments
- Use lap desks with cork that allows work to be secured with pushpins
- Use tables that adjust to wheelchair heights
- Provide two sets of books for school and home
- Tape assignments, lectures, and activities
- Provide notes via peer or teacher
- Allow for alternative assessments via presentations, portfolios, etc.
- Use communication boards with pictures, symbols, numbers, or words
- Use colored objects that are easy to handle to indicate responses to polar questions as true/false, yes/no, etc.
- Allow for extra time

# ORTHOPEDIC IMPAIRMENT

## Definition

Part 300: orthopedic impairment means a severe orthopedic impairment that adversely affects a child's educational performance. The term includes impairments caused by congenital anomaly (e.g., clubfoot, absence of some member, etc.), impairments caused by disease (e.g., poliomyelitis, bone tuberculosis, etc.), and impairments from other causes (e.g., cerebral palsy, amputation, and fractures or burns which cause contractures).

## Prevalence

Approximately 1% of students with disabilities have orthopedic impairments.

## Characteristics

### Osteogenesis imperfecta

(OI) literally means imperfectly formed bones. People with OI have an error (mutation) in the genetic instructions on how to make strong bones. As a result, their bones break easily.

### Hydranencephaly

Hydraencephaly is a rare neurological condition in which the brain's cerebral hemispheres are absent and replaced by sacs filled with cerebrospinal fluid.

### Three main types of Cerebral Palsy:

• Spastic CP is where there is too much muscle tone or tightness. Movements are stiff, especially in the legs, arms, and/or back. Children with this form of CP move their legs awkwardly, turning in or scissoring their legs as they try to walk. This is the most common form of CP.

• Athetoid CP (also called dyskinetic *CP*) can affect movements of the entire body. Typically, this form of CP involves slow, uncontrolled body movements and low muscle tone that makes it hard for the person to sit straight and walk.

• Mixed CP is a combination of the symptoms listed above. A child with mixed CP has both high and low tone muscle. Some muscles are too tight, and others are too loose, creating a mix of stiffness and involuntary movements.

More words used to describe the different types of CP include:

• Diplegia—This means only the legs are affected.
• Hemiplegia—This means one half of the body (such as the right arm and leg) is affected.
• Quadriplegia—This means both arms and legs are affected, sometimes including the facial muscles and torso.

## Etiology

Possible causes of hydranencephaly include prenatal stroke; prenatal drug exposure; prenatal infections, and death of twin in utero.

Most cases of osteogenesis imperfecta (commonly known as "brittle bone disease") are caused by a dominant genetic defect. Some children with OI inherit the disorder from a parent. Other children are born with OI even though there is no family history of the disorder. In these children, the genetic defect occurred as a spontaneous mutation.

## Teaching Tips

- Learn more about CP. The resources and organizations at the end of this publication will help you.

- This may seem obvious, but sometimes the "look" of CP can give the mistaken impression that a child who has CP cannot learn as much as others. Focus on the individual child and learn firsthand what needs and capabilities he or she has.

- Tap into the strategies that teachers of students with learning disabilities use for their students. Become knowledgeable about different learning styles. Then you can use the approach best suited for a particular child, based on that child's learning abilities as well as physical abilities.

- Be inventive. Ask yourself (and others), "How can I adapt this lesson for this child to maximize *active, hands-on* learning?"

- Learn to love assistive technology. Find experts within and outside your school to help you. Assistive technology can mean the difference between independence for your student or not.

- Parents are experts, too. Talk candidly with parents. They can tell you a great deal about their daughter or son's special needs and abilities.

- The team must combine the knowledge of its members to plan, implement, and coordinate the child's services.

- *Physical therapy* (PT), which helps the child develop stronger muscles such as those in the legs and trunk. Through PT, the child works on skills such as walking, sitting, and keeping his or her balance.

- *Occupational therapy* (OT), which helps the child develop fine motor skills such as dressing, feeding, writing, and other daily living tasks.

- *Speech-language pathology* (S/L), which helps the child develop his or her communication skills. The child may work in particular on speaking, which may be difficult due to problems with muscle tone of the tongue and throat.

The Osteogenesis Imperfecta Foundation suggests the following:

- Don't be afraid to touch or hold an infant with OI, but be careful. Never lift a child with OI by holding him or her under the armpits. Do not pull on arms or legs or lift the legs by the ankles to change a diaper. To lift an infant with OI, spread your fingers apart and put one hand between the legs and under the buttocks; place the other hand behind the shoulders, neck, and head.
- Do not feel guilty if a fracture does occur. Children must develop and fractures will occur no matter how careful you are.

# MULTIPLE DISABILITIES

## Definitions

Part 300: multiple disabilities means concomitant impairments (such as mental retardation-blindness, mental retardation-orthopedic impairment, etc.), the combination of which cause such severe educational needs that they cannot be accommodated in a special education program solely for one of the impairments. The term does not include deaf-blindness.

## Prevalence

Approximately 2% of students receiving special education services have multiple disabilities. In the 2000–2001 school year, a reported 122,559 students with multiple disabilities received special education services.

## Assessment

Multiple Disabilities Classification includes the manifestation of two or more disabilities (such as mental retardation-blindness), the combination of which requires special accommodation for maximal learning. Assessments for both disabilities are necessary.

## Etiology

Many of the factors that cause sensory impairment can also cause other impairments. These include:

- Diseases like meningitis
- Syndromes that cause developmental disabilities (such as Down Syndrome)
- Birth trauma, particularly for premature babies

In addition, it can be difficult to recognize early signs of illness or disability among children with multiple disabilities, which can result in permanent sensory impairment (for example, middle ear infections left untreated).

## Characteristics

A wide range of characteristics may be evident including, but not limited to:

- Limited speech or communication
- Difficulty in basic physical mobility
- Tendency to forget skills through disuse
- Trouble generalizing skills from one situation to another
- A need for support in major life activities

## Teaching Tips

Incorporate a variety of components to meet the considerable needs of individuals with multiple disabilities. Programs should assess needs in four major areas: domestic, leisure/recreational, community, and vocational. Instruction should include expression of choice, communication, functional skill development, and age-appropriate social skills training.

Related services and a multidisciplinary approach are crucial. Appropriate people such as speech and language therapists, physical and occupational therapists, and medical specialists need to work closely with classroom teachers and parents.

# Resource B

## *Functional Behavior Assessment*

Student Name: ___*Sam Smith*___   Date Initiated: ___*January 23, 2006*___

DOB: ___*3/26/91*___   Grade/Teacher: ___9___

Classification: ___*Emotionally Disturbed*___   Program Placement: ___*12:1+1*___

### Identified Student Strengths (Use Behavioral Terms):

*Sam is a very polite and respectful young man. He enjoys a positive rapport with adults and seeks out friendships with his peers.*

### Identified Selected Problem Behavior (Use Behavioral Terms):

*Sam needs to improve his organizational skills. He is not always prepared for class and tests or quizzes. Sam does not always complete his homework.*

### Identification of Targeted Behavior (observable, measurable, and well defined—What is the specific behavior that you want to increase or decrease):

*Sam needs to improve his level of effort in school as evidenced by the following:*

- *Complete homework*
- *Prepare for tests/quizzes*
- *Participate actively in lessons*
- *Helping peers*

## Method(s) of data collection (check all that apply):

| X | Internal documents | X | Classroom Observation |
|---|---|---|---|
| X | Student Interview | X | Parent Interview |
| X | Psychological Evaluation | | Educational Evaluation |
| X | Teacher Consultation | | Counselor Interview |
| | Other: | | Other: |

List target behavior that most interferes with the student's functioning in the educational setting. Estimate or directly observe the frequency, intensity, and duration of each:

## Baseline Data

| Behavior | Frequency | Intensity | Duration |
|---|---|---|---|
| Lack of organizational skills: poor preparation for school | Daily | Moderate | Throughout the school day |

Observe and identify the environmental factors that seem to cause and maintain the targeted behavior. List the consequences that have been attempted:

| Settings<br>Where does the target behavior seem to occur | Classroom |
|---|---|
| Interventions Attempted<br><br>Planned ignoring, curriculum modification, classroom modification, time away, reprimands, ISS/OSS, physical intervention, parent conference, superintendent's hearing, etc. | Active listening<br>Guided practice completing an agenda book<br>Parent conference<br>Counseling |
| Educational Impact<br><br>How is the target behavior disrupting the educational process of the student or other students | When Sam is not prepared or organized, he loses valuable instructional time that prevents him from obtaining his academic goals |

## What seems to be the function of the target behavior?

| | | |
|---|---|---|
| X | Affective Regulation/Emotional Reactivity<br>*Anxiety, depression, anger, poor self-concept* | *History of depression and anxiety* |
| | Cognitive distortion *Distorted thoughts, inaccurate attributions, negative self-statements, erroneous interpretation of events* | |
| X | Reinforcement<br>*Antecedent*<br>*Behavior*<br>*Consequence* | *Antecedent: difficult work*<br>*Behavior: does not complete assignments*<br>*Consequence: avoids the difficult work and possible feelings of inadequacy* |
| X | Modeling<br>*Poor decision-making skills, ineffective problem-solving skills, delayed or maladaptive emotional development, insufficient coping strategies* | *Ineffective problem-solving skills*<br>*Delayed emotional development* |
| X | Family Issues<br>*Poor social skills* | *Sam currently has a very supportive home.* |
| X | Psychological/Constitutional<br>*Physiological, personality characteristics, developmental disabilities, temperament, inadequate attention span, poor impulse control* | *History of ADHD*<br>*Poor impulse control* |
| | Communicate need<br>*Inability to communicate with verbal cues* | |
| X | Curriculum/Instruction<br>*Instruction, curriculum, environment, poor academic skills, cognitive ability* | *Sam needs a supportive and structured educational environment.* |
| | Love and Belonging<br>*The need to be loved and accepted by groups, families, and loved ones* | |
| | Power<br>*The need for achievement and feeling worthwhile; desire for respect and recognition within a group; competitive desire to win* | |
| | Survival/Safety<br>*The need for things that keep us psychologically and physiologically healthy and safe such as food, clothing, shelter* | |
| | Freedom<br>*The need to form our own space; sense of independence and autonomy* | |
| | Fun<br>*The need to enjoy ourselves and seek pleasure* | |

# HYPOTHESIS STATEMENT

Write a hypothesis regarding the function of the behavior.

*When x (trigger) occurs, the student does y (behavior) in order to z (function).*

*When Sam is in a less-structured environment, he becomes disorganized and does not prepare for school in a possible attempt to excuse himself from difficult work.*

# Resource C

## BEHAVIOR INTERVENTION PLAN

| Student | Lorelle |
|---|---|
| Grade | 2 |
| Date | October 31, 2008 |

The team recognizes that this student may manifest behavior that does not conform to the usual rules and regulations of the school. However, it also recognizes that a standard of discipline must be maintained for the protection of all students and to minimize disruption to the educational process. Therefore, this Behavior Intervention Plan has been developed. Nothing in this plan is intended to prevent school authorities from taking whatever emergency or immediate steps necessary to maintain a safe environment.

| Target Behavior | Disruptive and off-task behaviors |
|---|---|
| Replacement Behavior | On task; following the teacher directions the first time without incident |

| Intervention Strategy | Consequences (positive and/or negative) | Assessment/ Data Collection (method and schedule) | Person(s) Responsible for Implementation | Dates Implemented |
|---|---|---|---|---|
| Alternative working site within school | Allow Lorelle to concentrate; provide a safe environment for Lorelle to regulate emotions and achieve academic success | Daily observations | Classroom Teacher; Special Education Teacher | 10/31/08 |
| Put student in leadership role in classroom | Provide opportunity to experience success Decrease amount of transition time, which leads to off-task behaviors | Daily observations | Classroom teacher | 10/31/08 |
| Alternate working space within the classroom | Allow Lorelle an area in which to work where stimuli is reduced | Daily observations | Classroom teacher | 10/31/08 |

# Resource D

Sample PLEP Responses

| Academic | **Strengths** |
|---|---|
| | Has improved in the area of proofreading and identifying proper paragraphing in writing |
| | Can organize thoughts into an essay with an introduction, body, and conclusion |
| | Benefits from assistance in editing written work |
| | Can decode unfamiliar words |
| | Can comprehend grade-level material that is read silently |
| | Can complete multistep math problems involving fractions |
| | **Weaknesses** |
| | Has a limited sight word vocabulary |
| | Cannot decode unfamiliar words |
| | Cannot compute basic math facts |
| | Does not have math facts automatized |
| Social | **Strengths** |
| | Independent and confident when interacting with peers |
| | Helpful to teachers and peers |
| | Good listener—does not interrupt/offers valuable and appropriate feedback |
| | Honest in deeds and words |
| | Happy/content |
| | Well liked by others |
| | Demonstrates caring attitude toward others |
| | Mature compared to same-age peers |
| | Patient when needs are not immediately met |
| | Appropriate and pleasant sense of humor |
| | Polite/uses manners in most situations |
| | Interacts positively with peers during structured/unstructured times |
| | Demonstrates a good sense of judgment and decision-making skills/considers consequences of behaviors |

| | |
|---|---|
| | **Weaknesses** |
| | Rude in responses toward others |
| | Tattletale frequently |
| | Quick to anger |
| | Name calls |
| | Worries in excess |
| | Stubborn |
| | Complains excessively |
| | Hard to please |
| | Forgetful |
| | Immature when compared to same-age peers |
| | Disruptive |
| |     Interrupts lessons |
| |     Shouts out answers |
| |     Is out of seat frequently |
| |     Is noisy during quiet times |
| | Withdrawn |
| | Depressed |
| | Aggressive |
| | Victim/scapegoat |
| | Attention seeking |
| | Mood swings |
| | Does not demonstrate prosocial behaviors for an academic setting |
| | Demonstrates little or no interaction with teachers |
| | Difficulty accepting constructive criticism |
| | Overreacts to frustrating situations |
| **Physical** | **Strengths** |
| | Demonstrates age-appropriate motor and sensory development, health, vitality and physical skills |
| | **Weaknesses** |
| | Delayed gross motor skills as evidenced by the inability to skip, jump, hop |
| | Poor penmanship as a result of delayed fine motor skills |
| **Management** | **Strengths** |
| | Responsible |
| | Independent |
| | Follows directions |
| | Cooperative |
| | Creative |
| | Positive thinker |

*(Continued)*

(Continued)

|  | |
|---|---|
|  | Works in a group situation for ___ minutes |
|  | Works independently for ___ minutes |
|  | Can transition from class to class with little/no assistance |
|  | Can transition from lesson to lesson with little/no assistance/support |
|  | Completes work on time |
|  | Self-directed |
|  | Able to plan long-term assignments with minimal assistance |
|  | Self-motivated, focused |
|  | Good effort/willingness to learn |
|  | Consistent effort |
|  | Benefits from reminders and prompts to complete assignments on time |
|  | Seeks assistance needed to complete assignments |
|  | Receives assistance constructively and positively |
|  | Seeks support from teachers as needed |
|  | Not resistant to receiving help |
|  | Benefits from 1:1 support to get started |
|  | Can follow a daily schedule with little/no reminders |
|  | Maintains a well-organized notebook system |
|  | **Weaknesses** |
|  | Irresponsible |
|  | Incomplete work |
|  | Doesn't follow directions |
|  | Poor participation |
|  | Poor study habits |
|  | Avoids work |
|  | Inconsistent in efforts to complete work on time |
|  | Lack of effort contributes to incomplete work or late work |
|  | Rarely completes assignments or studies outside of classroom |
|  | Rarely completes assignments without supervision |
|  | Applies minimal effort toward schoolwork |
|  | Resistant to receiving help |
|  | Tends to put little time into schoolwork leading to poor test grades |
|  | Has received low test grades in academic courses due to lack of preparation |
|  | Has a tendency to rush through assignments, which hinders accuracy and retention of material |
|  | Needs to check assignments daily for accuracy and completion |

# Resource E

## SELF-CONTROL GOALS

The student will identify, explore, and practice appropriate methods of handling frustration and anger such as: appropriately ask for staff support in order to remain in class, speak using manners and a polite tone of voice, and accept consequences for behavior without emotional outbursts when encountering an upsetting or frustrating situation.

The student will maintain appropriate, social behavior by: following staff directions the first time, refraining from engaging in negative behaviors of peers, and ceasing disruptive behavior in all situations.

The student will identify and explore antecedents to and consequences of violent behavior such as: responding to all situations in a nonviolent manner by refraining from using threats, respecting physical space, and using a polite tone of voice in all situations.

The student will continue to adhere to rules and procedures and remain focused on the task at hand by using such strategies as moving to a less stimulating area of the room in stimulating situations.

The student will maintain focus on academic tasks and refrain from becoming involved with negative peers as evidenced by the ability to explore and identify the reasons for a desire to become involved in the negative behavior of peers during counseling sessions.

The student will adhere to the rules and regulations and remain focused on the task at hand by demonstrating the ability to: move to a less stimulating area of the room, continue to work independently, accept adult support and redirection, and refrain from involvement in negative peer issues during stimulating situations with less adult support.

The student will describe orally or in writing the actions of self and others that trigger strong emotional response during periods of reflection on previous interactions with others in counseling.

## EFFORT GOALS

The student will maintain focus on task and ask for teacher assistance when needed and complete all classroom assignments and homework on time with an 80% level of accuracy in all classroom situations.

The student will work for the entire class period, initiate work, work to completion, work to teacher expectations, and complete all assigned work in all classroom situations.

# BEHAVIOR GOALS

The student will explore and identify verbally or in writing long- and short-term goals to assist him/her in focusing on personal issues and motivations, and in focusing on personal issues at each opportunity when negative peer issues arise or during a crisis situation that is occurring within the environment.

The student will choose not to involve themselves in others' negativity by moving to a quiet area of the room, asking for adult support, and refocusing on the task at hand and identified goals during crisis situations.

## Interpersonal Skills

The student will identify, explore, and practice appropriate and positive methods of communication and will respond appropriately when spoken to, listen without interrupting, and offer opinions in a nonhostile manner when engaging in peer interactions.

The student will initiate age-appropriate interactions and conversations with peers using a positive tone of voice, taking turns in conversations, maintaining appropriate topics of conversation, using manners, refraining from instigating and name calling, and using appropriate nonverbal communication skills when in social situations.

The student will discuss verbally aspects of healthy, age-appropriate relationships in response to exploring aspects and characteristics of healthy relationships; evaluating their own relationships and make efforts to change unhealthy aspects in counseling sessions.

The student will respond appropriately and in a respectful manner by refraining from making negative comments, threats, inappropriate body language and facial expressions when given a staff request.

The student will maintain appropriate physical and social boundaries with adults and peers as evidenced by keeping an appropriate physical distance, using a normal tone of voice, listening without interrupting, and refraining from talking about topics that are explicit in nature when engaging in social situations.

The student will maintain appropriate conversation skills in social situations with peers as evidenced by: looking at whomever is currently speaking, using appropriate affect and remaining attentive to the conversation, introducing appropriate topics of conversation, avoiding topics related to drug or gang activity or topics that are overly personal, maintaining the conversation with questions that express interest, and waiting for natural conversation breaks to begin speaking during conversations with peers and adults.

## Anger Management Goals

The student will seek adult assistance in a nonviolent manner by using an appropriate tone of voice and physical proximity, and by removing him/herself from a harmful situation when encountering a situation when student feels the need to defend him/herself.

The student will promptly and appropriately ask for a time out to explore, identify, and utilize coping skills such as refraining from using inappropriate language to express feelings and take time to gather thoughts before reacting to effectively deal with difficult situations when encountering a difficult situation.

## Coping Goals

The student will explore healthy and effective coping mechanisms as alternatives to self-harm such as seeking adult assistance and guidance, developing positive self-talk, setting realistic expectations and effectively communicating needs and emotions during counseling sessions.

The student will apply healthy coping skills to assist her in appropriately dealing with problems by not reacting in an angry or depressive manner after identifying emotional state and antecedents to feelings; choosing a positive means of coping via exploration and practice; and asking for staff support if necessary during counseling sessions.

The student will identify and explore ways to maintain appropriate behavior in frustrating situations such as following staff requests the first time; effectively communicating needs; distinguishing between needs and wants; and remaining calm and patient when needs are not met during counseling sessions.

## Self-Esteem Goal

The student will identify positive traits about him/herself and respond appropriately to compliments and praise, make positive self-statements, and articulate positive goals during counseling sessions.

## Conflict Resolution Goals

The student will verbally articulate and communicate an understanding of appropriate and healthy ways to handle a conflict including: active listening without interrupting, negotiation, mediation, brainstorming possible solutions to conflicts, speaking within the topic without placing blame or verbal attacks, and respecting physical space during counseling sessions.

The student will verbally express effective methods to appropriately deal with an accusation such as looking at the person, refraining from glaring, maintaining appropriate physical distance and demeanor, maintaining a calm voice and affect, asking the person to specify what you are being accused of, honestly self-reporting your behavior and apologizing if the behavior is true in counseling sessions.

# Resource F

## SAMPLE INDIVIDUALIZED EDUCATION PLAN

### Middle school student IEP generated after initial review to determine ED classification

| Date of CSE/CPSE Meeting:<br>*Date of Meeting* | Purpose of Meeting:<br>*Initial Review* |
|---|---|
| **Student Name:** *John Doe*<br>*(fictitious student)* | **Date of Birth:** *Student DOB* |
| **Age:** *Student Age* | **Telephone:** *Student Phone Number* |
| **Address:** *Student Address* | **Student ID #:** *Student ID Number* |
| **Male** ____X____ **Female** _____ | **Current Grade:** 7 |
| **Dominant Language of Student:**<br>*English* | **Interpreter Needed:** *no* |
| **Current Classification:**<br>*Emotionally Disabled* | **Previous Classification:**<br>*None* |
| **Racial/Ethnic Group of Student (optional information):** | **Date of Initiation of Services:** *day after BOE mtg.*<br>**Projected Date of Review:** *+ 1 year, – 1 day from date of meeting*<br>**Date for Reevaluation:** *+ 3 years, – 1 day from date of meeting* |
| **Medical Alerts:**<br>*List any concerns (e.g., bee allergies, food allergies, asthma, etc.)* | |
| **Parent/Guardian's Name and Address:** *Parent/Guardian name and address* | |
| **Telephone:**<br>*Parent Phone Number* | **County of Residence:**<br>*Parent county of residence* |
| **Dominant Language of Parent/ Guardian:**<br>*Parent Language* | **Interpreter Needed:** *yes/no* |
| **Second Parent/Guardian's Name and Address:**<br>*if second parent, list here* | |
| **Telephone:** | **County of Residence:** |
| **Dominant Language of Parent/ Guardian:** | **Interpreter Needed:** |

# TRANSCRIPT INFORMATION FOR SECONDARY STUDENTS

| Credential/Diploma Sought: | *Regent's* |
| --- | --- |
| Expected Date of High School Completion: | *2011* |
| Credits Earned to Date: | *0—John is in 7th grade* |
| Commencement-level State Tests Passed: | *N/A* |

# PRESENT LEVELS OF PERFORMANCE AND INDIVIDUAL NEEDS

## Current functioning and individual needs in consideration of:

- the results of the initial or most recent evaluation, the student's strengths, the concerns of the parents, the results of the student's performance on any state or districtwide assessment programs;

- the student's needs related to communication, behavior, use of Braille, assistive technology, limited English proficiency;

- how the student's disability affects involvement/progress in the general education curriculum; and

- the student's needs as they relate to transition from school to postschool activities for students beginning with the first IEP to be in effect when the student turns age 15 (and younger when deemed appropriate).

1. **Academic/Educational Achievement and Learning characteristics**: Address current levels of knowledge and development in subject and skill areas, including activities of daily living, level of intellectual functioning, adaptive behavior, expected rate of progress in acquiring skills and information, and learning style.

| **Present Levels:** | *Current Testing (indicate date, testing administrator and school/agency)* |
| --- | --- |
| | *Wide Range Achievement Test—III*<br>  *Reading Composite 90 SS, 25th percentile*<br>  *Arithmetic Composite 74 SS, 4th percentile*<br>  *Spelling 81 SS, 10th percentile* |
| | *John is currently a 7th grade student in a 12:1+1 program and preparing for a Regent's Diploma. Academic and behavioral difficulties support John being classified as a student with an emotional disability.* |
| | *Current testing indicates that John is a student functioning in the low average range of cognitive abilities. Based on the results of these tests, John's achievement appears to be commensurate with his ability. This suggests that John is capable of completing grade-level work.* |

|  | *John demonstrates the abilities necessary to complete his class work. Current teachers report that he is able to read and comprehend the written materials to complete assignments and answer questions. He has the ability to convey thoughts into written word. He demonstrates limited competency in math. He has demonstrated that he has some knowledge in science and social studies.*<br><br>*John needs to further improve his spelling and reading comprehension. He has the ability to demonstrate an understanding of basic skills math.* |
|---|---|
| **Abilities:** | • *can complete grade-level classwork*<br>• *can read, summarize, and comprehend material presented in a 7th grade curriculum*<br>• *can compute basic skills math and complete assignments involving simple fractions* |
| **Needs:** | *John needs to:*<br>• *improve written language skills and spelling*<br>• *improve ability to compute higher order math computations*<br>• *increase his content knowledge in social studies and science* |

2. **Social Development:** Describe the quality of the student's relationships with peers and adults, feelings about self, social adjustment to school and community environment, and behaviors that may impede learning.

| **Present Levels:** | *John has a history of leaving home without permission, curfew violation, physical and verbal aggression, disrespect, drug use, and assault.*<br><br>*John has shown tremendous improvement in his interpersonal abilities. He has developed a positive rapport with teachers and his incidences of aggression have greatly decreased. John is described as a fun-loving child, full of zest and vigor. He has a good sense of humor. John has demonstrated that he can use appropriate language, tone of voice, and respectful tones when communicating with staff and peers. John can be pleasant and cooperative and most often enjoys his classes.*<br><br>*John is an extremely social young man. This sociability often interferes with his ability to learn as well as creates a disturbance for the learning of his peers. John enjoys to horseplay and rough house with his peers in a "joking" manner. However, this behavior has created extremely unsafe situations for others. John seems to become overly impulsive and hyper at these times. John presents as "pouting" when corrected by his teachers for these behaviors and will not communicate verbally. He will, however, maintain nonverbal communications such as nodding his head and using hand gestures. When upset, John can become challenging, disrespectful, argumentative. At these times, he uses inappropriate language, raises his voice, and does not follow directions.* |
|---|---|
| **Abilities:** | • *fun-loving, good sense of humor*<br>• *can be polite and respectful*<br>• *enjoys a positive rapport with staff*<br>• *cooperative* |

| Needs: | John needs to: |
|---|---|
|  | • *use class time to learn; find appropriate times to socialize with peers* |
|  | • *reduce the physical amount of horseplay* |
|  | • *develop age-appropriate anger management skills as evidenced by* |
|  | using appropriate tone of voice |
|  | using appropriate language |
|  | communicating his frustrations and thoughts verbally and in a respectful manner without intimidation and threats |
|  | maintaining appropriate and respectful physical space |

**3. Physical Development**: Describe the student's motor and sensory development, health, vitality, and physical skills or limitations that pertain to the learning process.

| Present Levels: | *John's history includes diagnoses of Attention Deficit Disorder, Learning Disorder, and Conduct Disorder. He experiences environmental allergies.* |
|---|---|
|  | *John demonstrates good fine-motor coordination.* |
|  | *John is slightly overweight.* |
| Abilities: | *John appears to be in good physical health* |
|  | *Good motor coordination* |
| Needs: | *John needs to* |
|  | • *Make healthy food and exercise choices* |

**4. Management Needs**: Describe the nature and degree to which environmental modifications and human or material resources are required to address academic, social, and physical needs.

**A functional behavioral assessment** should be completed for any student who demonstrates behaviors that impede learning. A functional behavioral assessment becomes the basis for positive behavioral interventions, strategies, and supports for the student.

| Present Levels: | *John demonstrates many strengths that will result in his academic success. He seems to enjoy many of his classes and puts forth good effort. His current grades are all in the high 80s and 90s. John works well 1:1, can work independently and in groups. He is able to ask for assistance when needed and completes his assignments in a timely manner. John responds well to praise and encouragement. John can respond to verbal and nonverbal prompts for redirection and refocusing behaviors.* |
|---|---|

| | |
|---|---|
| | *John demonstrates behaviors that limit his instructional time and prevent him from accessing his curriculum. He is often late to class as he is socializing and horseplaying in the hall. He sometimes chooses not to follow classroom procedures. Some teachers report that he does not complete assignments on time and is disruptive during lessons. John is easily influenced by the negative behaviors of his peers.* |
| **Abilities:** | • *Puts forth good effort*<br>• *Can ask for assistance when needed*<br>• *Works well 1:1, in small groups and independently*<br>• *Responds well to praise and encouragement*<br>• *Can be redirected when off-task* |
| **Needs:** | *John needs to:*<br>• *Improve his level of effort to be consistent in all classes*<br>• *Develop self-control to avoid being influenced by negative peers*<br>• *Follow all classroom procedures at all times* |

# MEASURABLE POSTSECONDARY GOALS

For students beginning with the first IEP to be in effect when the student turns age 15 (and younger if deemed appropriate), identify the appropriate measurable postsecondary goals based upon age-appropriate transition assessments relating to training, education, employment, and, when appropriate, independent living skills.

| Postsecondary Education/ Training: | *John will seek postsecondary education and/or vocational training that best matches his interests and abilities.* |
|---|---|
| **Employment:** | *John will seek full-time, competitive employment in the field that best matches his interests and abilities.* |
| **Community Living:** | *John will become an independent and contributing member of society.* |

# MEASURABLE ANNUAL GOALS

* For students with severe disabilities who would meet the eligibility criteria to take the New York State Alternate Assessment, the IEP must also include short-term instructional objectives and benchmarks for each annual goal.

**Annual Goal:** What the student will be expected to be able to do by the end of the year in which the IEP is in effect.

**Evaluative Criteria:** How well and over what period of time the student must demonstrate performance in order to consider the annual goal to have been met.

**Procedures to Evaluate Goal:** The method that will be used to measure progress and determine if the student has met the annual goal.

**Evaluation Schedule:** The dates or intervals of time by which evaluation procedures will be used to measure the student's progress.

| Annual goal: | *John will independently analyze, synthesize, and evaluate experiences, ideas, information, and issues presented by others in a written paragraph using proper standard grammar and spelling* | |
|---|---|---|
| Evaluation Criteria: | *4 out of 5 trials* | |
| Evaluation Procedures: | *Teacher observations; Weekly lesson review; Practice tests* | |
| Evaluation Schedule: | **1st quarter** | *e.g., goal not met due to time* |
| | **2nd quarter** | *e.g., goal not met due to time* |
| | **3rd quarter** | *e.g., goal progress noted* |
| | **4th quarter** | *e.g., goal achieved* |

| Annual goal: | *John will independently apply mathematics in real-world settings, solving problems through the integrated study of number systems, geometry, algebra, data analysis, probability, and trigonometry* | |
|---|---|---|
| Evaluation Criteria: | *4 out of 5 trials* | |
| Evaluation Procedures: | *Teacher observations; Weekly lesson review; Practice tests* | |
| Evaluation Schedule: | **1st quarter** | |
| | **2nd quarter** | |
| | **3rd quarter** | |
| | **4th quarter** | |

| Annual goal: | *John will demonstrate emotional self-control by independently following the rules and regulations and remain focused on the task at hand in stimulating situations with less adult support* | |
|---|---|---|
| Evaluation Criteria: | *4 out of 5 trials* | |
| Evaluation Procedures: | *Teacher observation; internal documents* | |
| Evaluation Schedule: | **1st quarter** | |
| | **2nd quarter** | |
| | **3rd quarter** | |
| | **4th quarter** | |

# SPECIAL EDUCATION PROGRAMS AND RELATED SERVICES/PROGRAM MODIFICATIONS

| Special Education Programs/ Related Services | Ratio | Frequency | Duration | Period | Location | Start Date |
|---|---|---|---|---|---|---|
| Special Class Size Counseling | 12:1+1 ---------- Individual | 5 ------------ 2 | 5 hours ------------ 40 minutes | Weekly --------- Weekly | Special location Special location | Day after BOE mtg. |

## Extended School Year Services Yes *X* No

| Special Education Programs/ Related Services | Frequency | Duration | Location | Initiation Date |
|---|---|---|---|---|
| 12:1:1 | Daily | 6 weeks | Special location | First day of summer session |

| Program Modifications/ Accommodations/ Supplementary Aids and Services | Frequency | Duration | Location | Initiation Date |
|---|---|---|---|---|
| Functional Behavioral Assessment | Daily | Throughout each day | Classroom | Day after BOE mtg. |

| Assistive Technology Devices/Services | Frequency | Duration | Location | Initiation Date |
|---|---|---|---|---|
| N/A | | | | |

| Supports for School Personnel on Behalf of Student | Frequency | Duration | Location | Initiation Date |
|---|---|---|---|---|
| N/A | | | | |

# TESTING ACCOMMODATIONS

The following individual appropriate accommodations are necessary to measure the academic achievement and functional performance of the student on state and districtwide assessments. Recommended testing accommodations will be used consistently:

- in the student's education program,
- in the administration of districtwide assessments of student achievement, consistent with school district policy, and
- in the administration of state assessments of student achievement, consistent with State Education Department policy.

**Individual Testing Modification(s):**

| Accommodation Name | Accommodation | Specifications/Conditions |
|---|---|---|
| *Flexible schedule/timing* | *Extended Time* | *Time & ½* |
| *Flexible Setting* | *Separate setting* | *Small group* |
| *Other* | *Calculator* | *Any math test not measuring computation* |

**Participation in State Assessments**

[X]  The student will participate in the same state assessments that are administered to general education students.

 [X]  Graded: The student will take the state assessment with his/her grade level peers.

 [ ]  Ungraded: The student will take the state assessment based on chronological age because his/her instructional levels in English and mathematics are three or more years below the grade-level coursework of the student's nondisabled peers.

[ ]  The student will participate in the New York State Alternate Assessment (NYSAA) for Students with

Severe Disabilities.

Explain why the state assessment(s) administered to general education students is not appropriate for the student and why the alternate assessment selected is appropriate for the student:

---

**Participation in Districtwide Assessments**

[X]  The student will participate in the same districtwide assessments that are administered to general education students.

□ The student will participate in the following alternate assessment for districtwide assessments.

Explain why the districtwide assessment(s) administered to general education students is not appropriate for the student and why the alternate assessment selected is appropriate for the student.

**Removal from the general educational environment** occurs only when the nature or severity of the disability is such that, even with the use of supplementary aids and services, education cannot be satisfactorily achieved.

☐ **Explanation of the extent, if any, to which the student will not participate in general education programs, including extracurricular and other nonacademic activities:**

*The student is currently attending the campus school of the residential treatment center. The student's educational program may take place in an alternative setting on the Hopevale campus if deemed necessary.*

☐ *The student will not participate in the general education physical education program, but will participate in specially designed or adapted physical education.*

**Language other than English exemption**

X *No*        ☐

☐ *Yes, the student's disability adversely affects the ability to learn a language, and the student is excused from the language other than English requirement.*

# PARTICIPATING AGENCIES FOR STUDENTS WHO REQUIRE TRANSITION SERVICES

*Participating Agencies* that have agreed to provide transition services/supports (before the students leave the secondary school program):

| | |
|---|---|
| **Agency name:** | |
| **Telephone number:** | |
| **Service:** | |
| **Implementation date if different from IEP implementation date:** | |

# COORDINATED SET OF ACTIVITIES LEADING TO LONG-TERM ADULT OUTCOMES

If any of the following areas are *not* addressed, explain why:

| Coordinate Set of Activities | Activity | School District/ Agency Responsible | Date |
|---|---|---|---|
| **Instruction:** | *John will be offered the opportunity to pursue the curriculum and receive individualized instruction.* | *Home School* | *Day after BOE mtg.* |
| **Related Services:** | *Related services are listed in Section IV of this document.* | *Home School* | *Day after BOE mtg.* |
| **Employment/ Postsecondary Education:** | *The Guidance Department will work with John to identify colleges and/or vocational training programs with supported education options.* | *Home School* | *Day after BOE mtg.* |
| **Community Experience: (if appropriate)** | *John will be provided a list of organizations that support his interests, abilitie,s and needs* | *Home School* | *Day after BOE mtg.* |
| **Activities of Daily Living:** | *N/A* | *N/A* | *N/A* |
| **Functional Vocational Assessment:** | *N/A* | *N/A* | *N/A* |

# SUMMARY OF SELECTED RECOMMENDATIONS

| | |
|---|---|
| **Classification of Disability:** | *Emotionally Disabled* |
| **Recommended Placement—Sept.–June:** | *Home School* |
| **Extended School Year (ESY) Services:** | *Yes* |
| **Recommended Placement—July and August:** | *Home School* |
| **Transportation Needs:** | *N/A* |

# REPORTING PROGRESS TO PARENTS

| | |
|---|---|
| State manner and frequency in which progress will be reported: | • *Quarterly annual goal progress reports*<br>• *Quarterly report cards*<br>• *Mid-quarter progress reports*<br>• *Summer school report cards*<br>• *Treatment meeting reports* |

# COMMITTEE PARTICIPANTS

**The list of names below indicates attendance/participation at the committee meeting and not necessarily agreement with the IEP recommendations developed at the meeting (see signatures on attached page):**

| Name | Professional Title | Committee Member Role |
|---|---|---|
|  | CSE Chairperson | CSE Chairperson |
|  | School Psychologist | School Psychologist |
|  | School Counselor | School Counselor |
|  | ELA Teacher | Regular Education Teacher |
|  | Special Education Teacher | Special Education Teacher |
|  |  | Parent Member |
|  | Secretary | CSE Secretary |
|  |  | Parent |
|  |  | Parent |
|  |  | Student |

*General and Special Education Teachers must be teachers of the student. If student does not have a General Education Teacher, a teacher that would otherwise teach the student must be selected.

# Recommended Reading and Additional Resources

## ARTICLES

Feil, E. G., Severson, H. H., & Walker, H. M. (1995). Identification of critical factors in the assessment of preschool behavior problems. *Education and Treatment of Children, 18,* 261–271.

Fitzsimmons, M. K. (1998). Functional behavior assessment and behavior intervention plans. (ERIC EC Digest E571). Reston, VA: Council for Exceptional Children. (http://ericec.org/digests/e571.htm)

Flannery, K. B., O'Neill, R. E., & Horner, R. H. (1995). Including predictability in functional assessment and individual program development. *Education and Treatment of Children, 18,* 499–509.

Forum at NASDSE, June 1998. Available from 703.519.3800 (voice) or 7008 (TDD).

Functional behavioral assessment: State policies and procedures from Project

Gable, R., Hendrickson, J. M., & Sasso, G. M. (1995). Toward a more functional analysis of aggression. *Education and Treatment of Children, 18,* 226–242.

Gable, R. A., Quinn, M. M., Rutherford, Jr., R. B., & Howell, K. W. (1998). Addressing problem behaviors in schools: Use of functional assessments and behavior intervention plans *Preventing School Failure,* 4(3), 106–119.

Iwata, B. A., Pace, G., Kilter, M., Cowdery, G., & Cattalo, M. (1990). Experimental analysis and extinction of self-injurious escape behavior. *Journal of Applied Behavior Analysis, 23,* 11–27.

Iwata, B. A., Vollmer, T. R., & Zarcone, J. R. (1990). The experimental (functional) analysis of behavior disorders: Methodology, applications, and initiations.

In A. C. Repp & N. N. Singh (Eds.), *Perspectives on the use of nonaversive and aversive interventions for persons with developmental disabilities* (pp. 301–330). Sycamore, IL: Sycamore Press.

Nelson, J. R., Roberts, M. L., Mathur, S. R., & Rutherford, R. B. (1999). Has public policy exceeded our knowledge base? A review of the functional behavioral assessment literature. *Behavioral Disorders, 24,* 169–179.

O'Neill, R. E., Horner, R. H., Albin, R. W., Sprague, J. R., Storey, K., & Newton, J. S. (1997). Functional assessment and program development for problem behavior (2nd ed.). Pacific Grove, CA: Brooks/Cole Publishing Company.

Quinn, M. M., Gable, R. A., Rutherford, Jr., R. B., Nelson, C. M., & Howell, K. W. (1998, January). *Addressing Student Problem Behavior: An IEP team's introduction to functional behavioral assessment and behavior intervention plans* Available from the Center for Effective Collaboration and Practice(888.457.1551). E-mail: center@air-dc.org. Web Site: http://www.air-dc.org/cecp/ceep.html.

Rutherford, R. B., & Nelson, C. M. (1995). Management of aggressive and violent behavior in schools. *Focus on Exceptional Children, 26,* 1–16.

Scott, T. M., & Nelson, C. M. (1999). *Using functional behavioral assessment to develop effective behavioral intervention plans: A ten step process.* Manuscript submitted for publication.

# BOOKS

## Attention Deficit Hyperactivity Disorder

*Shelley: The Hyperactive Turtle* by: Deborah M. Moss
Shelley is a young hyperactive turtle who faces difficulties due to his inability to sit still and his frequent behavior problems, which lead to problems at school and on the bus, at home and with friends, eventually leading to a poor self-image and depression. After a visit to a neurologist, he no longer thinks of himself as a bad turtle and his condition gradually improves.

*Eagle Eyes* by: Jeanne Gehert, M.A.
Designed for ages 6–12, this is a book addressing ADD. Ben has attention deficit disorder (ADD) and this story focuses on his family and the journey they take to help Ben control his movement and thinking. The story involves a doctor who works with the entire family to help ensure that Ben is successful.

*Help is on the Way: A Child's Book About ADD* by: Marc A. Nemiroff and Jane Annunziata
This colorful book provides information to kids about the nature of ADD and various strategies for coping with ADD.

*Eddie Enough!* by: Debbie Zimmett
Eddie has had a particularly rough day at school. He has had trouble paying attention, he bumps into things, and some kids in his class make fun of him. After he visits the doctor and learns he has ADD, his parents and teachers help him come up with strategies for improving his days at school.

*A.D.D. not B.A.D.* by: Audrey Penn
For ages 5–9, this book offers an explanation of age-appropriate behaviors and insight into ADD from the perspective of a student and his teacher.

*Learning to Slow Down & Pay Attention.* A Book for Kids about ADHD by: Kathleen G. Nadeau
For students ages 7–12, this book explains to kids what ADHD is and how they can deal with it.

The "Putting on the Brakes" Activity Book for Young People With ADHD by: Patricia O. Quinn
For students 9–13, this book contains various activities that kids can do to help them stay on task and concentrate on one task.

*Thumbs Up, Rico!* by: Maria Testa
Rico is a boy with Down syndrome who loves basketball. The story describes his relationship with a neighborhood boy named Caesar, his older sister Nina, and his art class.

## Autism/Asperger's/PDD

*Joey and Sam* by: Illana Katz and Edward Ritvo
Sam is 5 and has autism, and Joey is his 6-year-old brother. They describe an ordinary day at home and at school, showing how they are different and alike.

*All About My Brother* by: Sarah Peralta
An eight-year-old girl offers insight into autism through the world of her younger brother who is nonverbal.

*Asperger's Huh? A Child's* Perspective by: Rosina Schnurr
Children ages 6–12. Meant to help children better understand Asperger's Disorder in simple terms.

*The ADHD Autism Connection* by: Diane M. Kennedy
This book offers insights into the number of similarities between ADHD and Autism in children.

*My Friend with Autism* by: Beverly Bishop
A book that helps children understand autism, and that is written from a child's point-of-view. This book includes a lesson and acts as a coloring book too.

*Helping Children with Autism Learn: Treatment Approaches for Parents and Professionals* by: Bryna Segal
This book looks at autistic learning disabilities and autistic learning styles, and what makes the world of an autistic child different.

*Looking After Louis* by: Lesley Ely and Polly Dunbar
Designed for ages 7–8, this book takes a look at a boy with autism and how his classmates help become part of his world. Louis has autism but through imagination, kindness from his classmates, and a special game of soccer with his class, he overcomes some of the barriers that students may face with autism. Instead of trying to fit into the world of his class, they take the approach to enter his world.

*Teach Me Language: A Language Manual for Children with Autism, Asperger's Syndrome, and Related Developmental Disorders* by: Sabrina Freeman, Lorelei Dake, and Isaac Tamir
This book is designed for parents and therapists who teach language to children with autism, Asperger's, and related developmental disorders.

*My Friend with Autism. A Coloring Book for Peers and Siblings* by: Beverly Bishop
Ages 7–11. Meant for anyone who comes in contact with an autistic child, including young classmates, neighbors, church members, and professionals. The book explains in two ways what autism is and how the behavior of autistic children can be different:

## Mental Retardation/Down Syndrome

*Be Good to Eddie Lee* by: Virginia Fleming
Interactions between neighborhood children and a boy with Down syndrome.

*I Can, Can You?* by: Marjorie W. Pitzer
Ages 4–10. Contains pictures of children with Down syndrome performing various tasks such as eating spaghetti, laughing, taking their bottle, and swimming. The pictures of these children model behavior that other children with Down syndrome can also do.

*How About a Hug* by: Nan Holcomb A young girl with Down syndrome includes the details of a typical day in her life. While her daily activities require a degree of concentration and don't go perfectly smoothly, she is surrounded by helpful, supportive, and affectionate friends, family and teachers, all of whom she agrees to hug when they offer.

*Buddy's Shadow* by: Shirley Becker
Buddy, a 5-year-old boy with Down syndrome, purchases a puppy.

*We'll Paint the Octopus Red* by: Stephanie Stuve-Bodeen
Emma is a little girl who has a new baby brother with Down syndrome.

*What's Wrong with Timmy?* by: Maria Shriver

When Kate meets Timmy, a boy who is mentally disabled, she is full of questions. After talking with her mother, Kate realizes that she and Timmy have a lot in common and they become fast friends.

*Where's Chimpy?* by: Berniece Rabe

Misty, a young girl with Down syndrome, misplaced her stuffed monkey and reviews her day with her father to try to remember where she left him.

*Charlsie's Chuckle* by: Clara Widess Berkus

Charlsie, a 7-year-old boy with Down syndrome, has an infectious laugh and enjoys bicycling around his neighborhood. On one such excursion he inadvertently wanders into a disputatious city council meeting and brings humor and harmony to the argumentative adults.

*Cookie* by: Linda Kneeland

Molly, a 4-year-old girl with Down syndrome, has difficulty talking. Her frustration with communication difficulties is relieved when someone comes to teach her sign language.

*The Hangashore* by: Geoff Butler

Newfoundland story of a young man with Down syndrome who displays courage and kindness toward a judgmental government official.

*My Sister is Different* by: Betty Ren Wright

Carlo tells us what it is like to have an older sister with mental retardation.

*My Brother, Matthew* by: Mary Thompson

David describes life with his younger brother, who was born with a mental disability

*Taking Down Syndrome to School* by: Jenna Glatzer

Nick talks about living with Down syndrome. He tells about playing with friends, going to school, and working with his speech therapist.

## Learning Disability, Reading Disability, Dyslexia

*Kevin's Story* by: Dvora Levinson, Ph.D.

Kevin exhibits reading problems and is referred for testing with a psychologist who explains reading and learning disabilities to him and his family.

*Charlie's Challenge* by: Ann Root and Linda Gladden

Charlie excels at some school activities but struggles with other school activities. After his doctor determines that he has a learning disability, his teacher implements some learning strategies that help Charlie's performance and confidence.

*The Survival Guide for Kids with Learning Disabilities* by: Gary Fisher PhD and Rhoda Cummings, EdD

Designed for ages adolescent to young adult, this book is for a young person with a learning disability and some of the questions surrounding their learning difference. The book answers many of the common questions that arise and also helps the young person better understand themselves.

*The Don't-Give-Up-Kid and Learning Differences* by: Jeanne Gehret, M.A.

Designed for age 8, this book is about Alex who has reading problems and this makes him the target of a lot of teasing from others in his class. Alex is aware of his different learning style but he also realizes that his hero Thomas Edison faced similar problems.

Together Edison and Alex work at trying new solutions to try to create something that no one would ever expect. In the end, they succeed and create their dream of finding a solution to learning disabilities that no one else could have created.

*Happy Birthday Jason* by: C. Jean Cutbill and Diane Rawsthorn
Children learn an understanding of Jason and his disabilities to realize that they are not so different.

*The Alphabet War: A Story About Dyslexia* by: Diane Burton Robb
Probably meant for kids 9–13. Tells the story of a boy who has dyslexia and the struggles both emotionally and intellectually he has to endure.

*Reach for the Moon* by: Samantha Abeel, Charles R. Murphy, & Williams, Roberta
A combination of the poetry and prose of a gifted 13-year-old with a learning disability, and the watercolors that inspired her words.

*Dyslexia* by Dr. Alvin Silverstien, Virgina Silverstien, and Laura Silverstien-Nunn
Designed for ages 7–10, this is a book about dyslexia. It takes a look at what dyslexia is, how it occurs and what the brain does. It also talks about who gets this disability, how it becomes diagnosed, and how to receive help once the diagnosis is made.

*Taking Dyslexia to School* by: Lauren E. Moynihan
Matt explains his dyslexia and tells about strategies he uses in school. Includes a list of tips for teachers.

## Cerebral Palsy

*Patrick and Emma Lou* by: Nan Holcomb
Three-year-old Patrick has cerebral palsy. He is having a hard time managing his new walker, but with the help of a new friend, Emma Lou, who is six and has spina bifida, they both discover something very important about each other.

*Rolling Along: The Story of Taylor and His Wheelchair* by: Jamee Riggio Heelan
A young boy learns he can be independent and mobile with a new wheelchair.

*Howie Helps Himself* by: Joan Fassler
Although he enjoys life with his family and attends school, Howie, a child with cerebral palsy, wants more than anything else to be able to move his wheelchair by himself.

*A Smile from Andy* by: Nan Holcomb
Andy, who has cerebral palsy, is very shy. One day he meets a girl who helps him discover something that he can do to reach out to others in his own special way.

*Can't You Be Still?* by: Sarah Yates
Ann, who has cerebral palsy, attends school for the first time.

*Andy Opens Wide* by: Nan Holcomb
Andy, a young boy with cerebral palsy, is frustrated by his inability to open his mouth wide enough for his mother to feed him easily.

*Different Is Just Different!* by: Karin M Schwier
For preschoolers to grade 3, this book is about a five-year-old boy who meets a woman in a wheelchair and others who are different from himself.

# WEB RESOURCES

## Early Childhood

National Institute for Urban School Improvement
http://www.urbanschools.org/

The National Research Center on Learning Disabilities (NRCLD)
http://nrcld.org/
Conducts research on the identification of learning disabilities; formulates implementation recommendations; disseminates findings; and provides technical assistance to national, state, and local constituencies.

Culturally and Linguistically Appropriate Services
http://clas.uiuc.edu/
Collects and describes early childhood/early intervention resources that have been developed across the United States for children with disabilities and their families, and the service providers who work with them.

American Academy of Pediatrics
www.aap.org

Center for Early Education and Development (CEED)
http://education.umn.edu/CEED/default.html

Circle of Inclusion
www.circleofinclusion.org

Division for Early Childhood (DEC)
Council for Exceptional Children
www.dec-sped.org

Early Childhood Outcomes Center
www.the-eco-center.org

First Signs, Inc.
www.firstsigns.org

National Center for Early Development & Learning
www.fpg.unc.edu/%7Encedl

National Child Care Information Center (NCCIC)
www.nccic.org

National Early Childhood Technical Assistance Center (NECTAC)
www.nectac.org

Research and Training Center (RTC) on Early Childhood Development
www.researchtopractice.info

ZERO TO THREE: National Center For Infants, Toddlers, and Families
www.zerotothree.org

# ELECTRONIC JOURNALS

The Special Ed Advocate
http://wrightslaw.com/
William & Mary University
http://www.wm.edu/TTAC
Click on *Articles* and under Challenging Behaviors, find information on crisis information; also other valuable information.

American Psychological Association: *Prevention & Treatment Journal*
http://www.apa.org/prevention
APA's site on prevention issues and you can subscribe to their FREE Prevention & Treatment journal.

## For Counselors

American School Counselor Association
www.schoolcounselor.org

American Counseling Association
www.counseling.org

The Center for School Counseling Outcome Research
http://www.umass.edu/schoolcounseling
Dedicated to improving the practice of school counseling by developing the research base that is necessary for responsible and effective practice.

The Center for Mental Health Services (CMHS)
http://www.mentalhealth.samhsa.gov/cmhs/default.asp
The Federal agency within the U.S. Substance Abuse and Mental Health Services Administration (SAMHSA) that leads national efforts to improve prevention and mental health treatment services for all Americans.

American Academy of Child and Adolescent Psychiatry
http://www.aacap.org
Great handouts for parents & teachers

National Institute of Mental Health
http://www.nimh.nih.gov/publicat/adhd.htm
Informative booklet on ADD: Decade of the Brain; Drop Adhd.htm for full listing of offerings.

National Organization for Rare Disorders, Inc.
http://www.rarediseases.org
Good information on rare childhood diseases.

Center for the Future of Children
http://www.futureofchildren.org
Journal on the Web

Priory Lodge Education
http://priory.com
Many good psychology references and general psychology information.

Psychiatry Matters.MD
http://www.psychiatrymatters.md

Mental Health Network
http://www.mentalhealth.com
Information on a wide variety of mental health disorders.

Internet Mental Health Resources
http://www.med.nyu.edu/Psych/src.psych.html

American Academy of Child and Adolescent Psychiatry
http://aacap.org
Great handouts for parents & teachers

The American Academy of Experts in Traumatic Stress
http://www.aaets.org/tnesp.htm

American Society for Suicide Prevention
http://www.afsp.org

## For Parents and Families

ERIC National Parent Information Network (http://www.npin.org)
A wealth of information for parents and educators working with parents.
www.npin.org

Federal Resources for Educational Excellence (FREE)
(http://www.ed.gov/free)
A rich resource on teaching and learning, including A Parent's Guide to the Internet.

U.S. Dept. of Education Publications and Productions
http://www.ed.gov/pubs
Publications for parents, plus educational research, improvement reports and studies, partnerships, and family involvement.

Parents' Page
http://www.cse.ucla.edu/CRESST/pages/info-parent.htm
Excellent source on assessment, specifically for parents.

National Parent Teachers Association
http://www.pta.org
Information on programs and advocacy to help children achieve.

Administration for Children and Families
http://www.acf.dhhs.gov
Good source of information and statistics on a broad range of federal programs for children and families

Information on Disabilities
http://ericec.org

PACER
http://www.pacer.org
Information for parents of children with disabilities

Kids Together
http://www.kidstogether.com
Good site for parents and kids on special education issues.

Adolescent Directory Online
http://education.indiana.edu/cas/adol/adol.html
Online electronic guide to information regarding adolescent issues and secondary education; including a page for teenagers

Children's Partnership
http://www.childrenspartnership.org
Parent's guide to the information superhighway

Download Worksheets for Students
http://www.freeworksheets.com
For those students who may need some extra help on a vast variety of subject areas. Would have been great for summer…but I just found it.

EduPlace
http://www.eduplace.com
Great links to other sites

Family
http://www.family.com

Family Education
http://www.familyeducation.com

National Parent Teachers Association
www.pta.org
Information on programs and advocacy to help children achieve.

GuidanceChannel.com
http://www.guidancechannel.com
Check out the monthly column by NASP writers on various topics of interest.

Homework Heaven
http://www.homeworkheaven.com

Kidsource
http://kidsource.com

MetLife
http://www.metlife.com
Good information on family issues.

National Parent Information Network
http://www.npin.org

Net Mom
http://www.netmom.com

Parent Soup
http://www.parentsoup.com
Parent Soup for parenting tips; EXCELLENT

Positive Parenting
http://www.positiveparenting.com

School Work
http://www.schoolwork.org

Talking with Kids
http://www.talkingwithkids.org
Information on tough topics that we need to talk to kids about, for parents, teachers, and anyone who works with kids.

## For Psychologists

International School Psychology Association
http://www.ispaweb.org

National Association of School Psychologists
http://www.nasponline.org

Sandy Steingart's School Psychology Resources
http://www.schoolpsychology.net

Global School Psychology Network
http://www.dac.neu.edu/cp/consult
A professional development community for school psychologists. Run by Lou Kruger at Northeastern University.

Positive Behavioral Interventions and Supports
http://www.pbis.org
Lots of good info on FBA and behavioral intervention.

## For Teachers

Encyclopedia Britannica
http://www.britannica.com
Free, extensive access to the world's largest encyclopedia. ERIC Clearinghouse on

Disabilities and Gifted Education
http://ericec.org

USA Today Newspaper Education Page
http://www.usatoday.com/educate/home.htm
Great synopsis of what is new in education

Teacher Net
http://www.teachernet.com
Lots of info for teachers

Education Week
http://www.edweek.org/ew/index.html
A nonprofit, tax-exempt organization based in Washington, D.C. with the primary mission to help raise the level of awareness and understanding among professionals and the public of important issues in American education. Local, state, and national news and issues from preschool through the 12th grade are covered.

National Education Association
http://www.nea.org/index.html

Education Advocacy
http://www.pdkintl.org

The Alternative Education Resource Organization (AERO).
http://www.edrev.org
A nonprofit organization founded in 1989 to advance learner-centered approaches to education.

Bartleby
http://bartleby.com
Free books and great reference materials.

Center for Future of Teaching and Learning
http://www.cftl.org
Meta-analysis article on reading.

Intervention Central
http://www.vesid.nysed.gov/specialed/publications/policy/iep/attach1.htm
Extensive resource for academic and behavioral interventions

## Medical

American Medical Association
http://www.ama-assn.org
American Medical Association site.

America's Doctor
http://www.AmericasDoctor.com
Real MDs with real advice. Always get a second opinion

Cancer Page
http://www.cancerpage.com
Background information and links.

Dr. Andrew Weil's Site
http://www.drweil.com
A Web site by Dr. Andrew Weil's "alternative" medicine site.

Dr. C. Everett Koop's Site
http://www.drkoop.com
An informative and up-to-date Web site by C. Everett Koop, former U.S. Surgeon General, and has many good ideas on better health for all, infants through adults.

Center for Health and Health Care in Schools (CHHCS)
http://www.healthinschools.org

InteliHealth
http://aetnaushc.com
A wonderful site on all health issues by Aetna Insurance and John Hopkins Medical School.

Kid's Health
http://kidshealth.org
Great resource on health and behavior management issues; also updates pediatricians on various childhood illnesses.

MedScape
http://www.medscape.com
Sign up for access—free—all areas of medicine covered. Weekly e-mail updates.

Merck Manual
http://www.merck.com
Medical resource—now online free.

American Red Cross
http://www.redcross.org

## Parent Groups & Support

Beach Center on Disabilities
www.beachcenter.org

PACER Center
www.pacer.org

Parent to Parent—USA
www.p2pusa.org

Technical Assistance Alliance for Parent Centers
www.taalliance.org

### Special Education

Special Education Resources on the Internet (SERI)
http://seriweb.com
A collection of Internet accessible information resources of interest to those involved in the fields related to Special Education.

The Office of Special Education Programs (OSEP) http://www.ed.gov/about/offices/list/osers/osep/index.html
Dedicated to improving results for infants, toddlers, children, and youth with disabilities ages birth through 21 by providing leadership and financial support to assist states and local districts.

Council for Exceptional Children
http://www.cec.sped.org

Academy for Educational Development
http://www.aed.org
All your special education and regular education needs.

Assistive Technology
http://www.webable.com

Brain Injury Association, Inc.
http://www.biausa.org

Center for Applied Special Technology
http://www.cast.org
Comprehensive resources on technology. Also add /bobby to the URL and you can search for sites that are accessible to the disabled.

CHADD Home page
http://www.chadd.org
Guide to ADHD and other related disorders

Ed Law
http://www.edlaw.org
Education law IDEA, Section 504

Federal Resources for Educational Excellence
http://ed.gov/free
Click on—"educational technology"

LD Online Site
http://www.Ldonline.org

LRP Site
http://www.lrp.com/ed
Special Education Law

National Information Center for Children and Youth with Disabilities
http://nichcy.org

Neuropsychology Central
http://www.neuropsychologycentral.com
TBI and general brain information.

Recordings for the Blind and Dyslexic
http://www.rfbd.org

Asperger Site
http://www.asperger.com

Circle of Inclusion
http://www.circleofinclusion.org
Information about inclusion of disabled from birth to 8 into early childhood settings.

Federation for Children with Special Needs
http://fcsn.org
Great site on special education issues

TBI Glossary
http://www.neuroskills.com

# References

Aiken, L. (2000). *Psychological testing and assessment* (10th ed.). Boston, MA: Allyn & Bacon.

Allen, J. M., & LaTorre, E. (1998). The school counselor's role in special education. In C. Dykeman (Ed.), *Maximizing school guidance program effectiveness: A guide for school administrators and program directors* (pp. 117–122). Greensboro, NC: ERIC/CASS.

American Psychiatric Association. (2000). *Diagnostic and statistical manual of mental disorders DSM-IV-TR* (4th rd.). Alexandria, VA: Author.

American School Counselor Association, (2006) . Examining disability and giftedness in the schools. *Professional School Counseling Journal* (Special edition), 10(1).

Arc, The (2004). Introduction to *mental retardation*. Retrieved September 10, 2008, from: http//www.thearc.org/NetCommunity/Page.aspx?pid_33

Baker, B., & Brightman, A. (2004). *Steps to independence: Teaching everyday skills to children with special needs* (3rd ed.). Baltimore, MD: Paul H. Brookes Publishing Company.

Barnett, D. W., Daly III, E. J., Jones, K. M., & Lentz, Jr., F. E. (2004). Response to intervention: Empirically based special service decisions from single-case designs of increasing and decreasing intensity. *The Journal of Special Education, 38*, 66–79.

Bateman, B., & Linden, M. (1998). *Better IEPs: How to develop legally correct and educationally useful programs* (3rd ed.). Longmont, CO: Sopris West.

Bender, W., & Shores, C. (2007). *Response to intervention: A practical guide for every teacher.* Thousand Oaks, CA: Corwin Press.

Bley, N. S. & Thornton, C. A. (2001*). Teaching mathematics to students with learning disabilities* (4th ed.). Austin, TX: Pro-Ed.

Bowen, M., & Glen, E. (1998). Counseling interventions for students who have mild disabilities. *Professional School Counseling, 2(1)*, 16–25.

Braddock, D. (1987). *Federal ploicy toward mental retardation and developomental disabilities.* Baltimore, MD: Paul H. Brookes Publishing Company

Brown, D. (2000). *Learning a living: A guide to planning your career and finding a job for people with learning disabilities, attention deficit disorder, and dyslexia.* Bethesda, MD: Woodbine House.

Casbarro, J. (2008). *Response to Intervention.* Port Chester, NY: National Professional Resources, Inc.

Crockett, J., & Kauffman, J. (1999). The concept of the least restrictive environment and learning disabilities: Least reflective of what? Reflections on Cruickshank's 1977 guest editorial for the Journal of Learning Disabilities. In D. P. Hallahan & B. K. Keogh (Eds.), *Research and global perspectives in learning disabilities: Essays in honor of William M. Cruickshank* (pp. 147–166). Mahwah, NJ: Lawrence Erlbaum.

Disability Categories: State Terminology, Definitions and Eligibility Criteria. (2004, February). *Project FORUM at NASDSE*, pp. 83–84. Available from http://www.nasdse.org/forum.htm

Erford, B. (2003). *Transforming the school counseling profession.* Upper Saddle River, NJ: Prentice Hall.

Ferguson, D. (1995). The real challenge of inclusion: Confessions of a "rabid- inclusionist." *Phi Delta Kappan, 77*, 281–287.

Finn, C., Jr., Rotherham, A., & Hokanson, C., Jr. (Eds.). (2001). *Rethinking special yeducation for a new century.* New York: Thomas B. Fordham Foundation.

Frantz, C., & Prillaman, D. (1993). State certification endorsement for school counselors. *Remedial and Special Education, 22(4)*, 214–222.

Fuchs, L. S. (2003). Assessing intervention responsiveness: Conceptual and technical issues. *Learning Disabilities Research & Practice, 18(3)*, 172–186.

Gearheart, B., Mullen, R., & Gearheart, C. 1993). *Exceptional individuals: An introduction.* Pacific Grove, CA: Brooks/Cole Publishing Company.

Gillam, S., Hendricks, M., George, J., & Baltimore, M. (2003). The utilization of technology to assist collaborative efforts among school counselors and special educators with the implementation of IDEA 1997. *Journal of Technology in Counseling, 3*(1). Retrieved September 6, 2005, from: http://jtc.colstate.edu/Vol3_1/Gillam?gillam.htm

Greer, B., Greer, J., & Woody, D. (1995). The inclusion movement and impact on counselors. *School Counselor, 43,* 124–132.

Greene, G., & Kochhar-Bryant, C.A. (2003). *Pathways to successful transition for youth with disabilities.* Columbus, OH: Merrill-Prentice Hall.

Greene, R.W. (2001). *The explosive child: A new approach for understanding and parenting easily frustrated chronically inflexible children* (4th ed.). Baltimore, MD: Paul H. Brookes.

Hallahan, D., & Kauffman, J. (2006). *Exceptional learners: An introduction to special education* (10th ed.). Boston, MA: Pearson.

Halpern, A. (1993). Quality of life as a conceptual framework for evaluating transition outcomes. *Exceptional Children, 59,* 486–498.

HEATH Resource Center. (2006). *The counselor toolkit.* Washington, DC: The George Washington University.

Howe, K., & Miramontes, O. (1992). *The ethics of special education.* New York: Teachers College Press.

Jordan, D. (2001). *A guidebook for parents of children with emotional or behavior disorders* (3rd ed.). Minneapolis, MN: PACER.

Kauffman, J. (2002). *Education deform: Bright people sometimes say stupid things about education.* Lanham, MD: Scarecrow Education.

Kauffman, J., & Hallahan, D. (2005). *Special education: What is it and why do we need it?* Boston, MA: Allyn & Bacon.

Kochhar-Bryant, C. (2003). Coordinating systems and agencies for successful transition. In G. Greene & C. Kochhar-Bryant (Eds.), *Pathways to successful transitions for youth with disabilities* . Columbus, OH: Merrill-Prentice Hall.

Kochhar-Bryant, C., & Basset, D. (2003). *Aligning transitions and standards-based education.* Columbus, OH: Merrill/Prentice Hall.

Korinek, L., & Prillaman, D. (1992). Counselors and exceptional students: Preparation versus practice. *Education and Supervision, 32*(1), 3–11.

Lewis, R., & Doorlag, D. (2003). *Teaching special education students in general education classrooms* (6th ed.). Upper Saddle River, NJ: Merrill-Prentice-Hall.

Miller, J. A. (1999). *The childhood depression sourcebook.* New York: McGraw-Hill. Milsom, A., & Peterson, J. (Eds.).

NASDSE (1998). *Guidance on functional behavioral assessments for students with disabilities.* Retrieved August 8, 2008 from: http://www.vesid.nysed.gov/specialed/publications/policy/functionbehav.htm

National Technical Assistance Consortium for Children and Young Adults Who Are Deaf-Blind, The (2004). *Annual deaf-blind census.* Monmouth: Teaching Research Division.

O'Leary, E., & Paulson, J. (1991). *Developing and writing transition services within the IEP process.* Unpublished manuscript.

O'Neill, R. E., Horner, R. H., Albin, R. W., Storey, K., & Sprague, J. R. (1990). *Functional assessment and program development for problem behavior: A practical handbook.* Pacific Grove, CA: Brooks/Cole.

Scarborough, J., & Deck, M. (1998). The challenges of working for students with disabilities: A view from the front lines. *Professional School Counseling, 2*(1), 10–15.

Schmidt, J. (2003). *Counseling in schools: Essential services and comprehensive programs* (4th ed.). Boston, MA: Allyn & Bacon.

Sciarri, D. (2004). *School counseling: Foundations and contemporary issues.* Pacific Grove, CA: Brooks/Cole Publishing Company.

Stone, L., & Bradley, F. (1994). *Foundations of elementary and middle school counseling.* White Plains, NY: Longman Publishers.

Studer, J. (2005). *The professional school counselor: An advocate for students.* Belmont, CA: Brooks/Cole.

Turnbull, A., Turnbull, R., Shank, M., & Leal, D. (1999). *Exceptional lives: Special education in today's schools* (2nd ed.). Upper Saddle River, NJ: Merrill.

U. S. Department of Education. (2002).*Twenty-fourth Annual Report to Congress.* Washington, DC: Author.

Watson, D., & Taff-Watson, M. (Eds.), (1993). Second edition. *A model service delivery system for persons who are deaf-blind.* Arkansas: University of Arkansas.

Witt, J. C., Daly, E. M., & Noell, G. (2000). *Functional assessments. A step-by-step guide to solving academic and behavior problems.* Longmont, CO: Sopris West.

Zigmond, N. (2003). Where should students with disabilities receive special education services? Is one place better than another? *Journal of Special Education, 37,* 193–199.

**CORWIN PRESS**

The Corwin Press logo—a raven striding across an open book—represents the union of courage and learning. Corwin Press is committed to improving education for all learners by publishing books and other professional development resources for those serving the field of PreK–12 education. By providing practical, hands-on materials, Corwin Press continues to carry out the promise of its motto: **"Helping Educators Do Their Work Better."**